D1090407

Critical Essays on Marcel Proust

*Critical Essays on
World Literature*

Robert Lecker, General Editor
McGill University

Critical Essays on Marcel Proust

Barbara J. Bucknall

G.K. Hall & Co. • Boston, Massachusetts

Library of Congress Cataloging-in-Publication Data

Critical essays on Marcel Proust.

(Critical essays on world literature)
Includes index.
1. Proust, Marcel, 1871–1922—Criticism and
interpretation.   I. Bucknall, Barbara J.   II. Series.
PQ2631.R63Z545987   1987   843′.912   87–19
ISBN 0-8161-8833-5

CONTENTS

INTRODUCTION

There seems to be no limit to the number of books that have been, are, and can be written about Proust. Here is another one, but it is certainly not the last. It is my conviction that what Proust meant when he said we would be the readers of ourselves (*RTP* 3:1033) was that his work was quite deliberately written on so many different levels opening onto so many different types of interpretation that every reader would see what Proust had written in a different way, both individually and in the course of their existence. When Proust presents as a childish misconception the narrator's notion that each spectator at the theater is at the center and sees a different stage (*RTP* 1:446) this is, in fact, ironically true. Even though there is only one stage each of us sees a different one, where the human comedy is concerned, while believing ourselves to be at the center of the theater, that is in the best possible position for viewing what is going on.

It is because of this that a collection of this nature to which many people have contributed can be of interest. So far as possible, I have put together views which represent different aspects of Proust and from different angles. I have begun with three articles, one of which is a review in the traditional sense, while the other two come very close to that category because they represent initial reactions. The first is the reader's report that Jacques Madeleine wrote for the publisher Fasquelle in 1912, after having read the manuscript which Proust had submitted and which was still in a fairly embryonic state as compared to the complete *A la recherche du temps perdu;* however, one can recognize in Madeleine's report many elements that were to reappear in *Du côté de chez Swann*.

It is clear that Madeleine was in a state of complete exasperation when he wrote this report, because Proust's work was so entirely different from what he expected a book to be. I rather imagine that Anatole France was his notion of what a good writer should be, and no one could be less like Anatole France than Proust, even though (or rather because) Proust admired him. Where was the clear and accurate presentation of characters so that the reader knew exactly what to think of them and what to expect? Where was the deliberate limitation of the number of characters so that their interrelations could be clear and distinct as in the Cartesian tradition?

1

Where was the curtailing of description so that every word would count without fatiguing the reader? Where were the little signposts in the text to let us know exactly what was negated and what affirmed by the author's ironic smile? Where was the even, steady pace, leading clearly in a definite direction? Where was the appeal to a cultivated intelligence which perceived that it was not being expected to rise more than a few degrees above its customary level? And, to conclude, where was the pleasurable relaxation found in reading it? Instead of all these positive aspects, Madeleine saw almost nothing in Proust's work but their repugnant opposites. He did admit, however, to having noticed some remarkable insights by the way.

What is particularly interesting about this reader's report is that the attitude expressed remains typical of many people who attempt to read Proust to this day. My students are very liable to complain about having to read Proust. One of them even said in horror, "But with Proust you have to read *every word!*" It all becomes a question of the sheer effort you are willing to put into reading a book, particularly when you do not know exactly where you stand with it. Nevertheless, I do not think I would call the instinctive anti-Proustians fools as Jacques Rivière did. What is involved is not lack of intelligence so much as one's expectations of literature.

The review of *Du côté de chez Swann* that Paul Souday published in *Le Temps* on 10 December 1913 is considerably more flattering than Madeleine's report. The general tone of the review, however, is patronizing and condescending, and he infuriated Proust by taking the typographical errors with which this volume abounded as evidence that Proust was ignorant of grammar.[1] He also objected to Proust's long, complex sentences, which he considered awkward. Neither did he see any sign of structure in this first volume, for which he may be forgiven (although not by Proust), as *A la recherche du temps perdu* is constructed on such an immense scale that *Du côté de chez Swann* gives one very little idea beforehand of the connections to be made between certain themes in this volume and the subsequent ones. Far from suspecting the existence of these connections, Souday considered that much of *Du côté de chez Swann* consisted of padding.

Souday, who was after all a respected critic of his time, was not entirely imperceptive. He noticed the affinity between Proust and certain English authors of the nineteenth century, although he considered this unfortunate. Proust got rapped over the knuckles for being un-French, which is as much as to say that he was not conforming to the latest French literary stereotypes. No wonder Jacques Rivière went back to the classics as a way of reminding people that there was more than one French literary tradition into which Proust might be expected to fit!

Souday also praised Proust for his poetic and sensitive descriptions and had the taste to select for quotation certain passages that have become anthology pieces. He did suppose, however, as did some other people at the time, that Proust was simply narrating his own childhood memories rather than doing something more creative. It took Rivière to proclaim that what was at issue was self-analysis rather than total recall.

Style as an expression of personal vision, which is such a Proustian concept, is the subject of the article Rivière published in the *Nouvelle Revue Francaise* (or *N.R.F.*) under the title "Marcel Proust et la tradition classique" ("Marcel Proust and the Classical Tradition") in February 1920. It was a kind of postscript to a brief article by Rivière commenting on the award of the Goncourt Prize to Proust for his *A l'ombre des jeunes filles en fleurs*. As editor of the review, Rivière is leaping to the defense of an *N.R.F.* author, but Proust had become an *N.R.F.* author initially because of Rivière's appreciation of his work. Rivière understood the structure of Proust's work from the start, and it may very well be to him that Proust alludes when he says that people who can read a book and understand it are rare (*RTP* 3:894).

In the article we include here, Rivière is obviously aware that he has to defend the bestowal of the Goncourt Prize on Proust on a great many different fronts simultaneously. This leads to some appearance of confusion, since, as Proust's lone defender, he is taking on simultaneously the heirs of realism, romanticism, and symbolism, the admirers of Barrès and the avant-garde. Laying about him in all directions while keeping a cool head, he maintains that Proust is both modern and classical because he represents a break with every kind of superficiality, emotionalism, and woolly-mindedness, and a return to real in-depth psychological analysis such as was practiced by Racine.

The comparison to Racine must have come as a surprise to people in 1920. They may even have wondered whether this was not some excessive piece of flattery, such as was practiced by Proust when he compared the aristocratic aesthete Robert de Montesquiou to Corneille (*EA* 408) and then went on, as if Montesquiou were the equal of Baudelaire, to compare Baudelaire to Racine. Proust must have felt deeply flattered by the comparison of his own writing to that of Racine. But as Rivière analyzes in detail *why* Proust is like Racine, it becomes apparent that flattery is not what is intended, but a simple statement of the facts.

This is in spite of the enormous difference between Proust's bulk and the stringent limitations that Racine imposed on himself with his concision and concentration in vocabulary, emotional expression, physical action, and the number of characters involved in a play. One would have to be a formalist to suppose that this made an essential difference to the basic similarity Rivière perceived between these two analysts of the human heart who had begun by analyzing themselves. The differences of form make no difference to the acuity of their perception or to the precision with which they impale jealousy, vainglory, hatred, fruitless self-condemnation, and an emotion which calls itself love but is at the furthest possible remove from friendship or affection. The differences could then be subsumed under the principle that Proust states in *Le Temps retrouvé* when he says: "But—as Elstir had found with Chardin—you can make a new version of what you love only by first renouncing it" (*RTP* 3:1043; *RTPK* 3:1102).

Jumping ahead over a fairly lengthy period during which Proust continued to be the object of disparaging comments as well as praise, we come to the chapter on Proust and Bergson in *Le Progrès spirituel dans l'œuvre de Marcel Proust* by Henri Bonnet. This book was first published in 1946–49, after having been presented as a doctoral thesis in 1944. This book was republished in 1979 under the title *Le Progrès spirituel dans "La Recherche" de Marcel Proust*, but I feel that its proper place, chronologically speaking, lies here. It indicates a growing recognition of Proust not only as a psychologist and stylist but as a deeply philosophical thinker. However, in spite of Proust's disclaimer to E.-J. Bois in 1913, there seems to have been from the outset an assumption that since Bergson was a philosopher and Proust a novelist, anything that Proust was apt to say of a philosophical nature must have come to him from Bergson.

Because of his professional interest in philosophy, Bonnet felt bound to consider with some care the assumption that Bergson influenced Proust. He subjects it to a careful scrutiny, taking first the similarities between the ideas of the two men, which he perceives as being caused to a considerable extent by a common cultural background, and then the differences, which he perceives as essential. For him there can be no question of an influence but only of certain coincidences at times between two brilliant and original thinkers who were marked by their epoch.

Influence-hunting no longer enjoys the popularity it once did, but these carefully reasoned pages can still be read with profit. It can still be worth bearing in mind that *A la recherche du temps perdu* can be read for its clearly rational thought just as much as for some rather more subterranean processes. There is in Proust a tendency to produce maxims rather in the style of La Rochefoucauld, and these maxims are frequently true. For instance, when Proust demonstrates that we always get what we want on condition we stop wanting it or, again, that we stop wanting something once we have got it, this is true not only of the high-strung narrator but of many other people as well.

This is the kind of thing that Bonnet might consider to belong to the realm of psychology rather than philosophy. Yet it is true that Bergson is a psychologist himself to a considerable extent, a fact that Bonnet would by no means deny, since he says more than once that Bergson made philosophical discoveries by searching "the inner depths." Bergson's insistence on quality as a leading motif of his philosophical work was, Bonnet says, arrived at in this way. Of course we have already noticed that Jacques Rivière said that Proust owed the power and authority of his writing to profound self-analysis, so it is apparent that Bergson and Proust used a very similar method.

It would, however, be rather paradoxical to see evidence of an "influence" in the ordinary sense of the word, in the act of two men searching their own inner depths—which is, or so I believe, the reason no writer who has received the full impact of Proust ever writes anything like him. One might cite Samuel Beckett as an example. Nothing could be further, in its style, from *A la recherche du temps perdu* than *Waiting for Godot*,[2] and yet Samuel Beckett's little book on Proust, first published in 1931, shows how much Beckett appreciated Proust.

This leads us on to Philip Kolb's brief but insightful article on "Proust's Protagonist as a 'Beacon,' " published in 1965. In this article Kolb begins by pointing out that the narrator is a curiously vague and shadowy figure for a protagonist and that his very vagueness encourages the reader to identify with him. Kolb implies, in his last sentence, that after having identified with the narrator in his search for what will give real joy and meaning to his life, the reader will also rejoice with him in his discovery of his artistic vocation and at least some will treat him as a guide in this respect.

Leading up to this joyful revelation are the four "beacons," Vinteuil the musician, Bergotte the writer, Elstir the artist, and La Berma the actress, all votaries of art. Kolb discusses how and why they differ from the remarkable individuals in other areas, such as politics and philosophy, who are held up for our admiration in Proust's unfinished novel, *Jean Santeuil*.[3]

Kolb also comments in this article on the importance of religious terms as applied by Proust to things of beauty. This was indeed what most struck me when I first started studying Proust under his guidance at the University of Illinois, and more than one critic has felt it necessary to use some kind of religious or at least spiritual language when discussing Proust's most elevated passages.

It is highly unusual, however, to speak of Proust in terms of alchemy, as does Victor E. Graham in an article also published in 1965, "Proust's Alchemy." Unusual as it is, it has a very distinctive charm, which does full justice to Proust's poetic side. It also fits in with the curious mixture of religious and magical terms that often characterize Proust's references to some higher sphere. For example, when the narrator enters the church of Combray, he is so impressed by its beauty and the antiquity of some of the things it contains that he feels as if he were in a valley visited by the fairies (*RTP* 1:61), which is not an idea that would occur to an average church-going boy. And when Swann hears the Vinteuil sonata again at Madame de Saint-Euverte's and feels he is being visited by supernatural beings, it is of genies, mermaids, and goddesses that he thinks (*RTP* 1:347–48), rather than of the angels that the Vinteuil septet represents for the narrator, considerably further on (*RTP* 3:260).

Kolb exercises his usual discretion when he speaks of the religious element in *A la recherche du temps perdu*, but it is possible to exaggerate it, and some people do. But alchemy, being a craft that is to one side of religion rather than in conflict with it, fits in fairly well with Proust's distinctly syncretist approach to the supernatural. It also fits in with certain psychological methods—and Victor Graham does say that alchemy is "a philosophy of life"—although with none that Proust would ever have heard of. Carl Gustav Jung, for instance, published a book on alchemy entitled *Mysterium Coniunctionis*, which one would have to be something of an alchemist oneself to read, but which is intended to provide insights into psychology.[4] After all, it does seem fairly clear that whatever school of psychology one is involved with, its aim is not to destroy those parts of one's personality that are viewed as regrettable or inferior but to transmute them into something positive. For Graham, the base elements of life are transmuted by the philosopher's stone, which in Proust's case is art, into the wished-for gold.

Georges Cattaui once called Proust a Sufi (or Islamic mystic),[5] but was then persuaded to abandon the idea, and in my own *Religion of Art in Proust*,[6] I claimed that I saw Proust as being similar to a Mahayana Buddhist. Whether one calls him an alchemist, a Sufi, or a Buddhist hardly matters in fact. What is actually involved is the attempt to pinpoint in terms that will have some meaning for us the fact that Proust's approach to his art was intensely spiritual but in a way for which we have no generally accepted term in the Christian tradition.

Proust probably had no specific term for it, either, as it brings together so much that the Christian tradition (if we exclude the Gnostics) sees as separate—for instance spirituality and sex, ugliness and beauty, greatness and pettiness, the comic and the tragic—and presents them as being mutually supportive rather than exclusive. It may indeed be for this reason that the metaphor, which brings together things that we normally think of as widely separate, was of such essential importance to Proust. The opposing sets of images—in this case based on water and fire—which Graham delineates would also fall into this category.

Nicholas Kostis, whose article "Albertine: Characterization Through Image and Symbol" was published in 1969, implies in a footnote that he feels Graham has not gone sufficiently far in his book on Proust's imagery[7] into the sea imagery Proust associates with Albertine. I am not sure that it is a question of not going far enough; I see it rather as a question of these two critics reading images (sometimes different images) in different ways. In his book Graham tries to account for Proust's imagery in general, whereas Kostis, in this particular article, concentrates on the imagery surrounding one particular character, Albertine, and comments on it in terms of the function of Albertine in the narrator's experience of love.

Kostis divides his article into three sections, one in which the narrator sees Albertine as a rose, one in which he perceives her mobility and mystery in terms of the sea, and one in which he sees her fugitive nature in terms of birds, particularly sea gulls. And why should he not? So many poets have seen the women they loved as roses that Proust is obviously appealing to a strong heterosexual tradition when he compares Albertine to a rose. However, after a while, flowers also come to stand for her lesbianism. The image of the sea also follows the same progression, for feminine mystery, seen in terms of the sea, becomes the mystery of Albertine's sexual preferences when it is not the mystery of the narrator's passion for a woman whose nature he has never grasped. And finally, where bird imagery is concerned, the narrator and Albertine are so far from being two turtle doves that she turns into a sea gull that flies away from him. In fact she was a sea gull from the start.

It is common practice nowadays to see Albertine as an Albert and equate her with Alfred Agostinelli. But, although it may seem paradoxical to say so, it may in fact be more appropriate for her to be a girl if we are judging the entire drama surrounding Albertine not in terms of what we surmise about Proust's own sexual preferences but in terms of literary structure. Proust insists so much that the narrator is physically incapable of giving Albertine any kind of sexual satisfaction, let alone the sexual satisfaction she craves, that his exacerbated jealousy, which amounts to emotional cannibalism, seems fully accounted for.

After all, if the narrator is shown as tormenting and persecuting a hapless young woman because he thinks the things she does are wicked, in the spirit of "blame the victim," while at the same time his attitude, because of his jealousy, is quite understandable, this constitutes an artistic success at the same time as an implicit plea for tolerance. But if he had been presented as a homosexual who resents the man he loves having relations with a woman, as suggested by Justin O'Brien,[8] whom Melvin Seiden quotes in a footnote in the next article in this collection, it would have been difficult to reconcile this with the pleas for tolerance and understanding toward homosexuals that Proust puts forward in the rest of a *A la recherche du temps perdu*, for the narrator might well have seemed to many of Proust's contemporaries to be as wicked as Iago. (It is perhaps not irrelevant to comment that Iago has been acted as a homosexual in recent years on the London stage.)

It is true that Morel, the lover of the Baron de Charlus, has a vicious character, but Proust never attempts to portray him from the inside, like the narrator, in order to make the reader participate in his emotions. At the same time the Baron de Charlus is consistently portrayed as a comic or rather tragi-comic, which means that when Morel does something objectionable to him we respond with heartless laughter or, at the most, with disapproval tempered by the smug feeling that the Baron de Charlus has brought it on himself. On the whole we hear far more about Robert de Saint-Loup, who continues to remain brave, affectionate, intelligent, and handsome, once he has made the switch from heterosexuality to homosexuality, than we do about Morel.

In this connection, Saint-Loup is the character whom Melvin Seiden mainly undertakes to discuss in his article "Proust's Marcel and Saint-Loup: Inversion Reconsidered," published in 1969. This article contains many comments on different critics who had previously approached the topic of homosexuality in Proust's work. In consequence the article is rather dense and complex, as there are so many opinions to respond to. Basically Seiden is deeply aware of Proust's ambiguity. He feels that the narrator is a homosexual who does not wish to admit the fact, but chooses to displace the guilt of homosexuality onto the admirable Saint-Loup. However, because Saint-Loup continues to be admirable in spite of this, he constitutes in his own person a defense of the moral values of homosexuals, even if the reader is expected to grieve over his degradation.

Melvin Seiden also has some comments to make about the tone of anti-Semitism that dominates the narrator's references to Bloch and his family, and denounces it as vulgar and brutal. He constrasts it with the tone of understanding and even wisdom with which the narrator refers to homosexuals. So this critic tackles two subjects that were of considerable emotional importance to Proust.

Up to this point, following the chronological order of the articles in the present collection has involved a connection in themes and subject matter from one article to the next, but now that we arrive at Sybil de Souza's article "Pourquoi le 'Septuor' de Vinteuil?" ("Why Vinteuil's Septet?"), which was published in 1973, there is a distinct break. This article, which deals mainly with the actual instruments used by the great composer, Vinteuil, is one of four I have selected to illustrate Proust's aesthetic theory and practice in detail. It is true that Kolb also discusses the subject, but the importance of the arts for Proust is something that I think cannot be sufficiently stressed. So much in his life was a cause of tension and strain that, even though the absurdity of some of the situations in which he found himself in his youth (e.g., listening to Robert de Montesquiou perorate) reduced him to helpless mirth, suffering was very familiar to him. His sensibility was so much more acute than that of most people that the slightest thing could cause him rage or anguish, but by the same token he could reach heights of joy that are equally unknown to most of us. And the charm of Sybil de Souza's article lies in the fervor with which she conveys the precise nature of the happiness that Proust found in music.

Many people compile lists of the names of famous composers to identify the sources on which Proust drew when he imagined the music of Vinteuil. Sybil de Souza really only discusses Debussy and Wagner. But she does this with an attention to detail that re-creates the impression one has on listening to their music. The comments on *Tristan und Isolde* are particularly apt, showing as they do for how many years Proust could treasure a particular sound that had brought him happiness. Indeed this search for happiness through things of beauty has long been recognized, since Henri Bonnet gave the subtitle *L'Eudémonisme esthétique de Proust* (Proust's aesthetic Eudaemonism) to the second volume of *Le Progrès spirituel dans l'œuvre de Marcel Proust* (Spiritual progress in the work of Marcel Proust), but it is a truth that bears repetition.

With the article by J. E. Rivers, "Proust and the Aesthetic of Suffering," which was published in 1977, we revert to the suffering that Proust so often felt and which was the reverse side of his capacity for joy. However, even though Rivers is able to produce quotations from Proust to support his conviction that the picture Proust paints is one of intense gloom, powerfully affecting even artistic creation, he does recognize that this gloom is not completely unrelieved.

Of course it is true that the social scenes in *A la recherche du temps perdu* are frequently cruel, because they show that each individual in a position of social power sets out to humiliate and subjugate the others in order to satisfy his or her own ego. Even if, like Eulalie, one does something as innocent as visiting a bedridden old lady (Aunt Léonie), this will not protect one from being drawn into the paranoid plots spun by the old lady for no other reason than to bring a bit of excitement into her life. Proust shows pride, envy, and the will to dominate as the principal factors of life in society. We commit so many sins that when we suffer we cannot say we have not deserved it. Hardly anyone is innocent, because the cruelty we exercise toward others, and which is worse than the ceremonials of sadism, is based on indifference (that is, a total lack of awareness) toward the pain we cause.

And yet the social scenes are permeated with an absurdity that is truly comic. In Proust's view of society, Molière and Racine join forces, particularly when Molière is quoted by the narrator's grandmother in a tragic context, that of the stroke she has just suffered in a restroom, while Racine is frequently quoted in a way that is comic and sometimes sacrilegious. Molière and Racine join forces in Proust's view of society, as Louise Jefferson points out in her article in this collection. But all the same, J. E. River's view of Proust's pessimism is not unjustified. How much of a taste one has for black humor must determine how far one finds Proust comic and how far one finds him tragic. "It only hurts when I laugh" could indeed have been Proust's slogan in many instances.

The following article, "Marcel Proust et l'architecture: considérations sur le roman-cathédrale" ("Marcel Proust and Architecture: Some Thoughts on the Cathedral-Novel"), by J. Theodore Johnson Jr., which was published in 1975–76, shows us how well informed Proust was on the subject of church architecture and more particularly of cathedrals. Johnson produces a wealth of documentary evidence to show that Proust not only published translations of Ruskin but truly soaked himself in Ruskin in a way that had a lasting effect on him. The same is true of his reading of Emile Mâle, which overflows into his correspondence. In fact one of the services performed by this article, although not as a main objective, is to show how useful Proust's correspondence is if we wish to understand what was going on "behind the scenes" of his work on *A la recherche du temps perdu*. And one of the things that Proust's correspondence makes apparent is the precision on which he insisted in getting every minute detail exactly and factually right. If his work may be compared to a cathedral, which is the purpose of Johnson's article, then Proust may be compared to one of those medieval workmen who put the utmost inventiveness and care into carving little figures, by way of decoration, which no one might ever consciously see, while at the same time he is the architect who has planned the whole structure and the quarry from which he draws his materials. The sheer scale of such an enterprise is daunting, and it is not surprising that Johnson's article is a long one.

A second article by Johnson specially commissioned for this section and written in 1984 deals with the subject of Proust and painting, with a wealth of scholarly detail about the painters alluded to by Proust. I do not think Proust would have objected to this approach, as, in spite of his negative view of a connoisseurship that remains sterile, he appreciated the history of art as a subject for study. If he had not done so, he would hardly have immersed himself in Ruskin and Mâle, nor would he have attributed connoisseurship in matters of art and architecture and even of fashion and furnishing to the great painter Elstir. In other words, being a connoisseur does not prevent one from being creative. In fact connoisseurship does seem to put one on a higher level, in Proust's eyes, than an aesthetic enjoyment which remains inarticulate, even though stopping short at connoisseurship prevents one from being creative. Proust did at one point consider working in a museum, when his parents were putting pressure on him to choose a career, and he had a great respect for art historians in various fields. It is not for nothing that he makes it an issue of some importance that Swann should be an art historian whose amateur status is largely due to the fact that he does not do it for a living. Swann is full of precise information on works of art, and Proust suggests very strongly that it is due to the deadening power of society that his feeling for art has either been destroyed or has been concealed by him in order to avoid appearing ridiculous. If he were to complete his abandoned study on Vermeer this would be a good thing, and when he sees Madame de Saint-Euverte's footmen in terms of paintings, this shows that the suffering caused by Odette has brought something back to life within him.

If we are to speak of bringing things to life, the theater is one of the lively arts and Louise M. Jefferson, in her essay on Proust and the theater, commissioned for this collection and written in 1984, shows very clearly just how lively Proust's descriptions of social and amorous encounters became as a result of his interest in the theater and particularly in dialogue. The social comedy is truly comic, in the tradition of Molière, which is as much as to say that it also has its darker side, as we have seen. Jefferson brings this out by the examples she give us, particularly of the oft-repeated scene in which a jealous lover forces his mistress into an avowal that, once made, he cannot tolerate. Is there not here some similarity to the end of Le Misanthrope, when Alceste offers total and exclusive love in solitude to Célimène, presumably with the intention of redeeming her, which he had expressed in act 1, and is in despair when she replies that she is willing to marry him but not to leave Paris? Is he perhaps capable of actually hanging himself, after having talked about it in choleric outbursts that no one took seriously? Proust's novel shows that Albertine actually did die after the narrator had made life unbearable for her, but of course Molière would never have put such a thing on the stage. His tragic possibilities are things one can only speculate about, but they are within the reach of our imagination. The novel is a better medium for the conjunction of the tragic and the comic, Molière and Racine, than the traditional stage. Perhaps Beckett is closer to Proust than he at first appears, as is Racine, once questions of style are set aside. But that just shows how many very varied views on Proust are actually justified.

The final article of this collection is "Death of My Grandmother / Birth of a Text" by Elyane Dezon-Jones, commissioned for this collection and written in 1984. It has a double interest, in that it deals with the various versions of certain episodes as Proust worked his way toward a final version and also with the narrator's grandmother, whom he loved far more than he ever loved Gilberte or Albertine (that is, if one takes the word *love* in its usual sense as a positive emotion). Dezon-Jones quotes from Proust's correspondence with his publishers and also utilizes Proust's Carnets, his Cahiers, the typescripts, the Gallimard galleys, the announcements put out by Gallimard for volumes to appear and extracts published in the *N.R.F.* In her quotations from the Cahiers, some words are crossed out and others substituted above the line. These are Proust's own doing and should not be mistaken for errors perpetrated by Dezon-Jones or the editor.

Dezon-Jones's idea that the grandmother had to die for the creative impulses of the narrator to be unleashed is distinctly original. A more traditional critic would say that the main pivot on which this article turns is the difficulty Proust experienced in stating his real views so long as his mother was alive. However Dezon-Jones does not make this suggestion, since she is concerned with the text itself, not with Proust's biography. This is the case with much recent French criticism, and it is a pleasure for me to be able to offer the reader a range of approaches to Proust which goes from initial incomprehension to some of the most recent developments, in what Larkin B. Price would call a "panorama."[9]

Now it only remains to elucidate a few abbreviations used in the course of this volume. This is a more difficult thing to do than one might anticipate, however, as the articles included in this collection represent different stages in the publishing history of the works of Marcel Proust, so different editions are referred to.

The abbreviations used most commonly are as follows: *RTP* for *A la recherche du temps perdu,* edited by Pierre Clarac and André Ferré, 3 vols. (Paris: Gallimard, 1954); *CSB* stands for *Contre Sainte-Beuve* in the various editions, while *EA* stands for *Essais et articles* in the Pléiade edition: *Contre Sainte-Beuve* preceded by *Pastiches et mélanges* and followed by *Essais et articles*, edited by Pierre Clarac with Yves Sandré (Paris: Gallimard, 1971); *JS* stands for *Jean Santeuil* and *PJ* for *Les Plaisirs et les jours* in *Jean Santeuil* preceded by *Les Plaisirs et les jours*, edited by Pierre Clarac with Yves Sandré (Paris: Gallimard, 1971). When people speak of the five-volume edition of Proust's work, these five volumes are what they mean.

A common way of referring to the early edition of Proust's correspondence is *Corr*. This refers to the *Correspondance générale* of Marcel Proust, edited by Robert Proust and Paul Brach, 6 vols. (Paris: Plon, 1930–36). *C.G.* is also used. *Cor.* is used to refer to the *Correspondance*, edited by Philip Kolb (Paris: Plon, 1976–).

I have used a couple of unfamiliar abbreviations in this edition. One is *RTPK*, which stands for the Kilmartin translation of *A la recherche du temps perdu*, which is what I have used consistently throughout this collection whenever an English translation was required, although I have been careful to keep the reference to the original French edition at the same time. The full bibliographical reference is: *Remembrance of Things Past*, translated by C. K. Scott Moncrieff and Terence Kilmartin, 3 vols. (New York: Random House and Chatto & Windus, 1981). I have also used *JSF* for the edition of *Jean Santeuil* by Bernard de Fallois.

In most cases the authors of previously published articles have stated clearly what editions they were using and explained their abbreviations. However, the abbreviations used in the book by Henri Bonnet, *Le Progrès spirituel dans "La Recherche" de Marcel Proust*, from which we include the already mentioned article on Proust and Bergson, are quite idiosyncratic. Where Proust is concerned, all his references are to the first Gallimard edition. *Sw.* stands for *Du coté de chez Swann*, *A l'.* for *A L'ombre des jeunes filles en fleurs*, *Sod.* for *Sodome et Gomorrhe*, *Pr.* for *La Prisonnière*, *A.D.* for *Albertine disparue* and *T.R.* for *Le Temps retrouvé*.

Some of his abbreviations of Bergson's titles perhaps need explaining. *L'Essai* is *Essai sur les données immédiates de la conscience* (Paris: F. Alcan, 1930) and *Les deux Sources* is *Les deux Sources de la morale et de la religion* (Paris: F. Alcan, 1934). Other editions of Bergson used by Bonnet are *L'Evolution créatrice* (Paris: F. Alcan, 1923), *Matière et mémoire* (Paris: F. Alcan, 1921) and *La Pensée et le mouvant* (Paris: F. Alcan, 1934), containing *La Perception du changement* and *L'Introduction à la métaphysique*.

Finally, there is one abbreviation of a periodical title which may present the reader with a problem: *BSAMP*, which represents the *Bulletin de la société des amis de Marcel Proust et des amis de Combray*.

I am afraid that there are marked discrepancies in spelling in this book. Unfortunately this was unavoidable, as the Kilmartin translation of *A la recherche du temps perdu* retains the English spelling of Scott Moncrieff, while American spelling is used in the text. When an English author, such as John Ruskin, is quoted, it is necessary to retain the English spelling also. Differences in capitalization are, however, slight.

BARBARA J. BUCKNALL

Brock University

Notes

1. In my translation of this article, I have left most of the sentences which Souday considers ungrammatical in the original French, as there would be no way of translating them without obliterating the mistakes.

2. J. E. Rivers, however, points out similarities, in the article "Proust and the Aesthetic of Suffering" included in this volume.

3. I have been unable, for reasons of space, to include an entire article on *Jean Santeuil* in this collection. However I am glad that I have been able to include these comments on it, if only to show by comparison the magnitude of Proust's final achievement, which indeed is Philip Kolb's purpose.

4. Carl Gustav Jung, *Mysterium Conjunctionis, An Inquiry into the Separation and Synthesis of Psychic Opposites in Alchemy*, translated by R.F. Hall, 2nd ed., Bollingen Series, no. 20 (Princeton: Princeton Univ. Press, 1970).

5. Georges Cattaui, *Marcel Proust: Proust et son temps; Proust et le temps* (Paris: Julliard, 1952), p. 171.

6. *Religion of Art in Proust* (Urbana: Univ. of Illinois Press, 1969), chap. 8.

7. Victor E. Graham, *The Imagery of Proust*, Language and Style Series, no. 2 (Oxford: Basil Blackwell, 1966).

8. Justin O'Brien, "Albertine the Ambiguous: Notes on Proust's Transposition of Sexes" *PMLA* 64 (December 1949).

9. Larkin B. Price, ed., *Marcel Proust: A Critical Panorama* (Urbana: Univ. of Illinois Press, 1973).

[Altogether, What Is It?]

Jacques Madeleine*

At the end of the seven hundred and twelve pages of this manuscript (at least seven hundred, for many pages carry numbers adorned with a supplementary two, three, four, five—after infinite spasms of affliction at being drowned in unfathomable developments and exasperated fits of impatience over the prospect of never again rising to the surface—one has no, I repeat absolutely no notion of what is going on. What is the purpose of all this? What does all this mean? Where does all this lead? It's impossible to know anything about it! It's impossible to be able to say anything about it!

The letter enclosed with the manuscript supplies some explanations. But whoever reads this volume will not have this letter in front of him.

The letter admits that nothing happens in these seven hundred pages, that the plot has not really begun, or has only begun in the last sixty pages, and in a way which is imperceptible to anyone who has not been previously informed, for the future main character only appears briefly in them, and then under the mask of an appearance contrary to the way in which he will reveal himself later on. And how could anyone tell that it is he? No one will ever guess who it is!

This whole first part, so the letter declares, is nothing but a "preparation," a "poetic overture!" A volume longer than one of Zola's longest novels is excessive as a preparation. And what is a worse misfortune is that his preparation does not prepare anything at all, and even more, does not give anyone any idea beforehand of what the letter informs us will happen, the letter alone. Even with the information supplied by this letter, one wonders constantly: but why is all this going on? But what is the connection? What? What after all?

This is really a pathological case, which all the distinguishing marks.

The way, which turns out to be easy, to become fully aware of it, and the only way, which turns out to be difficult, to give an idea of the work, is to follow the author step by step, groping along like the blind man one is.

The first part is itself divided into three parts:

*Reader's report to Fasquelle publishing company, © Fasquelle, first published by Henri Bonnet in *Le Figaro litteraire*, 8 December 1966. Translated by the editor.

Pages 1–17. A certain gentleman suffers frequently from insomnia. He twists and turns in bed, he rehashes in his half-sleep impressions and hallucinations some of which carry him back to the difficulties he had getting to sleep when he was a little boy, in his bedroom in his family's country home in Combray. Seventeen pages! in which one sentence (end of page 4 and page 5) has forty-four lines, where one gets out of one's depth.

Pages 17–74. A little boy cannot get off to sleep until his mamma has come to give him his goodnight kiss. She does not come when she is having someone to dinner. One of these "someones" is M. Vington. Several pages on M. Vington whom we shall never see again. Another of these "someones" is M. Swann. M. Swann is a close friend of the Comte de Chambord and the Prince of Wales; but he hides these lofty connections and is treated rather casually by the little boy's very middle class family. Mention is made of a Mme de Villeparisis, a close relative of the Maréchal de Mac-Mahon, with whom Swann frequently dines. There are many pages devoted to these two people, and after that to the old servant, Françoise. . . . And we are constantly treated to an analysis of the case of the little boy who cannot get to sleep until his mamma . . .

Finally, we hear the last of the childhood memories which pass through the sleepless nights of the gentleman.

Pages 75–82. But the same person dunks a cake in a cup of tea and here comes a fresh flow of memories rising to the surface.

Pages 82–221. It is Combray. It is aunt Léonie who for years, had not left her bedroom, then had not left her bed, and is now dead. She gets all the news of the village from old Françoise and from a pious old lady called Eulalie; she puts up, although with annoyance, with the talkativeness of her parish priest. There is a digression on an uncle Charles. There is another one, neverending, on old engravings. Then another one on a school friend, Bloch, who admires a contemporary great writer who is called Bergotte and who could be called Barrès because of certain aspects of the way he is described. Then a Monsieur Legrandin whom the family meets on their way from mass and whom we shall never meet again for the rest of the volume, after, however, he has been examined on every side in a very extensive number of pages. Then, a noble family and a noble lady by the name of Guermantes, on the subject of whom we hear the author hold forth inexhaustibly. Then Swann turns up again, but there is a coolness between him and the others because they cannot allow into their home the woman of ill repute whom he has married. Then M. Vington is mentioned again and we learn of his death. And we are present (pp. 187–190) at a scene of sadism in which Mlle Vington, before indulging in amorous pastime with a "girl friend" stimulates herself by providing the latter with a portrait of this deceased father for her to spit on. Then again, the Duchesse de Guermantes.

Finally this first part ends. On its own it would constitute a medium-sized volume. It is made up of the memories, of the whole childhood of the character who is talking, interrupted by a thousand subtle expositions, entangled with twenty narratives in which people appear only to disappear, so far as most of them are concerned, for good.

As for knowing where this is getting us, that's something else again!

This story, which takes up two hundred pages, relates events already fifteen years old, which have once been narrated to the little boy and which the grown man remembers in unbelievable detail.

Monsieur and Madame Verdurin have a salon whose chief ornaments are Dr. Cottard and his wife, a young pianist and his aunt, a painter and in addition a few other persons of no substance. One of their guests is a loose woman, Odette de Crécy, who brings Swann, already getting on in years, along with her. Swann is in love with Odette, who asks for nothing better than to be kept by him and achieves this without Swann realizing, even though he gives her three to ten thousand francs a year, that he is, in fact, keeping her. He does however come to realize something else, and that is that he is being shamelessly cuckolded. He is even completely dropped by her, but all the same he continues to send her money.

At the end, when all these obvious truths have become apparent to him and he has in addition perceived that Odette de Crécy never appealed to him and that she "was not his type," he leaves her.

Or rather we are led to believe that he leaves her. But it seems that this was not the case. For in the childhood memories of the first part we have seen Swann married to Odette de Crécy for already quite a long time and having had a daughter by her by the name of Gilberte.

This particular story here seems relatively simple. But in the manuscript it is interrupted by as many other completely different incidents and confused by as many other unbelievable digressions as we have seen in the first part. In it we find this sentence:

> In the regiment . . . I had a pal who was a bit like this gentleman. It didn't make the slightest difference what he was talking about—heaven knows what—this glass for instance, he could spout about it for hours on end; no, not this glass, that's stupid, but the battle of Waterloo or anything imaginable, and he aimed ideas at you along the way that you would never have thought of. [editor's translation]

Isn't the author afraid that people will apply this to him?

It really would be tempting! For hours on end . . . about this glass or the battle of Waterloo . . . He aimed ideas at you along the way that you would never have thought of . . . that is to say ideas which, it is quite true are not devoid of interest, ideas which are new, acute, full of observation and penetration, but which he aims at you for hours on end, along the way, that is to say without our having the slightest idea of where this way is taking us.

In addition this sentence happens to be a sample of all the other sentences. It is characterized by all the confusion and tangle that one already notices in the very letter which accompanies the manuscript and which makes it unbearable to read it for more than five or six pages.

And this "spouting" just goes meandering continually on. Swann goes, by chance on one occasion, into "high society." And that lasts for thirty pages (pp. 364 to 401). And there are three pages on the footmen lined up along the staircase and who remind him of "the predellas of San Zeno and the frescoes of the Eremitani," . . . Albrecht Dürer, . . . the stairs of the giants in the Ducal Palace, . . . Benvenuto Cellini, . . . the watchmen on the towers of a castle keep or a cathedral, . . etc. As much, to follow, on each guest. And it is inexhaustible and it becomes insane.

There are painful preparations like that at the beginning of Balzac's novels. But, once the characters have been presented, it's over and done with. The characters act. And they are characters.

Here, not at all. Swann will now slip back into the background. If there is anything useful in all this redoubtable jumble, one would really like to know what use he is or what he represents. Certainly he will not be spared us in the third part. And it is not to be hoped for that he will not inflict himself on us again in the second manuscript. We do know, however, from the letter, that he will not be the main character, that he will only be able to play an episodic role. What is more serious is that we remain in total ignorance of what the very character who rocks us to sleep at such length with his memories and his speculations will do in the book.

Pages 422–436. Fourteen pages on Briquebecq, where there is a church in the style of Persian architecture, on Venice, on Florence. . . .

Pages 436–471. About the Champs-Elysées and the public washroom. On the Champs-Elysées the little boy plays with little girls, one of which is Gilberte, the daughter of Swann and Odette de Crécy, who becomes the object of a grand passion on the part of the little boy.

Pages 472–520. M. de Norpois, or de Montfort, a diplomat, enters the picture. And the little boy goes to watch the acting of a Sarah Bernhardt who is called La Borma. Swann's marriage is discussed. So is the great writer Bergotte.

Pages 521–528. La Borma is discussed.

Pages 529–569. We get back again to the story of the little boy and Gilberte on the Champs-Elysées. Then the little boy is invited by the Swanns, first of all to attend children's tea parties which the little girl offers to her girl friends, then to visit Mme Swann herself, in whom the little boy takes a rather peculiar interest. However the respective parents continue to stay away from each other. The little boy is included in all the walks. He runs into the illustrious Bergotte.

After that we will hear no more, at least for the moment, about any of the preceding characters—about any of them no more about Swann or Gilberte or Bergotte than about all the others—with the possible exception of Mme de Villeparisis, who has been discussed at vague although extensive length five hundred pages earlier, and who now enters the scene without however doing anything.

Pages 569–655. The little boy goes to Bricquebecq with his grandmother. Interminable psychologizing on the journey, the hotel room, the Persian style church, the people in the hotel dining room, the rides in Mme de Villeparisis's carriage, etc.

Pages 656–672. A nephew of Mme de Villeparisis, sometimes named M. de Montargis, comes to Bricquebecq and strikes up a warm friendship with the little boy (in that connection, how old is the little boy? We never know).

Pages 672–675. The arrival of a brother or brother-in-law of Mme de Villeparisis is announced. His first name is Palamède; he could bear a princely title; he goes by the name of the Baron de Fleurus or de Charlus. We are given a description of him. We are told that he has beaten an "invert" who had propositioned him.

Pages 675–690. The Baron de Fleurus arrives. He is strange. He disconcerts the little boy by his behavior. He disappears.

Pages 691–706. The close friendship between the little boy and Montargis continues. Then Montargis goes away.

Pages 706–712. These few additional pages, on the stay at Bricquebecq. Then everyone goes away. And page 712 is the last one, though why that one rather than another?

The author concedes that his first volume could stop at page 633. It would cause no problem; and it would be of no advantage, for where 80 pages are concerned, out of so many . . . !

But all that could also be reduced by half, by three-quarters, by nine-tenths. And on the other hand, there is no reason why the author should not have doubled his manuscript or even have multiplied it by ten. When one takes into account the method of "spouting for hours on end, along the way" which he employs, writing twenty volumes is as normal as stopping at one or two.

Altogether, what is it?

For someone who has no outside information, it is a monograph on an unhealthy little boy with an unhinged nervous system and an exacerbated sensitivity, impressionability and meditative subtlety.

It is often uncommon. But too long, disproportionate. One can be quite sure that not a reader will be found who is sufficiently robust to follow the narrative for a quarter of an hour, all the more as the author does nothing to help him by the structure of his sentences—which leak in every direction.

And then what is the importance for the monograph on the morbid little boy, what is the importance of the interminable stories about Aunt Léonie, Uncle Charles, M. Legrandin and so many others? and the completely superfluous story of M. Swann? All that has no influence on the little boy's nervous disorder.

There all the same is all anyone can see who reaches the end of the present manuscript.

But does the letter let us know what the subjet is that the author claims to treat in his second volume or even in the two volumes?

We hardly need to take account of the very brief and contradictorily important appearance of the future "invert," the Baron de Fleurus.

However, there is one remaining question: Is the little boy intended later on to go along with the Baron de Fleurus? Nothing in the monograph indicates it. The letter only mentions a concierge and a pianist.

If the little boy does not become an invert, what is the use of the whole monograph? If he does—and one must hope he does, in the name of logic—there is a justification for its existence, but all the same there is a disproportion beyond anything one can imagine.

It is certain that—supposing one can endure reading it for more than a moment—it is certain that, in its details, there are many uncommon things and that one cannot accuse it of insignificance and lack of substance. . . .

But, in its entirety and even in each section, it is impossible not to become aware here of an extraordinary intellectual case.

Du côté de chez Swann   Paul Souday*

M. Marcel Proust, who is well known to admirers of Ruskin for his remarkable translations of *The Bible of Amiens* and *Sesame and Lilies*, has presented us with the first volume of a large-scale creative work: *A la recherche du temps perdu*, which will be composed of at least three volumes, because two others have been announced and should appear next year. The first already consists of five hundred and twenty pages of close type. What, we may ask, is the vast and serious subject which requires to be treated at such length? Is M. Marcel Proust covering, in his enormous work, the history of humanity or at least of a century? Not at all. He is narrating for our benefit his childhood memories. Was his childhood, then, filled with a great number of extraordinary events? Far from it: nothing in particular happened to him. Vacation walks, games on the Champs-Elysées constitute the basis of the narrative. People say that the subject matter is of little importance and that the entire interest of a book lies in the art of the writer. We can accept that. However we cannot help wondering how many folio volumes M. Marcel Proust would pile up and how many libraries he would fill if he got to the point of narrating his entire life.

*First published in *Le Temps*, 10 December 1913, reprinted in *Marcel Proust* (Paris: Simon Kra, 1927), pp. 7–16. Translated by the editor with the exception of quotations from *A la recherche du temps perdu*, which come from the Kilmartin translation.

Furthermore, this very lengthy volume is not easy to read. It is not only dense but also frequently obscure. This obscurity, to be quite honest, depends less on the depth of the thought expressed than on the extreme awkwardness of the elocution. M. Marcel Proust uses a style which is willfully overloaded, and some of his sentences, encumbered beyond belief with parenthetical clauses, recall the famous sentence about a hat, in which M. Patin, in life perpetual secretary of the Académie française, surpassed himself to the joy of several generations of schoolboys. M. Marcel Proust is quite happy to say: " 'That must be delightful,' sighed my grandfather, in whose mind nature had unfortunately forgotten to include any capacity whatever for becoming passionately interested in the Swedish co-operative movement or in the methods employed by Maubant to get up his parts, just as it had forgotten to endow my grandmother's two sisters with a grain of that precious salt which one has oneself to 'add to taste' in order to extract any savour from a narrative of the private life of Molé or of the Comte de Paris" [*RTPK,* 1:27] or again "And I would go and sit down beside the pump and its trough, ornamented here and there, like a Gothic font, with a salamander, which imposed on the rough stone the mobile relief of its tapering allegorical body, on the bench without a back, in the shade of a lilac-tree, in that little corner of the garden which opened through a service door, onto the Rue du Saint-Esprit, and from whose [in the original, "de laquelle," in the feminine, referring to a masculine noun and emphasized by Souday with an exclamation mark—ed.] neglected soil there rose in two stages, jutting out from the house itself, and as it were a separate building, my aunt's back-kitchen" [*RTPK,* 1:77]. I have chosen these examples from the shorter ones.

Add to this that incorrect expressions abound, that M. Proust's participles are, as a character in a play by Labiche observed, damned awkward customers, in other words that they don't agree; that his subjunctives are no more conciliatory or disciplined and do not know how to defend themselves against the audacious encroachments of the indicative. Here is an example: ". . . Certains phenomènes de la nature se produisent assez lentement pour que . . . la sensation même du changement nous est (*sic*) épargnée." Or again: ". . . Quoiqu'elle ne lui eût pas caché sa surprise qu'il habitait (*sic*) ce quartier . . ."[1] The poor subjunctive is one of the chief victims of the crisis the French language is going through; a number of authors, even respected ones, do not know how to handle it; poets whose plays are acted in subsidized theaters and practicing critics confuse *fusse* with *fus, eusse* with *eus, bornât* with *borna,* and recently one of our distinguished colleagues quoted, in order to make fun of it as a piece of monumental cacography, this sentence by the premier, M. Doumergue, which is irreproachable: "Je ne crois pas que l'honorable M. Barthou s'attendît à être renversé."[2] One cannot imagine, unless one reads them carefully from beginning to end, how badly written most of our new books are. It is clearly apparent that our young people no longer know any French. The language is disintegrating, is being transformed into a shapeless dialect and is slipping into barbarism. It is high time to react. People used to smile at the efforts of the editor of a review who corrected on the proofs all the solecisms of his contributors. It was not, or so it appears, a sinecure. We are beginning to miss this courageous grammarian. And we might well wish that every publishing house should employ as proofreader some old professor who really knows his syntax.

However M. Marcel Proust has, without a doubt, a great deal of talent. It is precisely for this reason that one must deplore the fact that he is spoiling such outstanding gifts with so many errors. He has a luxuriant imagination, a very discriminating sensibility, a love of landscape and the arts, and an acute sense of realistic observation which frequently turns to caricature. In his copious narrations there is something of Ruskin and of Dickens. He often has more to say that he can comfortably express. This overabundance of minute details and this insistence on proposing explanations for them are frequently met with in English novels, in which the sensation of life is produced by a kind of assiduous cohabitation with the characters. As Frenchmen and Latins, we prefer a more synthetic approach. It seems to us that the big volume of M. Marcel Proust has no real structure and that it is as overextended as it is chaotic, but that it contains precious elements which the author could have used to form an exquisite little book.

A prodigiously sensitive child loves his mother in a way and to an extent that seem almost morbid. Being alone terrifies him, and so that he can at least get to sleep, his mother has to come and give him a kiss when he is in bed. If she cannot or will not come, so as not to desert her guests, for instance, what goes on is a real drama, almost a death agony. "Once in my room I had to stop every loophole, to close the shutters, to dig my own grave as I turned down the bedclothes, to wrap myself in the shroud of my nightshirt . . ." [RTPK, 1:30]. But this curiously constituted child is only studied in a few quite moving pages. As we read on we will find little more on these night fears or this imperious and frantic filial affection. Other memories come crowding in on us, evoked by the taste of a cup of tea and "one of those squat, plump little cakes called 'petites madeleines,' which look as though they have been molded in the fluted valve of a scallop shell" [RTPK, 1:48]. This taste was that of the morsel of madeleine which aunt Léonie gave the little boy on Sundays at Combray, many years ago.

> The sight of the little madeleine had recalled nothing to my mind before I tasted it . . . the shapes of things including that of the little scallop-shell of pastry, so richly sensual under its severe, religious folds, were either obliterated or had been so long dormant as to have lost the power of expansion which would have allowed them to resume their place in my consciousness. But when from a long-distant past nothing subsists, after the people are dead, after the things are broken and scattered, taste and smell alone, more fragile but more enduring, more unsubstantial, more

persistent, more faithful, remain poised a long time, like souls, remembering, waiting, hoping, amid the ruins of all the rest; and bear unflinchingly, in the tiny and almost impalpable drop of their essence, the vast structure of recollection. [*RTPK*, 1:50–51]

What we are faced with here is not an association of ideas or even of images, but of purely sensory impressions. And M. Marcel Proust, like so many other contemporary writers, is above all an impressionist. But what sets him apart from so many others is that he is not solely or even principally visual: he is high-strung, sensual and dreamy. His tendency to meditation sometimes gets him into difficulties. He lingers dreamily and at enormous length over the character and destiny of very insignificant beings, a fussy old aunt, mad about pepsin and Vichy water, a machiavellian and devoted old housekeeper, an old parish priest who has no use for antique stained glass and is devoid of all artistic feeling. A few lines would have sufficed to sketch in these silhouettes. Certain episodes with unpleasing sexual connotations do not have the excuse of being necessary. What a lot of thinning out M. Proust could advantageously have done in his five hundred pages. But there are some very appealing descriptions which are hardly ever limited to the mere reproduction of an object and which are magnified, for the most part, by the aspiration of an aesthete or poet.

> The hedge [of hawthorns] resembled a series of chapels, whose walls were no longer visible under the mountains of flowers that were heaped upon their altars; while beneath them the sun cast a checkered light upon the ground, as though it had just passed through a stained-glass window; and their scent swept over me, as unctuous, as circumscribed in its range, as though I had been standing before the Lady-altar, and the flowers, themselves adorned also, held out each its little bunch of glittering stamens with an absent-minded air, delicate radiating veins in the flamboyant style like those which, in the church, framed the stairway to the rood-loft or the mullions of the windows and blossomed out into the fleshy whiteness of strawberry-flowers. [*RTPK*, 1:150]

And that is eminently Ruskinian. His readers will also appreciate the mounting astonishment and the emotions of the child when he sees for the first time in flesh and blood the Duchesse de Guermantes, whose family descends from Geneviève de Brabant and whom he had pictured to himself up till then "in the colours of a tapestry or a stained-glass window, as living in another century, as being of another substance than the rest of the human race" [*RTPK*, 1:191]. And here is the explanation of the title which belongs to this first volume:

> For there were, in the environs of Combray [the little town where the child and his parents spend their vacations] two "ways" which we used to take for our walks, and so diametrically opposed that we would actually leave the house by a different door according to the way we had chosen: the way towards Méséglise-la-Vineuse, which we called also "Swann's

way" because to get there we had to pass along the boundary of M. Swann's estate, and the "Guermantes way . . . [*RTPK*, 1:146] The Méséglise way with its lilacs, its hawthorns, its cornflowers, its poppies, its apple-trees, the Guermantes way with its river full of tadpoles, its water-lilies and its buttercups constituted for me for all time the image of the landscape in which I should like to live . . . [*RTPK*, 1:201].

But after two hundred pages devoted to these memories and to anecdotes about the grandfather, the grandmother, the great-aunts and the servants, we definitely set out a little too far along "Swann's way;" an enormous episode, occupying at least half the volume and filled no longer with childhood memories but with facts of which the child was largely unaware and which must have been pieced together later on, expounds in minute detail the love of this M. Swann the son of a stockbroker, rich and very much at home in high society, a friend of the Comte de Paris and the Prince of Wales, for an adventuress of whose past he is ignorant and whom he long believes to be virtuous, with a naiveté which seems most unlikely in a Parisian of his standing. She is unfaithful to him, tortures him and ends up by getting him to marry her. It is not positively boring, but it is a little banal, in spite of a rather excessive amount of coarseness, and in spite of Swann's notion of comparing his mistress to Botticelli's Zipporah in the Sistine Chapel. And what a lot of episodes in this one episode! What a crowd of walk-on parts, society people of every kind and ridiculous Bohemians, whose idiocies are put on display with excessive detail and prolixity! Finally the last part shows the young hero of the story madly in love with his little playmate of the Champs-Elysées, Gilberte, the daughter of M. Swann (whom the parents of the little boy no longer see because of his absurd marriage). This is, I think, the connecting link with the following volume, which we await with cordial feelings, but also with the hope of discovering in it a little more order, concision and sobriety of style. Readers will appreciate the melancholy conclusion of the present volume: a stroll taken by the adult author, twenty years later in the Bois de Boulogne, where he finds no trace of what had charmed him so much before. He feels nostalgic for the horse-drawn carriages and the elegance of former years; cars and hobble-skirts revolt him. "The reality that I had known no longer existed . . . the memory of a particular image is but regret for a particular moment; and houses, roads, avenues are as fugitive, alas, as the years" [*RTPK*, 1:462].

Notes

1. Certain natural phenomena come into being sufficiently slowly that we are spared the very sensation of change. [Editor's translation] . . . Although she had not concealed from him her surprise that he should live in this neighbourhood . . . [Editor's translation].

2. I do not believe that the honorable M. Barthou had any expectation of being overthrown [Editor's translation].

Marcel Proust and the Classical Tradition

Jacques Rivière*

When I was writing the few lines that people may have read in our last issue on the Prix Goncourt, I still had only a very imperfect idea of the storm that would be raised by the distinction accorded to Marcel Proust's book. The choice of the ten jurors seemed to me so appropriate that I could not, in spite of everything I knew, expect such a furious outburst of protests.

However, now I think it over, I can see quite well that these protests could be foreseen. At bottom they are perfectly normal. They are what always greets the first attempt to recognize a great work. They represent the ritual punishment of anyone who attempts, in the area of the things of the mind, to perform an act of simple and elementary justice.

If I had retained some doubt about the importance of *A la recherche du temps perdu* I would have been relieved of it by the little riot we have just witnessed. Only masterpieces have the privilege of uniting from the start such a consonant chorus of enemies. Fools never start a revolution unless they have been insulted in some really forceful and cruel way.

. . .

I should really have liked not to write about Proust except in the way in which he writes himself, that is to say slowly, pleasurably, and in detail. I had begun, six months ago, a study on his novel to which I wished to devote, for lack of other qualities, all my patience. Under the pressure of recent events, all I can show of it today is an extract, with the proviso of correcting later on by other considerations what is perhaps too exclusively technical in those which I am about to present to my readers.

I cannot treat as a simple accident the fact that Proust has seen principally ranged against him the upholders of "revolutionary art," all those who, vaguely confusing politics and literature, imagine that daring always goes in the same direction in both areas, that in the second as in the first the only possible initiative is *forwards*, that the inventor is always the one who goes further than the others—all those who view literary innovation as an emancipation and who greet as one further step towards Beauty each desertion of a rule which had been respected up till then, each fresh restriction to be dropped, each precision the fewer to be supplied. One of them, not without ingenuousness, has applied to Proust the epithet "reactionary." And how would he have understood that in literature one can have revolutions that move *backwards*, revolutions which consist of doing things that are less overwhelming, less imposing, less free, less sublime, less moving, less concise, less "brilliant" than the case had been before? How would he have understood that it is of a revolution of this kind that

*First printed in *La Nouvelle Revue Française*, February 1920, pp. 193–200. Permission to reprint kindly given by Alain Rivière. Translated for this volume by the editor.

we stand in need today, and that it is for this revolution that the "reactionary" Proust has in fact just given us the signal?

I shall attempt one day to analyze in detail the reasons that have turned our XIXth century into a period of serious lack of energy as regards all psychological literature. Today I shall only present the fact which seems to me to be incontrovertible. From Stendhal on, there becomes apparent a continuous crumbling of our faculty, which is yet so ancient and inveterate, for understanding and conveying feeling. Flaubert represents the moment when the trouble becomes perceptible and alarming. I do not mean to say that *Madame Bovary* and *L' Education sentimentale* imply no knowledge of the human heart; but neither of these works leads us any further into it, nor do they open up for us new aspects viewed *in direct confrontation*. There is in the author a certain heaviness of the intelligence as regards the emotions; it follows them awkwardly; it does not disentangle them anymore; it no longer knows how to capture them in their capriciousness and their nuances. I think that this accounts for the impression of marking time that these books give us, even though they are so strongly "marching onward," while their style, as Marcel Proust so rightly used to remark, makes us think of a moving walkway.

A more advanced stage of the malady from which our psychological sense suffered in the XIXth century can be studied to advantage in the first works of Barrès. A great attempt of a writer on himself; numerous and precise arrangements for proceeding to an investigation of his emotions which are intended to be as subtle and penetrating as possible: result, absolute zero. There is not, in the *Culte du Moi*, the smallest embryo of psychological discovery; it really is the "unknown God" who is worshipped in it, from one end to the other. In spite of all his good intentions, in spite of all the apparatus with which he surrounds himself, Barrès fails to overcome the hermetic inner night with which he is afflicted.

In any case, everywhere around him, at this time self understanding is at a low ebb. Never have people talked so much about intuition and never have people been so incapable of it; at least so far as subjects of thought are concerned. Symbolism teaches not only poets but also novelists a certain delightful way of only approaching oneself in a dream. What is involved here is above all being blind. The effort to be made, if there is one, is exactly the reverse of clear-sightedness: the better to make the reader vibrate, the usual thing is to touch on the emotions intended to ravish him only from the outside and with a kind of drunken circumspection; one has to squeeze them, wring them, make them yield all their juice; but above all one must not penetrate them, tackle them, dissolve them. The writer, whoever he may be, strives above all to give an inclusive picture; he is only happy when he manages to restore in a general way, by suggestion, by a caress, a moment of his soul; he only has the feeling of having done his work when he has contrived to submit to himself, just as he is and in total ignorance, for an instant.

The psychological novel is impregnated with lyricism; it is no longer a branch of the study of the passions; it is no longer used to portray characters; with a few very rare exceptions, it is no longer supposed to be anything but a collection of "impressions" on the soul, of "introspective landscapes."

At first glance Proust can seem to to have done nothing other than bring this genre to perfection. Is he not an amazing evocator of sensations and feelings? What else is he trying to do than bring back to life under the eyes of the reader his whole inner past?

Doubtless; but we have to take into account the way he does it. He is not counting for this on any magic wand. He has no intention of making his soul "arise" before us "from the depth of the waters" like an entire, fully equipped island. A la recherche du temps perdu: this title says everything; it signifies a certain labor, diligence, method, undertaking; it signifies a certain distance between the author and his subject, a distance that he will have to cross unceasingly through memory, through reflection, through intelligence; it implies a need for awareness; it announces a decisive conquest of the reality which is his goal.

And in fact Proust drops from the very start all the literary techniques which belong in the slightest way to enchantment. He deprives himself, even with a certain severity, of music; it is visible that he does not wish to suggest but to rediscover.

He captures feelings and characters through detail; he does not renounce all claim to show their outline and profile; but he knows that this must not and cannot be achieved in any other way than slowly. Nibble at first. He is a gnawer: he will pile up a lot of debris before one is able to understand that that isn't what it is, that these are rather the building materials for a vast and magnificent construction.

I cannot say how moving I find his renunciation of all emotional effects, his patience, his diligence, his love of truth. He takes up his pen by the right end; first of all he sketches a little part and then the rest comes along of its own accord, little by little. He also makes me think of those machines which swallow so mathematically the piece of cloth or the piece of paper which has been inserted into them only by the edge.

Nothing appears in his work except from the inside; he has no intention of repeating the echo of lost Time; he only attempts to restore its contents to it, little by little. And the same thing is true in particular of each emotion he has experienced, for every character he sees again. He immediately looks for their nuances, their inward diversity; it is only by dint of discovering the difference between them that he hopes to recall them to life.

M. Jacques Boulenger has commented very subtly in *L'Opinion* that Proust only portrayed characters "by retracing the reflection that they left within him" and that he thus went in search of their image as if in the depths of an inner mirror. We have to understand the entire significance of this proceeding. However hard one tries, there is no really profound description of characters unless it is based on a close and sound self-knowledge. Before turning outwards with some chance of success, it is necessary that analysis should have deeply bitten inwards. At least that is the law amongst us, in France. What was lacking in Flaubert and all the novelists of his school was knowing first of all how to grasp themselves. Because they chose to be objective from the start and directly, they condemned themselves to place *subjects* simply before themselves, but without animating them, without diversifying them, without shedding an inward light upon them.

Proust sees all things, and even external ones, from the angle from which he sees himself. And as he has adopted in himself the habit of refraction, his gaze, from the very start, specifies and reduces things to their constituents. In this way he succeeds, by never separating any being from its detail, in always showing it to us as something entirely concrete, as nourished within as without, at once astonishing and familiar.

It is with the great classical tradition that he resumes contact in this way. Does Racine do anything else than go in search of other people by looking within himself? Having sent one day his intelligence in pursuit of his sensibility, little by little, through everything that the one gains over the other, he becomes a creator. And in this way only. Nothing by him is brought into being all at once. It is by understanding, it is by analysis, it is by awareness that he brings different beings into existence. And if these beings themselves become clear before the eyes of the reader or the spectator, it is thanks to the continuation in them of this progress of the intelligence. From the very outset the poet has turned his back on their totality, he has refused to consider the aspect which they might have taken on; the only thing he wanted was to drink them in, to enter into their souls as he began by entering into his own, that is to say completely armed with attention. Where do Hermione, Néron, Phèdre come from, as we grasp their nature little by little, if not from the center of the feelings between which we are made to see them divided? There is no *creation* here, in the strict sense, but only invention, that is to say something *found*, perceived, clarified, a recognition, so to speak, of other people's awareness.

Proust takes up this method on a larger scale, more slowly, more minutely, less dramatically. He rediscovers, in all he does, the way to the inward parts. And not, according to the Bergsonian style, through an effort of concentration and sleep, but on the contrary by a peaceful unfolding of lucidity and discernment. As naturally as a poet projects images before himself, forgetting himself, Proust examining his own depths, inquires, explores, divines, recognizes and little by little arrives at an understanding of people and things; his mind gently devours whatever is obscure or opaque in them, destroys in them everything that escapes perception, everything that would tend to give one simply a general impression; thus he *invents* them, by no other means than drawing up an *inventory* of them, by nothing more than the calm perpetuity of the attention he accords them. In order to produce them he demonstrates them. On the page on which he writes, it is their palpability that he attempts and goes in search of through ten thousand words. He refuses to accept their shadows as such: they too must be full of characteristics that one can and must grasp: for lack of anything better he will people them with hypotheses.

In this way he works in the opposite direction to all romanticism which has consisted without pause of making people believe in things without showing them. We can expect from his intervention, so far as literature is concerned, an immense deflation. It will become impossible, for some time now on, to interest people by showing them things in the lump, to touch people's imagination directly; the writer will no longer be able to ask for that faith of the senses which has been appealed to in a more and more tyrannical way. He will have to explain himself, he will have to put his cards on the table. And then one will be able to see that great things are the ones in which there are the most small things, that depth is in inverse ratio to grandiloquence and that genius is not perhaps as different as people have come to think from judgment and preciseness.

By helping us to get rid of the failure to separate ideas and feelings, Proust helps us to get rid of the enigmatic and the unverifiable. He sends grist to the mill of our reason and sets our reflective faculty going again. Thanks to him, we are freed from that kind of sensual complicity or mystical conversation which was tending to become the only relationship in which we could find ourselves involved with a writer. We find ourselves taking pleasure again in understanding; it is our pleasure once more to learn something about ourselves, to feel ourselves grasped and defined, to recognize ourselves as more extensively susceptible to being put into words than we had believed ourselves to be.

The great and modest advance through the human heart that the classics had set going, begins again. "The study of feelings" makes progress once more. Our eyes are opened once more to inward truth. Our literature, suffocated for a moment by the ineffable, becomes openly once more what it has always been, in its essence: a "discourse on the passions."

Proust and Bergson   Henri Bonnet*

At the same time as Proust has been equated with the mystics and often for very similar reasons, he has also been equated with Bergson. On this point a fair degree of unanimity has been established. There are few

*From Le Progrès spirituel dans "La Recherche" de Marcel Proust (Paris: A. G. Nizet, 1979), 396–420. Reprinted in the editor's translation by kind permission of the author and publisher. Quotations from A la recherche du temps perdu come from the Kilmartin translation. All other quotations have been translated by the editor.

critics who express reservations on this subject. This is an important consideration and it is worth examining.

In this instance the suggestion has been made that Proust was not only similar to Bergson but was influenced by him. *L'Essai sur les données immédiates de la conscience* appeared in 1889 and *A la recherche du temps perdu* in 1913. This influence seems very probable when one compares the two works and their dates. Proust was personally acquainted with Bergson, who was his relative by marriage and who visited his house. And when Proust published his first translation of Ruskin, Bergson gave a report on it before the Académie des Sciences. Thibaudet, in *L'Encyclopédie française*, vol. 17, informs us that Proust "ignorait" [i.e. ignored or was ignorant of— ed.] Bergson. In whatever way one interprets the word "ignorer," this statement is untrue, as we can tell from Proust's correspondence and from the charming reminiscences of Fernand Gregh (*L'Age d'or*). In 1910 he wrote to his friend G. de Lauris (*Revue de Paris,* May–June 1938, 736): "I am happy that you should have read Bergson and liked him. It is as if we had been together on a great height. I am not yet acquainted with *L'Evolution créatrice*[1] (and because of the great value I attach to your opinion I am going to read it immediately). But I have read enough to Bergson and the parabola of his thought is already sufficiently describable after one generation that, whatever *Evolution créatrice* may have followed, I can, when you say Bergson, know what you mean."

Nevertheless Proust refused to agree that there had been any "direct suggestion" from Bergson to him (*Corr.* 3:195—Letter to C. Vettard: "For there has not been, so far as I can judge, any direct suggestion"). And his statement on the matter is not to be overlooked. Doubtless, and he does not dismiss this hypothesis, Bergson's influence could have affected him unwittingly. We will even make so bold as to say that his mind, from having to assimilate the ideas of the great philosopher, must have received some kind of imprint from them. But if Bergson's influence has been as strong as some suppose, it is certain the person chiefly concerned could hardly have failed to notice it!

Then again, the existence of *Les Plaisirs et les jours* seems to settle the question. We have seen that in this work Proust's ideas are in the process of formation. Most of his themes are indicated. The importance of memory, in particular, of time and most of all of the inner life are already considered worthy of note, involuntary memory is foreshadowed, and the action of society on the individual and the existence in each one of us of a social personality have already been discovered. It is almost certain that Proust had not read *L'Essai sur les données immédiates de la conscience* when he wrote *Les Plaisirs et les jours*. Bergson's book came out in 1889, the year when Marcel Proust accomplished his volunteer military service in Orleans. Furthermore, he declared to J.-L. Vaudoyer that *Les Plaisirs et les jours* had been written "in high school" when he was seventeen, "although published later."[2] At the age of seventeen, that is to say in 1888. It is moreover improbable that Proust read *L'Essai* immediately on publication. M. Charles Blondel (*La Psychographie de Marcel Proust*, 186) thinks he sees in the style of an R. de Montesquiou letter written in 1893 the trace of the influence of Bergson. In this letter Proust praises the noble soul of his correspondent, which ". . . prevents us," he says, "from foreseeing what form your future works will take, as is always the case when there is a spontaneous upsurge, a living spring, a true spiritual life, that is to say freedom." The hypothesis is probable. But this sentence might just as well reflect the influence of another philosopher who came before Bergson, that is Guyau of whom he might have heard through his mentor Darlu earlier and whom he sometimes discussed (as well as two other philosophers of that time, Ribot and Tarde) with his friend R. de Billy.

To continue, may not certain resemblances between Bergson and Proust be explained by shared influences? Bergson was only about ten years older than Proust. Both of them were equally steeped in the intellectual atmosphere of the years from 1880 to 1890, which are numbered among the finest years of symbolism. Now symbolist poetry is the revelation of the qualitative and of the importance of the inner life, of subjective life, of the unconscious. It is even a reaction against the scientific claims of the Parnassian school and the realist and naturalist novel, just as Bergson's philosophy is a reaction against the excesses of an unbounded trust in the possibilities of science. So far as Proust is concerned, it is not to be doubted that this influence had a real effect on him. In high school, he felt grateful to those of his teachers who admired or at least were aware of Leconte de Lisle and Léon Dierx. By the age of twenty he had read Baudelaire, Mallarmé, Verlaine, H. de Régnier and Maeterlinck, as one can tell from his correspondence and the epigraphs in *Les Plaisirs et les jours*. He was acquainted with Wagner and admired him. In November 1892 he contributed to *Le Banquet* a short but meaningful review of *Tel qu'en songe* by Henri de Régnier (reprinted in *Chroniques*). "*Tel qu'en songe*," he writes, "reserves for people who do not like poetry a disappointment which is even crueller than the inevitable disappointment which is inseparable for every intelligent person from reading a poem. For generally poetry contains more or less in solution foreign elements which suit its intentions." This is the idea, so typical of Baudelaire and Mallarmé, that poetry often contains impure, unpoetic elements, which the real poet must eliminate. In 1896 he protested, in *Contre l'obscurité*, against certain excesses of symbolism. But symbolism, like every literary movement, had its extremists, and Proust remained faithful throughout his life to Baudelaire, whom he was to name in a 1922 article, "the greatest poet of the nineteenth century" (*A propos de Baudelaire*).

His sensibility and his art are those of a Symbolist. "The influence that they exerted on him, says Marie-Jeanne Durry, "or rather the affinities which exist between them, are truly essential." The style of *Les Plaisirs et les jours*, as Mme M.-J. Durry rightly points out, is full of rather "formalist" reminiscences of symbolism. "But later will come the deep harmonies" ("Marcel Proust," an article which appeared in the collection of articles and documents published by the press of the *Revue du Capitole*, 152). To conclude, his aesthetic is essentially symbolist. The idea that art is a way of knowing things at first hand is at least potentially implicit in the aesthetic of Baudelaire, Mallarmé, and the Symbolists. In fact this is the essential characteristic which allows us to distinguish between them and the Parnassians on the one hand and the Romantics on the other. And it is a truth which, in his turn, Proust *demonstrated* in *Le Temps retrouvé*.

So it seems that for a hypothetical influence of Bergson on Proust we have to substitute the unquestionable influence of the symbolist era. Besides, as M. Valéry Larbaud points out, ". . . through this the parallels between Proust and Bergson are much more easily explained." "Has it not been said," he adds, "that Bergson formulated the latent or underlying philosophy of symbolism?" (Preface to *L'Esthétique de Marcel Proust* by Emeric Fiser, 12). M. Emeric Fiser adopted on his own behalf the opinion of M. Valéry Larbaud on the symbolist character of Proust's creation and aesthetic in his thesis *Le Symbole littéraire et Marcel Proust* (Corti, 1941). He has established, with the aid of valid proofs, the relationship which exists between the aesthetic concepts of Wagner, Bergson, Baudelaire, Mallarmé, and Proust. The resemblances which have been noted between the philosopher and the novelist may thus be explained in a far more convincing manner, not by some influence of one on the other, even though there is no reason to exclude it in toto, but by a single influence by which they both may be supposed to have been affected and which they would have breathed in in the intellectual circles in which they lived.

This way of seeing things provides at the same time an explanation of the resemblances which exist between Bergson and Proust. Both of them, in short, in their respective domains, felt obliged to address similar subjects and problems—problems of their time: the unconscious; life in society with its relationship to the individual and to the deep inner life of the artist and creator; the role of intelligence; time. Having coincided with each other in their choice of subjects, they did sometimes interpret things in the same manner and draw similar conclusions. This circumstance is not to be considered odd if one takes into account that the philosopher in Bergson is also very open to artistic phenomena and gifted with a remarkable talent for expression—and that the novelist or poet in Proust is very preoccupied with philosophical problems and possesses a keen intelligence.

However, besides these resemblances, there are, particularly from the psychological point of view, some considerable divergences which we have already indicated in the preceding pages. The principal one concerns the structure of the inner life which Bergson presents as continuous and Proust as discontinuous. But let us set the differences aside for a moment. Let us concentrate on the similarities, the areas of agreement, while leaving ourselves free to return to the subject later on for the necessary finishing touches. The points on which great minds are in agreement have a particular claim on our attention, and an examination of them will perhaps be rich in lessons for us.

Bergson's philosophy is one which has had the good fortune, like every philosophy which is fairly profound, to go beyond the restricted world of specialists, to concern the larger public of cultured people in general and the literati in particular. To wonder to what this success is due is to wonder what the profound message brought by this philosophy to humanity consists of. Now what Bergson has brought us and what people have taken pleasure in discovering in him is the revelation of a universe richer than the one in which we ordinarily live. It is the revelation of quality. He has given a philosophical basis to quality by pointing out to us that it is the very stuff of reality.

This quality is something which he quite naturally discovered in our own inner depths. His first book is the affirmation of the qualitative character of the slightest psychological phenomena, ranging from the most subjective feeling to the most objective sensation. He has revealed qualitative differences where we thought we could only perceive quantitative differences. He has shown us how habit, social life, and language substitute within us quantity for quality, what is homogenous for what is heterogenous, what is abstract for what is real. Bergson even extended his thesis to the point where he called into question the intensive character of psychic states, which is as much as to say that he totally denied the right of the quantitative to enter our inner life. A mistake, perhaps! For that means, in sum, reducing us to consider states of consciousness as something abstract. The doctrine of the *élan vital* which he was to put forward later on does not seem to us to agree with the thesis according to which there is no difference of intensity between states of consciousness.

But this revelation is completed by another from which it cannot, in any case, be dissociated: as he affirms the reality of quality, Bergson affirms the reality of change. In fact quality cannot become static without losing its qualitative character. A quality which would not change would be quality which repeats itself, and quality is something which can only exist once. This seems to be the secret point of view of Bergson on this subject.

However, we shall have a better chance of grasping the innermost thinking of the great philosopher if we observe that he must have proceeded not from quality to change, but from change to quality. It seems to be fairly certain that the origin of his entire system must be sought in a reflection on movement. It was at Clermont-Ferrand, between October 1883 and the year of 1888, that Bergson had his day of November 19. Joseph Desaymard, one of his former students in this city of the Auvergne, informs us that it was at the end of a course in which he had presented to his high school students the arguments of the Eleatic philosophers that the ruling idea of his doctrine became clear to him. (*La Pensée d'Henri Bergson*, 11, quoted by Chevalier in his *Bergson*, 51—Plon, 24th edition). Now we know that it was by examining the sophism of Zeno of Elea that Bergson drew the conclusion that it is impossible to explain movement by dividing it into fragments. In one sense, one can say that all of Bergsonism issued from this irrefutable observation, from this pure intellectual intuition, that *a moving object does not stop at any of the points through which it passes.* Movement is an indivisible continuity in progress. It forms a whole which cannot be taken apart. To take it apart means reducing it to quantity and rendering it permanently unintelligible. But how can one grasp movement in its indivisible continuity? There is only one way: that is to go down into our inner depths, espouse this movement, and relive it. To a movement which has been relived in this way Bergson gives the name of absolute movement. "When I speak of an absolute movement," he says, "what I am doing is attributing to the moving object an inner being and, in a way, moods . . ." (*Introd. à la métaphysique*, 202). Thus the possibility of understanding movement is linked to the existence of a qualitative and continuous heterogeneity and to the possibility of grasping it through introspection. And so it is that Bergson is led from the idea of movement to the idea of a heterogenous, qualitative, creative duration about which he said to Hoffding that it was the point from which he had set out and to which he had constantly returned. Now duration is nothing other than quality in the continuity of a movement. And it is because such a quality exists in us that we can intuit it at a certain psychological depth (". . . there is hardly anything other in the human soul than progressive developments", *Essai*, 99), that we can understand physical movement in what is absolute in it.

It is in this way that Bergson conceived the idea of a quality of a very original kind, since what is involved is a quality in movement, a dynamic quality.

But this is not all: the qualitative character of quality is affirmed, it is not explained. It can only be explained by memory. It is because the past accumulates within us and affects the present at every instant that there is no state within us which is not different from all the others. In fact since the past is an incessant accumulation, its action is at each moment different from itself. "Let us take the most stable of inner states, the visual perception of a motionless external object. Even though the object remains the same, even though I look at it from the same side, from the same angle, the perception I have of it is nevertheless different from the one I have just had, even if it is only because my perception is a moment older. My state of mind, as it advances along the path of time, swells continually with the duration it gathers; one could say that it grows as it goes on, accumulating substance from itself." (*Evol. créat.*, ii). An important consequence results from this role played by memory, and that is that this absolute movement which is constituted by duration is a movement with a definite direction; any turning back is in any case impossible; duration is therefore not only unpredictable (for one cannot foresee the qualitative) but in addition irreversible. A continuous and irreversible movement is nothing other than real time. So it is not only the comprehension of movement in its indivisibility that we recover when we descend into our own depths, it is the reality of time.

These psychological discoveries are completed by a metaphysical statement. In his intuition of psychological continuity he has the impression that he has reached the very ground of being. This indivisible progression which constitutes our underlying self is the very progression of nature—not of that inert nature which derives solely from quantity and geometry and which is a lesser nature—but of real, living nature. All organized beings, whether vegetable or animal, are drawn onwards, like our minds, in a great movement which is unpredictable because whatever changes qualitatively cannot be foreseen and irreversible because whatever changes while continually increasing cannot return to its point of departure.

Bergson's philosophy, in consequence, takes on the aspect of a philosophy of dynamism. (A dynamism which is, besides, characterized less by the concept of force than by the concept of qualitative change). Together with concrete movement or duration, as he has defined it, it is reality itself, which a basically mathematical, static metaphysics (Kantian philosophy: ". . . this type of universal mathematics which is however what science consists of . . ."; *Introd. à la métaphysique,* 250) had banished that he reintroduces into philosophy. This point of view is new. Other philosophers had certainly discovered the dynamic character of reality before him and even based their philosophy on it. But no one had ever emphasized the irreversible, unforeseeable nature of duration. Everything flows, Heraclitus had said. Bergson states more precisely: Everything flows *in a certain direction.* When one views the world, when one views reality from this angle, all philosophical and psychological problems appear unquestionably renewed. It would go beyond the bounds of this present study to consider whether Bergsonism really dissipates, as it undertakes to do, a certain number of metaphysical difficulties and problems—and whether it is true that our retrospective views of reality are unjustifiable. At least it draws our attention in a useful way to the manner in which the concepts which we used to present to ourselves as given are actually formed. And furthermore, there is an area in which its success is certain: thanks to it, in psychology, everything which is of a genetic order has new light shed on it; in particular the problem of invention.

Invention is the outstanding example of unforeseeable activity. It is nothing other than the revelation to consciousness of absolute movement, of the duration that exists within us, that is to say of the qualitative in its pure state. There are treasures within us. It is within himself that the inventor of whatever kind he may be: artist, scientist,[3] metaphysician, finds the riches which constitute the seed of invention; it is within himself that he discovers the initial creative shock. It is there that is to be found the emotion which is the origin of all great creations. "There are emotions which engender thought," writes Bergson in *Les Deux Sources de la morale et de la religion,* "and invention, although of an intellectual order, can have some sensibility as its substance" (39). And a little further on he is even more explicit: "Creation means, above all, emotion" (41).

The process which allows us to enter into contact with our own inner depths is called intuition by Bergson and it is once more in terms of movement that he defines it. "Intuition," he writes, "starts out from movement, posits it or rather perceives it as reality itself and sees nothing more in immobility than an abstract movement grasped instantaneously by our minds on the more fundamental basis of mobility." Movement is also quality and duration. Intuition arrives at quality, duration or, as Bergson sometimes says, the absolute. It is not a mysterious faculty, nor one which is yet to be created, as one could believe from reading *L'Evolution créatrice;* it is the faculty which all creators use and of whose existence Bergson reminds those metaphysicians who may have forgotten it. It is not from a deductive or analytical process that invention arises, but from a movement of the mind. That does not mean, however, that it can arise without preliminary work; on the contrary, artistic intuition like metaphysical intuition springs from the accumulation of materials (*Introd. à la métaphysique,* 254) and it is extremely strenuous (*La Pensée et le mouvant,* 40). But creation is a word to which Bergson assigns a positive sense. One cannot reduce invention in any absolute way to the conditions which surrounded its birth or to already known elements. Movement has taken place. Besides, any work of genius is disconcerting to begin with. It is a progression of the same kind, in any case, as certain profound progressions which come into effect in the course of the evolution of life and societies (*Les Deux Sources de la morale et de la religion,* 79–80). This is because the very basis of being is progression, change[4] and duration—or also, if one wishes, invention, liberty.[5]

Such are the essential points of Bergson's doctrine. If we have reminded the reader of them, it is in order to show that there is nothing in them which one does not meet again, obviously in a different form, in Proust. He too treats quality as reality itself. He too invites us to find the true riches within ourselves and not outside ourselves in the life of society. He too attributes to invention an emotional origin, a capacity for completely renewing either things or our way of seeing them. Finally if the question of movement or change evades Proust in its technical aspect, at least he insisted on the importance of time and memory, on the unforeseeable nature of our inner life and the events of life in society (it is true that he does not explain this unforeseeable nature in the same way. We refer the reader to what we have already said on this topic at the end of book 2).

But the point on which the agreement of the philosopher and the writer is most striking is the doctrine of art. From many points of view the aesthetic doctrine of Proust, and principally what one might call Elstir's aesthetic as it is expounded in *A l'ombre des jeunes filles en fleurs* is the very aesthetic of Bergson. It is also the type of aesthetic which can be formulated after the symbolist experience.

Point number one on which agreement between them is complete: art has the qualitative as its object. Bergson in *Le Rire* says "the individual," which amounts to the same thing. "What the artist captures on his canvas is what he has seen in a certain place, on a certain day, at a certain time, with colors never to be seen again" (*Le Rire*, 165). And, to continue, art consists just as much for both of them of recapturing reality and translating it. It is a mode of knowing. Bergson, from this point of view, even attributes a far greater importance to art than Proust, for it constitutes for him almost the only mode of knowing the intuitive, or as he says *absolute*, reality of things.[6] To attain to this reality it is necessary to recapture our true impressions under the crust of notions of a social and utilitarian origin which have covered them over and hidden them from our eyes. But who wrote this sentence: "The names which designate things correspond invariably to an intellectual notion alien to our true impressions and compelling us to eliminate from them everything that is not in keeping with that notion"—and this argument: ". . . what one knows does not belong to oneself"? Bergson? No, it is Proust, (*A l'.*, 2:123, 128; *RTPK* 1:835, 898), but it could equally well be Bergson. The whole art of Elstir consists of stripping "himself when face to face with reality, of every intellectual notion" (*A l'.*, 2:128; *RTPK* 1:898), in order to recapture nature as it is, that is to say poetic. "But the rare moments in which we see nature as she is, poetically, were those from which Elstir's work was created:" (*A l'.*, 2:124. *RTPK* 1:894). But Bergson for his part wonders: What is the aim of art? "If reality," he replies, "struck our senses and our consciousness directly, if we could establish an immediate contact with things and with ourselves, I am convinced that art would be useless or rather that we would all be artists, for our souls would vibrate in unison with nature, etc . . ." (*Le Rire*, 153–154). And he adds, a little further on, "Thus, whether in the form of painting, sculpture, poetry or music, art has no other aim than to discard those symbols which have a practical utility, those generalities which are accepted by convention and society, and in short everythng which masks reality in order to leave us face to face with reality itself" (161). (See also *La Perception du changement*, 170–74): "So we may well say that it is a direct vision of reality that we find in the different arts; and it is because the artist gives less thought to utilizing his perception that he perceives a greater number of things."

And does not Bergson seem to announce Proust prophetically when he writes in the *Essai*: "If now some bold novelist, tearing the cunningly woven cloth of our conventional self, shows us beneath this apparent logic a fundamental absurdity, under this juxtaposition of simple states an infinite penetration of a thousand diverse impressions which have already ceased to be at the moment when we name them, we praise him for having known us better than we knew ourselves" (101). And in *La Pensée et le mouvant* in 1934, speaking of the difficulty which philosophy experienced at the time when he was writing the *Essai* in reentering "the flux of inner life," Bergson, who since that time had read Proust, makes a clear allusion to the latter which is like a discreet homage from the great philosopher to the great writer. "May one not say that the novelist and the observer of the social scene had gone further in this direction than the philosopher? Perhaps, but it was only in certain places, under the pressure of necessity, that they had broken through the barrier; not one of them had as yet had the idea of going methodically *in search of lost time*" (27–28).

In *Les Deux Sources de la morale et de la religion*, besides, at more than one point, we discover ideas that the philosopher seems to owe to Proust. For example, when he asks while analyzing the passion of love: "Is pleasure really its aim? *Or might it not equally well be suffering?*", one thinks of everything Proust has written about suffering in love. In the same way, this distinction which Bergson establishes between the two kinds of emotions, the one powerless and following on an idea, the other creative and without apparent cause, is singularly reminiscent of the distinction which Proust establishes between the voluntary memory or impression and the involuntary memory or impression. Involuntary memory also is of an emotional order and is the only one to be creative. This idea, in any case, is one of the most important in the Proustian "philosophy" and Proust could have subscribed without reserve to these reflections by Bergson: "Whoever undertakes literary composition has been in a position to recognize the difference between intelligence left to its own resources and intelligence consumed by the inner fire of a unique and original emotion, born from a coincidence between the author and his subject, that is to say from an intuition. In the first instance the mind works without any enthusiasm, combining ideas long since embedded in words, which society supplies in a solid state. In the second, it seems that the materials furnished by the intelligence are first melted down and that afterwards they solidify once more in ideas which are molded this time by the mind itself . . . , etc . . . " (43). Finally the explanation which Bergson gives us, still in this same work, of the understanding of a work of art which had not at first been understood, is exactly, but in new terms, the one that Proust had already put forward:[7] "In a financial speculation what makes the initial idea a good one is the success of the enterprise. Something of the same sort takes place in artistic creation, with this difference that success, if it finally comes to the work which at first had shocked people, *depends on a transformation of the taste of the public effected by the work itself . . .*" (74).

So many similarities, and on such important points, and sometimes even certain similarities in style, do not however permit us to conclude that Bergson influenced Proust, a least not in any very definite way. We do not wish to claim that a man of Proust's intelligence would have read Bergson without learning something from him—anymore, as we have seen, than Bergson read Proust without learning something from him. But Proust's approach to the subjects he treated, not to mention his deep-seated intellectual tendencies, were not fashioned in any way by Bergson. What is at issue here is the agreement of two great minds, and these agreements are not so very rare in the history of thought, nor so very surprising in themselves because they are simply the result of responding in the same way to the truth.

When E-J. Bois interviewed Proust in 1913, Proust told him that his book could be understood as an attempt at a series of novels about the unconscious: "I would not be at all ashamed," he added, "to say Bergsonian novels if I believed this to be the case, for in every epoch it happens that literature has tried—after the event of course—to attach itself to the reigning philosophy. But this would not be exact, for my work is dominated by the distinction between involuntary and voluntary memory, a distinction which not only does not figure in the philosophy of M. Bergson but is even contradicted by it."

We know that in *Matière et mémoire* Bergson distinguishes between two kinds of memory: a corporeal, mechanical pseudo-memory which he names *habit-memory* and an example of which he gives as the act of learning by heart, and true memory, the *individual memory*, precise, attached to a specific moment in time, unique and, above all, incapable of being repeated. Now Bergsonian memory originates in the will. Does Bergson not say, even in the *Essai*, that an effort of will suffices to plunge us into the depths of the inner self, into duration? (p. 105). This means that it is very different from Proustian affective memory which is primarily involuntary. This is why the distinction established by Bergson between habit-memory and pure memory is not subscribed to by Proust who tells us that his own distinction, that between voluntary memory and involuntary memory, "is the only true one" (*Lettres de Marcel Proust à René Blum*, 60). Besides this it is, according to him, "contradicted" by Bergson's philosophy. Unfortunately, he does not offer any further explanations and he leaves it to his commentators to explicate this point. Now Proust, as we believe, was not the kind of man to utter a word at random—particularly in an interview for which he seems to have prepared his terms and weighed them well.[8]

If we look closely at his question we perceive that the possibility of an involuntary affective memory, in the style of Proust, seems difficult to reconcile with the psychology of Bergson. According to this latter, the mind stores all our memories and these remain within us constantly at our disposal and constantly exerting pressure on the present. This action of our past memories is never identical because the mass of memories never ceases to grow. It is one of the reasons for which, as we have said, the present—at least in the deep inner self—is also never quite the same. In this deep inner self everything melts into everything. Obviously, in order to be able to talk about duration one is obliged to distinguish between a "before" and an "after." But Bergson does not let this consideration stop him; the lasting self, he observes, does not need ". . . to forget the former states; it is sufficient that in recalling these states it should not juxtapose them to the present state as one might juxtapose one dot to another but that it should organize them on its own terms, as it happens when we remember, melted together, as one might say, the notes of a melody" (*Essai*, 76). These notes succeed each other, but nevertheless we perceive them inside each other. "One can therefore," he concludes, "conceive of succession without differentiation . . ." (77). In short, Bergson opposes, in favor of duration, his conception of qualitative multiplicity to the usual quantitative conception of multiplicity. But in this purely qualitative succession in which the present never repeats the past, how can a moment of our past be resuscitated? How can one, even, distinguish "moments" in our past except under the effect of present needs on the (psychologically) abstract level of useful action. It is a fact that Bergsonian memory, even if it allows us to remember a unique moment of our past, can only do so in an abstract manner. There is no notion in Bergsonian philosophy of any possibility of *reliving* in the present a real moment of our past self: ". . . deep psychological facts," so Bergson himself says, "reach consciousness once only never to reappear" (*Essai*, 166). In Bergson's hypothesis, this concrete identity between two moments of our psychological life which is produced in Proustian involuntary memory cannot take place.

The only concrete action of the past, according to Bergson, is the global action which it constantly exerts on the present.[9] For Marcel Proust, on the contrary, the largest part of our past only exists for us, at each moment of our lives, in a virtual state. "It is, no doubt, the existence of our body, which we may compare to a vase enclosing our spiritual nature, that induces us to suppose that all our inner wealth, our past joys, all our sorrows, are perpetually in our possession. Perhaps it is equally inexact to suppose that they escape or return. In any case if they remain within us, for most of the time it is in an unknown region where they are of no use to us, and where even the most ordinary are crowded out by memories of a different kind, which preclude any simultaneous occurrences of them in our consciousness. But if the context of sensations in which they are preserved is recaptured, they acquire in turn the same power of installing alone in us the self that originally lived them" (*Sod.*, 1:178; *RTPK*, 2:784).

What is involved, as we have already observed, is that Proust does not conceive of the structure of the mind in the same way as Bergson. Without denying a certain continuity which one might call noumenal and which is deduced, inferred rather than directly perceived, he considers our phenomenal self as discontinuous and complex to the same extent as the body. It is even under those conditions, for him, that the qualitative can enter our life. It is contained in each of the instants of our life as in the cells of a honey-comb. Bergson connects quality with continuity and it is doubtless because this quality risks disappearing in continuity that he immediately associates change as closely as possible with it, so that for him lived, moving time, as we recognize it in ourselves, that is, duration, is quality *par excellence*. Proust, in contrast, connects quality with discontinuity and complexity. It seems to be explained by elements which compose it. His way of treating his subjects, borrowing in order to create a character, a village, or a piece of music diverse materials from diverse sources, drawing for example to create Vinteuil's Sonata on musical impressions which have come to him from musicians as diverse as Saint-Saëns, César Franck, Wagner, Schubert, Fauré (see the dedication of *Du côté de chez Swann* to M. J. de Lacretelle reproduced in M. Georges Gabory's *Essai sur Marcel Proust*), this way of composing proves that for him quality is obtained by addition, by the combination of simpler elements. And since it does not seem, in other respects, that the great laws of the mind which constitute one of his chief objects of research have only, for him as for Bergson, a practical value, relative to our needs, we must acknowledge that he considers the individual or the qualitative as in no way incompatible with the existence of universal laws and the most rigorous determinism.[10]

One may wonder whether Bergson by substituting a "qualitative" multiplicity, without parts, that is to say by substituting duration for distinct and quantitative multiplicity, is not causing purely and simply the idea of multiplicity to disappear. For Marcel Proust, in any case, there is no change except by substitutions of the elements or cells. Change is explained by the mechanistic hypothesis. There does not seem to be any other way of explaining it. But Bergson maintains the opposite, he invokes intuition and, to speak truly, he rejects the mechanistic method of explanation. A mechanistic psychology, that is to say a psychology which would present to us the concrete, living self "as an association of terms which being distinct from each other, are juxtaposed in a homogenous setting" would, he thinks, find itself confronted with "insurmountable difficulties" (*Essai*, 106). In particular, it would be unable to explain the problem of freedom and invention in its positive aspect.

It is not our place in this work to decide who is right. Let us limit ourselves to observing that this is a point on which a serious conflict separates the two thinkers. We are very close to the deep philosophical tendencies of the two men. They agree, as we have seen, on the value which it is appropriate to attach to spiritual realities and more particularly to the riches which lie within us. We have said above that Bergson had given a philosophical basis to quality. We might have done better to write, but it really comes to the same thing, that he had given a philosophical basis to introspection. It is constantly by introspection that Bergson proceeds in his investigation—and in full awareness of what he is doing, since duration, the qualitative, the real can never be grasped except by looking within ourselves. Proust arrives at the same conclusion. But having reached this point, the two thinkers diverge. There is in Proust, in fact, a Cartesian, a convinced mechanist. In contrast, the entire philosophy of Bergson is in a sense, as we know, an attempt to set limits to the claims of mechanism.

Bergson does not call in question the legitimacy nor the profundity of mechanistic explanations in the sciences which deal with inert matter.

There they even reach the absolute (*L'Evolution créatrice*, Introd., iv). But he maintains a separate place for the sciences of life and of the mind. In this domain the mechanistic explanations elaborated by the intelligence are no longer valid, or at least they no longer attain the real, the absolute. In order to know life and the mind, which are purely qualitative realities, one must use another method of investigation—that is intuition, which we have already discussed. The signs of such a division in the field of our knowledge are not to be found in Proust. For him determinism is universal. Psychological facts are treated by him according to positive methods. He seeks out the laws which govern them, and in his aesthetic he has expressly allotted a considerable place to the general laws which experience reveals to us.

Doubtless Proust was fully aware that our intelligence was limited. He is even in agreement with Bergson twice over on this point; first of all by recognizing his failure to foresee things—and secondly by recognizing that poetic invention has its source not in itself but in the instinct of the artist, his sensibility. Proust and Bergson are both in agreement in admitting that the new cannot be deduced from the known—and that in order to attain it one must place oneself within it from the start, by an operation of the mind that the one names intuition and the other instinct, and which, for the one as for the other, is not purely intellectual, but, from the start, of an affective or feeling kind.

It is for this reason that intelligence cannot be the faculty of poetic invention. The function of the poet consists of attaining something new, something qualitative. Proust is willing to agree, like Bergson (and he even seems in this instance to have borrowed this idea from Bergson) that intelligence cannot grasp quality.

However, this fact is not explained in the same way by the two of them. For Proust it is due to the discontinuity of life, while it is due to its qualitative continuity for Bergson. The failure of the intelligence is due for the former to the conditions (discontinuity) in which it operates. For the second it results from the *given*, from the (qualitative) nature of the objects which are subject to its interpretation. The failure is irremediable for Bergson. For Marcel Proust it can to a certain extent be overcome. For him the intelligence is the victim of an illusion which can be explained by a psychological law. But for all that he does not question its universal value nor the possibility of formulating everything in intellectual terms which are perfectly adequate for their object.

If the intelligence cannot grasp quality at least it is the intelligence which must finally express it. The intelligence is always the ultimate judge and it is not possible to dispute its competence. What separates Bergson from Proust in this instance is, in short, what one could call the anti-intellectualist tendency of the former. We do not believe that it would be fair to treat Bergson as essentially anti-intellectualist. Bergson's philosophy, like that of Descartes, is a philosophy which did not achieve a rigorous unity. Besides, Bergson did not wish to give his thought a too determinate form. He has even told us that he could not, that he should not do this. But there is in him an anti-intellectualist tendency as there is a voluntarist tendency in Descartes. To pinpoint this anti-intellectualist tendency is not easy.

We discover it in his claim to perceive the most profound means of investigation of reality outside the intelligence. It is in *L'Evolution créatrice* that this thesis is expounded most rigorously. In it intuition is identified with a sort of instinct, with a sympathetic power, and Bergson seems to yield to a sort of intuitivism of the unconscious, to the affective, irrational forces of the individual. But it is important to pay attention to the fact that Bergson himself has warned us (148) that he had exaggerated a little, in order to make himself clearer, the opposition which exists between instinct and intelligence. He also warns us that there exists around intelligence a kind of fringe of instinct or intuition (*Les Deux Sources*, 226), which if judiciously utilized will allow us to penetrate psychological phenomena. It is true that it is still instinct which is involved, and an instinct which is described as being different in nature from the intelligence. However, Bergson does not deny that in its own domain—that of the sciences which study inert matter—intelligence reaches the greatest possible depth. He even concedes that ". . . an intelligent being has within himself the wherewithal to go beyond himself" (164), and that instinct, which is capable of going further than intelligence, nevertheless remains inert and incurious. Consequently it needs intelligence to give it the necessary "jolt" to make it break free from the special object to which it is attached (193, 215).

It is nevertheless true that intelligence emerges from *L'Evolution créatrice* with a very diminished status.

But should we judge Bergson's conception of the intelligence by *L'Evolution créatrice* alone? Bergson seems to have hesitated, at bottom, between this narrow conception of intelligence and the intellectual life and another broader conception which sheds light on his philosophy but which he has never explicitly defined. In *L'Essai sur les données immédiates* does he not say that the deep inner self includes not only emotions and feelings but also ideas, the most profound and the most personal ideas—the superficial self, located in space, abstract, consisting, in contrast, of the ideas which we have not assimilated or "that we have neglected to maintain and which have dried up from neglect" (102–03).[11]

This very broad and in no way anti-intellectualist conception of the intelligence also seems to inspire Bergson's remarkable articles on *L'Effort intellectuel* in 1902 and on *L'Introduction à la métaphysique* in 1903. But with *L'Evolution créatrice* in 1907, Bergson suddenly makes up his mind and his way of seeing things becomes strangely narrower. What had happened? We will not attempt to elucidate this point in detail. But the discovery of instinct as an activity "sui generis" of life and of the mode of causality which characterizes it assuredly obliged Bergson to eliminate intelligence from our deep inner life and to limit it to a type of external and superficial activity. Suddenly intelligence was denied all comprehension of the phenomena of the inner life and indeed of life at all. Suddenly it was banished to the sharply defined precinct of clear consciousness—the domains of the subconscious and the unconscious becoming those of instinct.[12] That meant making intelligence into a superficial and even artificial faculty. Therefore in order to correct what was too rigid and too unreal in his conception, Bergson pointed out to us that "every real intelligence is penetrated by instinct" just as "every concrete instinct contains an admixture of intelligence" (*E. C.*, 148). It nevertheless remained true that this association, in either case, constituted a simple mixture of heterogenous elements whose "collaboration" was, moreover, left unexplained.

So it is that *L'Evolution créatrice* appears to be an anti-intellectualist work and that Bergson looks like an anti-intellectualist when one judges him by it. However, this anti-intellectualist position does not correspond in any way to certain deep aspirations of Bergson. In this intuition identified with an instinct which has "become disinterested, conscious of itself, able to reflect on its object and to expand it indefinitely" (192),[13] he will be on his guard not to see (as one might expect and as some have believed) an extra-intellectual or irrational faculty. In a letter to Jacques Chevalier, he declares that "by taking the word intelligence in the very broad sense which Kant attributes to it", he could "call intuition *intellectual . . .*" ("Nouvelles littéraires" of December 15, 1928—an issue dedicated to Bergson. M.-J. Chevalier dates this letter, obviously by mistake, April 28, 1929!) He adds: "But I would rather call it *supra-intellectual,* because I have felt it necessary to restrict the meaning of the word *intelligence,* and because I limit this name to the totality of the discursive faculties of the mind." Truth to tell, it is difficult to see what this intelligence which is broader than the one described in *L'Evolution créatrice* might be. By making intelligence different in nature from instinct, he has in any case assigned insurmountable limits to intelligence. But we must understand Bergson. What he wants is to know. What intelligence does not provide him with, he wants all the same to attain. He believes he can attain it with intuition, and it is in this sense that it is intellectual for him—and not because it would participate in the nature of intelligence. Bergson is restricted by the overly rigid opposition that he instituted between intelligence and intuition in *L'Evolution créatrice*.[14] Therefore he gives to intuition, which participates in the nature of instinct, even when it is intelligence which forces it to arise from its torpor, even when it is intelligence which prepares the ground for it,[15] the name of *supra-intellectual.*

Doubtless Bergson believed that he had resolved all these difficulties in *Les Deux Sources de la morale et de la religion,* where he puts forward a new hierarchy of the faculties of the mind. He establishes a distinction between three levels of the mind: 1) The infra-intellectual level, the level of pure statics, the level of habit and social existence.[16] 2) The level of intelligence. 3) The supra-intellectual level which is that of intuition. In this way Bergson finally places intelligence above social existence. Intelligence deserves this promotion for services rendered to intuition, for this kind of revolution which it was able to bring about by smashing the framework of social existence where consciousness had dozed off in order to march onward once more towards the supra-intellectual level. It is situated exactly midway between the infra- and the supra-intellectual, midway between immobility and movement. It is the gesture by whomever means to move; it is a preliminary gesture but not yet movement. But why does Bergson place above the intellectual level a supra-intellectual level? Because he has to explain movement, movement which is everywhere: in life, in the evolution of society, and in the mind. Because in movement there is something more than in the individual steps which seem to compose it. Intellectual explanations are necessarily explanations *a posteriori*. Intelligence always intervenes when everything has been accomplished and then, in a triumphant manner, it explains the whole by the parts, the effects by the causes. But in the movement which engenders everything one could not distinguish between the parts or between the effects in the causes. A new kind of music, a new way of feeling can easily be defined after the event. But it would have been impossible before they came into being to create them starting with the elements of which they are composed. That is because in the whole there is something more than in the parts. In the same way, the supra-intellectual contains "all the intellectuality one could wish," but it is in the manner of a unity which may be supposed to include and go beyond a multiplicity which cannot be considered as its equivalent (62; see also 270–71). For example a supra-intellectual, that is to say mystical, ethic, is not inexpressible in terms of intelligence for Bergson—no more than a scientific psychology is impossible, as he says in *Essai*. The real impediment is that it cannot be integrally expressed in this way. There is always something that evades reason. And this something is movement in its unity. Mystical ethics cannot be deduced from rational ethics. It can be demonstrated after the event, but its superiority "is lived before being represented and in any case it could not be demonstrated afterwards if it had not already been felt" (56). In short, Bergsonian philosophy consists in the last resort of maintaining that there is in the ground of being something which refuses to be reduced to analysis. Doubtless after the event everything can be reduced to intellectual terms. We can even believe that the reduction is total, but if we do we are mistaken, for the reality that one grasps by doing this is an inert and in short incomplete reality. To grasp it again in its completeness we must, thanks to intuition, rediscover in ourselves the unity of the creative movement.[17]

Here we come into immediate contact with what we have called, with the utmost caution, Bergson's anti-intellectualism. This element which cannot be reduced to analysis, even after the event, is certainly an irrational element. It is all very well for Bergson to consider the intuition, which grasps the real in its entirety, as a supra-intellectual faculty, but the word intellectual is nothing but a label. Bergsonism is not a total irrationalism, but it still considers that there is a residue of essential irrationality in every non-material reality.[18]

By dint of the same observation we also come into immediate contact with what separates him from Proust. For the latter too, it is quite true that truth cannot generally be attained directly by abstract intelligence, the intelligence which reasons and deduces. Deduction is not a fertile operation, nor one which allows one to invent anything. For that one has to turn to other forces: i.e. intuitive forces. Proust was aware of this as much in art as in the psychology of everyday life. Aesthetic truth is grasped by the instinct of the artist, in the coincidences from which arise involuntary memories and aesthetic truths. Even psychological truths are based on our own lives. And if intelligence perceives them more rapidly, and extracts them itself directly, at least it cannot create them ex-nihilo and it has to wait for life to pass by with its joys and sorrows to grasp them. Finally in our own lives we fail just as often to foresee what others will do and understand their motives as to tell what our own reactions will be. Even if reality is governed by necessity, Proust thinks, it is still not exactly predictable. (*Pr.*, 1:10. What is at issue is a mistake of Bloch's "His mistake was, however, perfectly excusable, for the truth, even if it is logically necessary, is not always foreseeable as a whole" *RTPK*, 3:1). However, reality is *governed by necessity*. That is to say that it can be understood. And it is not an evil for intelligence to be thwarted by it. It is, in fact, useful that it should be intelligence itself that realizes the importance of experience: that is how we arrive at knowledge (*A.D.*, 1:14). In the same way, in art, intelligence comes in at the end to translate what imagination and sensibility have discovered into "equivalents of intelligence." For Marcel Proust invention has not reached its culmination until what has been felt has been completely expressed. So with him there is no irrational residue, but a great movement towards total illumination.

It is because Bergson and Proust do not agree on this point that the problem of artistic expression does not present itself to them in identical terms. As the areas of obscurity which exist within us remain, in so far as they are qualitative, irreducible for Bergson, it follows that for him to express is always to falsify. Thus the only mode of expression which is possible for him is inadequate—that is suggestion. The artist presents what he has to say in such a way as "to make people suspect the extraordinary and illogical nature of the subject he projects." He has put into external expression something "of this contradiction of this mutual penetration" which constitutes the essence of inner life. It is only on this condition that he places us "in our own presence" (*Essai*, 101); even so he only succeeds imperfectly.

For Marcel Proust, art tends to expression as its goal. Far from truth being realized in confused sensation, it is with words that shed light on it that it enters the world. When the young Marcel wonders in *Du coté de chez Swann* what is hidden beneath the impressions he receives from the three steeples in the neighborhood of Combray, he perceives that it is words. Let us take another look at this already quoted passage from *Le Temps retrouvé:* "In fact, both in the one case and in the other, whether I was concerned with impressions like the one which I had received from the sight of the steeples of Martinville or with reminiscences like that of the unevenness of the two steps or the taste of the madeleine, the task was to interpret the given sensations as signs of so many laws and ideas, by trying to think—that is to draw forth from the shadow—what I had merely felt, by trying to convert it into its spiritual equivalent. And this method, which seemed to me the sole method, what was it but the creation of a work of art?" (*T.R.*, 2:24; *RTPK*, 3:912). Art for him—even though it has the qualitative as its object—aims at transporting onto the conscious level, the level of intelligence, the potentialities of obscure consciousness. Expression, as an ascent to consciousness, is a birth, not in the least a miscarriage as is to a certain extent the case for Bergson.[19]

What is inexpressible in intuition is a torment to Proust up to the time when he liberates himself through the work of art. His readers will remember that one day while he is taking a walk in the neighborhood of Combray what he sees has a very strong aesthetic and emotional effect on him. But at that moment he can only express it by shouting "zut, zut, zut!" and laying violently about him with his walking stick. "Thus it is that most of our attempts to translate our innermost feelings do no more than relieve us of them by drawing them out in a blurred form which does not help us to identify them" (*Sw*, 1:144; *RTPK* 1:169). To be unable to express oneself is for him a form of impotence. The power and value of an artist is revealed in his style. It is thanks to style, to its perfection that what is qualitative—and theoretically inexpressible in our impressions—can be revealed to clear consciousness.

Marcel Proust is a man who in the course of his whole life, never considered anything more important than truth. "Truth is always salutary," he says (*Corr.*, 3:30), which for him is as much as to say that it is thought. Bergson, whose mind showed in many ways an affinity with Proust's, did not show as much trust as Proust in pure thought, and that is another proof of the irrationalist tendency of his mind. In the last resort, it is as oriented towards action that he shows what he considers to be the highest form of mind. Mysticism is, in fact, "an entering into contact and in consequence a partial coincidence with the creative effort manifested by life" (*Les Deux Sources*, 235). It consists, in short, of getting once more into touch with the vital current which will carry it further and even up to God. When the soul arrives at this height, it discovers in itself "a superabundance of life," an "immense impetus" (248); and nothing is less surprising because it has reached the very sources of life. Mysticism finds its goal in action. Doubtless it is also truth. But it is a truth which is not self-sufficient and which carries away the one who possesses it in a great rush of proselytism. Mysticism is a form of love, a love which would like "with the help of God, to perfect the creation of the human species and to make of humanity what it would have been at the start if it had been able to take on its final form without the help of man himself" (51). So mysticism is more than a form of knowledge. Ecstasy, that is to say contemplation, is only a halfway stage in the ascent of the mystic (see pp. 246–48 in *Les Deux Sources*). The supreme object of the mystic is to raise the world and humanity up to a new being. He can only fulfill himself completely in action—in an action, moreover, which, if we interpret Bergson correctly, is not outward but inward and in a way organic.

This way of seeing things is completely foreign, if not opposed, to Proust's tendencies. Action for him is always more or less scattering and agitation. It leads to a loss of spirituality. It achieves nothing. Only thought has a real effect. But this way of looking at things was natural for a philosopher who had refused to suppose that the creative impulse, whether it be life, the progress of spontaneous consciousness or invention, could be fully expressed in ideas, subordinated to the law of conservation of energy and in sum reducible to the principle of identity. But by establishing that the movement which carries all beings along in their evolution is synthetic or as he says "creative," he abandons to a certain extent the postulate of universal intelligibility[20] to which Proust remains faithful.

M. E. Burnet put it very well when he said: "Proust belongs to the lineage of those great writers whose sensibility makes appeals to intelligence. To feel is to begin to understand. Proust is not at all mystical, he is an intellectualist" (*Essences*, 20).[21]

Notes

1. Published in 1907.

2. *Corr.* 4:38 and 35. It is true that in *Les Plaisirs et les jours* he declares that certain pages, that is the oldest ones, date from 1890–1891. But it is possible that he was making himself out to be older than he was out of a young man's dread of being underestimated.

3. On this point, see particularly the *Introduction à la métaphysique*.

4. See his two lectures "La Perception du changement" in *La Pensée et le mouvant*.

5. Bergsonian philosophy may be considered, in a sense, as a solution to the problem of the existence of synthetic judgments posited by Kant. It is being itself, duration or change, by whatever name one wishes to call it, which is synthetic. The problem of synthetic judgments vanishes of its own accord. Their legitimacy no longer raises any difficulty. In thinking synthetically, one thinks being itself, one thinks intuitively. And in *L'Introduction à la métaphysique* Bergson notes that precisely this is the way to get rid of the apparently irreducible opposition between thesis and antithesis "I shall never be able to imagine," he observes, "how one can envisage it from the dual point of view of the black and the white." "Doctrines which have a basis in intuition," he adds, "escape the Kantian critique precisely insofar as they are intuitive" (253).

6. However, he discerns, in *La Pensée et le mouvant* a task which is proper to philosophy. "But if literature," he remarks, "had as its function to undertake in this way the study

of the soul in the concrete, using individual examples, the duty of philosophy seemed to us to be to establish in this area the several conditions of immediate direct observation, of one-self by oneself" (27–28). But already in *Le Rire* he observed another distinctive characteristic of the philosopher: whereas the artist attains reality by a natural detachment "which is immediately manifested by an original manner, so to speak, of seeing, hearing or thinking," the detachment of the philosopher is "willed, reasoned, systematic" (158).

7. See p. 77 of [*Le Progrès spirituel dans "La Recherche" de Marcel Proust*].

8. M. Etienne Burnet, in the most profound study (for Floris Delattre's study, in the *Etudes Bergsoniennes*, seems to us to be really too one-sided), which has been made of the relationship between Proust and Bergson, (*Essences:* Marcel Proust et le Bergsonisme) reduces the Proustian distinction between the two memories to that of Bergson (181). Moreover he does not give any reason to support this thesis which Proust opposed beforehand, with good reason. M. Emeric Fiser, in a study on "the role of memory in the works of Marcel Proust and Henri Bergson" published after "L'Esthétique de Marcel Proust," considers that if involuntary memory has no place in Bergson's psychology, the reason for that is that the latter is essentially a psychology of action, directed towards the future and only appealing to the past "to the extent to which it is useful for the preparation of this future" (183). But this statement is only correct for the socialized "superficial self" and M. Fiser himself contradicts further on what he has just stated by pointing out that the case is not completely the same in the instance of duration, that is to say in the deep inner self. Let us add that it is only by adopting a disinterested attitude that the artist and the philosopher, according to Bergson, can reach the underlying reality. It is because it is determined by need that intelligence is relative. But it is possible to attain the absolute, precisely by making an effort to free oneself from need. From this point of view, therefore, Bergson's philosophy is in no way a philosophy of action. It is even quite the opposite. In another connection, M. Fiser is doubtless right to say that the conception of the real is not the same in Proust and Bergson and that in the latter it is directed towards the future (which does not necessarily mean towards action). What is real for Bergson is, in fact, whatever is in motion. But is the past, in contrast, the primordial reality for Proust? We do not think so. Reality for Proust, who in this is quite different from Bergson, is outside of *Time*.

9. Doubtless Bergson could have replied that by plunging into the depths of present duration we could discover this past in it, because its action makes itself felt in it without our being aware of the fact. But it is not in this way that involuntary memories appear. They are not at our disposal at any and every moment. They are bound to a "self" which they cause to be reborn in us. In short, contrary to what Bergson wanted, it seems that his "memory" is unable to send us back in duration, in time, while Proust's involuntary memory performs this operation extremely well.

10. In the deterministic hypothesis the qualitative can be understood very well. It takes the form of the point of intersection of an infinite number of causal series.

11. At the time when he writes *L'Essai* the two "selves" are coextensive to some extent, like the obverse and the reverse of the same coin. In reply to the reproach of doubling the self and thus reintroducing in us quantitative multiplicity, Bergson in fact states as follows: "It is the same self which perceives distinct states and which *then concentrating its attention to a greater extent* will see its states melt into each other as do icicles under prolonged contact with a hand" (105). It is we who underline.

12. That is why the terms "consciousness" and "intelligence" are no longer interchange-able as they were in *L'Essai* where he writes: "Consciousness tormented by an insatiable longing to make distinctions substitutes the symbol for reality, or else only perceives reality through the symbol" (97). *Consciousness* is here a synonym of *clear consciousness*. Later Bergson will say "intelligence"—for instinct in *L'Evolution créatrice* is a form of consciousness, of a different nature ("annulled" consciousness—and not simply "non-existent" (156), he specifies).

13. "That an effort of this kind is not impossible," he adds, "is already demonstrated by the existence in man of an aesthetic faculty juxtaposed to normal perception" (192).

14. And without doubt he clings to this distinction because it permits him to overcome the objection which Kant opposed to the possibility of metaphysics. Our intellectual knowledge, Bergson thinks, only becomes relative if it claims to represent life to us. Taking a block impression of inert matter, it can represent the latter faithfully. It cannot represent life, because that would be the equivalent of representing the stereotyper who took the impression (E. C., iv). It is to intuition that he will assign the mission of representing life. It is true that this theory does not accord very well with L'Introduction à la métaphysique, in which Bergson resolves the Kantian objection by recognizing that even scientific invention, like every other kind of invention, implies intuition.

15. See what Bergson himself said on this subject to the Société francaise de philosophie (Lalande's Philosophical Vocabulary (article: intuition). And in L'Introduction à la métaphysique he points out to us that intuition, which has "nothing mysterious" about it, springs from the accumulation of materials.

16. Which corresponds "symmetrically" in man to certain animal instincts" (62). Instinct seems to be situated on the infra-intellectual level. Intuition is instinct, but an instinct which has become conscious. On page 267, Bergson considers instinct a debased intuition. It seems that he "devalued" instinct in Les Deux Sources.

17. This is why, in L'Introduction à la métaphysique, Bergson points out that "from intuition one can proceed to analysis but not from analysis to intuition" (229).

18. It is in this residue that one can see the principle of the mysticism at which Bergson finally arrives in Les Deux Sources. His mysticism is certainly not any more total than his irrationalism. It has the same origin. It makes no difference for this mysticism to have no anti-intellectual intention (nor even any opposition to positive science), but a certain appeal to the deep inner life (see the interview conducted by H. G. in Les nouvelles littéraires of December 15, 1928). That is what it is, in spite of its author's intentions, for it is not sufficient to want a thing to be thus or so in order to make it into what one desires in actual fact.

19. And for M. Paul Valéry—so far as Bergson is concerned, however, none better than he, in L'Effort intellectuel, had shown how intuition, the dynamic schema, is transformed into invention, into precise images.

20. Perhaps this is why it is not true to say, like M. J. Chevalier in the issue of Les nouvelles littéraires quoted above, or like M. E. Burnet (Essences, 209), that Bergson's philosophical intuition can be equated with Descartes's intuition of certainty. Psychologically it is the same phenomenon—but Descartes considers it to be entirely rational—not so Bergson!

21. But he is not, in contradiction to what Burnet adds, an intellectualist "in the manner of Bergson"!

Proust's Protagonist as a "Beacon"   Philip Kolb*

"Ces grands novateurs sont les seuls vrais classiques et forment une suite presque continue."[1]

There are five characters in A la recherche du temps perdu whom Proust seems to place in a favored category and to view in a somewhat different light from the others. Critical studies have been devoted to some of

*From L'Esprit créateur 5, no. 1 (Spring 1965): 38–47. Reprinted by kind permission of the author and of the editor of the journal.

them individually, but these five characters have not, to my knowledge, been studied as a group, nor has their interrelationship been explored. The present study is an attempt to determine the nature and the significance of their relationship to one another.

The one about whom the least has been written, although the most problematical, is the protagonist. The first problem that he presents is the question of establishing his identity. According to the Webster-Merriam unabridged international dictionary, third edition, a protagonist is "the chief character of a novel or story in or around whom the action centers." By such a definition, the protagonist of Proust's novel would seem to be his narrator, since the plot of *Le Temps perdu* centers on the narrator's experiences in a quest that leads ultimately to the discovery of his true vocation.

Objections might, however, be raised. The narrator of this novel is so modest and unobtrusive that he seems at times to disappear from the scene altogether. That is precisely what he does during the episode of the first part entitled *Un Amour de Swann*, where events are recounted that occur before the narrator's birth. The novel does, of course, embrace his own story. And yet, in the course of thousands of pages, so few hints are interspersed about his physical appearance that it is impossible to imagine what sort of man he is, at least physically. We learn that he is frail and suffers from asthma and insomnia, but little else about him except his attitudes toward love and literature.

While he observes many people, he himself takes little part in their activities. Proust's reputation is based in part on the splendid portrait gallery with which he has endowed French literature. His gifts for characterisation have earned him a place alongside Saint-Simon, the great memorialist of Louis XIVth's court. Proust's characters, like Dickens', have entered, during the past fifty years, the vocabulary of the reading public. People are wont to refer familiarly to the domineering Mme Verdurin, eccentric old Aunt Léonie, the ambiguous Baron de Charlus, and many others. But it would hardly occur to us to characterize someone by comparing him to Proust's narrator. Alongside of his other characters, the narrator seems pale and elusive, scarcely a character at all.

Indeed, it has even been suggested that the real protagonist of Proust's novel is not a character, but Time. His general title *A la recherche du temps perdu* would almost seem to support such a contention. While the words "A la recherche" announce that the novel is a quest, the remainder of the title indicates that the object of that quest is Time, time that is past and seems to have been lost or wasted, although ultimately the narrator will find a means of retrieving his wasted years by making them live again in a novel. In Proust's own words, as expressed in an interview published in *Le Temps* in 1913, his novel can be characterized as an attempt to "isolate" the "invisible substance of time."[2] He accomplishes his aim by showing us the many ways in which the passage of time affects individuals as well as a whole society. Undoubtedly Time does play its role in an impersonal way. But we can hardly call Time the protagonist except in a figurative or allegorical sense. Proust himself, in the interview just quoted, speaks of it as a substance. Strictly speaking, Time is a major theme of his novel, closely interwoven with that of Memory. While such themes form an interlocking network serving as a sort of sub-structure of the novel, the work also has a plot and characters in the traditional sense. So it would seem more logical to seek the protagonist among those characters. The only one of them who seems to fit our definition is the narrator. If the novel's action is the narrator's quest of a vocation, as we have said, then the narrator is the one on whom "the action centers." In fact he is the only character who holds our attention from the very beginning of the novel to the end, even if somewhat intermittently and at times from a far-off corner. Ultimately, as we shall see, he does acquire a new stature and achieves a status that better befits his importance as a protagonist.

If then we agree to designate the narrator as the key character, the question arises why he is so much less vividly portrayed than the others. Several reasons might explain this apparent anomaly. In the first place, when we look about us, unless we use a mirror, the visual impression we receive will necessarily exclude our own image. Then, too, the narrator's lack of participation in the actions he describes is due at least in part to his resemblance to the author, a semi-invalid who led a sedentary life. As we know, Proust was almost completely bed-ridden during the period of his novel's composition. There is, however, another reason which is, in my opinion, all the more plausible because it is based on aesthetics. If such a master of portraiture presents his narrator with such vague and imprecise traits, we can be assured that he does so with a purpose. The vast accumulation of notebooks Proust used in planning the novel show conclusively that he left nothing to improvisation. His purpose in this instance was in all probability to allow his reader to identify himself more readily with the narrator. It is evident that the less we know of his physical characteristics, the easier it is for us to imagine ourselves in his place.

The resemblance between author and narrator should not be misinterpreted to mean that I equate the two. True enough, the novel is written in the first person singular, and, as we have seen, certain particularities of the author are attributable to the narrator. From the very first, readers have assumed the novel was autobiographical. Yet Proust repeatedly denied having any intention to write such a novel. He was visibly annoyed when Montesquiou, congratulating him on some excerpts published in the *Figaro*, referred to them as recollections of childhood.[3] Proust feared that this aspect of his novel would be misconstrued. It did indeed contribute to the legendary figure of Proust as a snob and a social climber, a spineless individual who had squandered his youth in idleness. One critic, writing anonymously about the Goncourt prize novelists, referred to his *Temps perdu* as a "series of autobiographical novels," and went on to complain of the author's lack of will power, as if no valid distinction exists between him and the narrator.[4] Even among more recent critics, such notions recur persistently.

What then is the truth? Today we have sufficient documented information about Proust to distinguish fact from fiction. As usual with Proust, the answer on this point is not a simple one. But we can say that if, on the one hand, his narrator resembles him like a brother, there seem to be enough fictional elements to justify Proust's disclaimer of having written an autobiography. Consider for instance the narrator's lack of will power. In Proust's childhood and youth, he unquestionably did consider himself wanting in this respect. At about twenty years of age, answering a drawing-room album questionnaire, he put down as his "chief failing" *(principal défaut)*: "ne pas savoir, ne pas pouvoir 'vouloir'."[5] His concern about the problem is underlined by the fact that he read and quoted Ribot's treatise on *Les Maladies de la Volonté*.[6] So Proust's own insecurity in this respect *is* autobiographical.

Does this confirm the notion of a weak-willed Marcel Proust, an invertebrate molleycoddle? If it appears so, then perhaps we need to examine the facts more closely. For it can be shown that there is a discrepancy in that assumption about Proust. To some extent, the error is due to a failure to take into account the chronology of Proust's development. In his childhood and even later, he did torment himself about his lack of will power. Possibly he had reason to be concerned. During his year of military service, he complained of a difficulty in concentrating on his work. And his hesitancy in selecting a career is well known, although the fault here lay principally in the ideas of his parents. In his twenty-fifth year, he finally started to write his first novel. Again the results were equivocal. For, on the one hand, he began writing with great rapidity, and, while his pace slackened after about eighteen months, he continued working for four years, and did not abandon the novel until he had accumulated more than a thousand pages. On the other hand, he had failed to complete the work, or to impose upon it any unity of plot or consistent structural pattern. It could therefore be claimed that Proust, at the age of 28, when he abandoned his unfinished novel, still had to cope with problems of self-discipline. There were mitigating circumstances, and what he had accomplished was not negligible; still, the net result was admittedly a failure.

He had lost a battle, not a war. For his situation would be totally different just one decade later. If we speak of the Proust of the years 1909 to 1922, the inescapable facts are these. Here was a neurotic individual, beset by numerous ailments, some perhaps imaginary, other undoubtedly real and serious, who, despite ill health and other torments, conceived the plan for an exceedingly complex, ingenious and original novel. He proceeded to carry out that plan, and in executing it, proved himself endowed with impressive powers of mental concentration, as well as the physical stamina needed for the sustained effort of setting down on paper the thousands of pages that went into the numerous rough drafts corresponding to the various stages in the composition of *A la recherche du temps perdu*. Such a man was certainly no effete, spineless creature. His novel could never have been written had its author not possessed vast sources of hidden energy and an indomitable will.

From these facts, it becomes evident that the narrator of *Le Temps perdu* must indeed be distinguished from its author. It is even more essential to avoid another misconception, the assumption that the ideas and opinions expressed by the narrator in the course of the novel coincide at all times with those of Proust. He has expressed himself on this matter. In a letter to Jacques Rivière, he explains his intention of tracing the evolution of his narrator's ideas; in doing so, he has traced his errors and blunders, but feels no compulsion to point out that they *are* errors or blunders. Only at the end of the work, once the narrator has learned the lessons of life, will the ideas and beliefs of the author be disclosed. Proust cites the example of the disillusioned scepticism expressed by the narrator at the end of *Du côté de chez Swann*, pointing out that the conclusion will be exactly the contrary.[7] Only at the end does the point of view of the narrator merge with that of the author, somewhat as a double image, viewed in a stereoscope, gradually becomes a single image as it comes into focus. Evidently then, it is necessary to use extreme care in attributing to Proust any idea expressed by his narrator before the novel's conclusion. The title of his volume, *Le Temps retrouvé*, makes his intent perfectly clear in that respect. The so-called wasted years were not irretrievably lost, since they are finally regained, and their lessons utilized, in the creation of a work of literary art.

If now we direct our attention to the Proustian portrait gallery mentioned earlier, I believe it possible to discern a difference in Proust's attitude toward two sets of characters. There is, on the one hand, the majority of characters, and, on the other, a separate little group seeming to belong to a favored category. In the first, larger group, we find a variety of persons whom the narrator observes with a relentless, penetrating gaze, subjecting them sooner or later to the subtly disintegrating effects of his satire. His treatment of the more select group, however, shows little of this tendency, and appears marked by restraint. This is particularly true of the four full-length portraits of Vinteuil, La Berma, Elstir and Bergotte. These four seem to stand apart and above the rest.

If such is the case, there must be a reason. Proust's intention, as I see it, is to present idealized portraits of these four artists. Let us review the elements of each character that conform to such a purpose.

Vinteuil is at first seen through the eyes of indifferent townspeople, who think him to be a sad, timid, insignificant piano teacher, exceedingly prudish although obliged to close his eyes to the scandalous conduct of his daughter. Only after his death is his full stature as a composer recognized. His music finally reveals his true nature to have been the very opposite of what it had seemed in the eyes of his neighbors. His true character is marked not by sadness, shyness and timidity, but is, on the contrary, infused with vigor, boldness and the joy of creative endeavor (Pléiade ed., 1954, III, 254–255). He exemplifies what Proust designated as his "pre-pared" characters, that is, characters who, according to plan, turn out to be quite different from what we had been led to suppose. Vinteuil's music is associated, at first anonymously, with the themes of love and memory, playing the role of catalyst in connection with Swann's love for Odette. But later in the novel, his music has a much greater importance. For it causes the narrator to meditate on the true nature of art, and to realize that through it alone can an artist achieve a sort of immortality. He feels that all the joys he has known are as nothing compared to the joy Vinteuil ex-pressed in his music. In such a manner, Vinteuil's music inspires the narra-tor to dedicate himself to his art, and prepares the novel's *dénouement*.

Elstir represents Proust's ideal of a modern painter. His originality consists in his ability to reveal a special universe, or to enable us to see through his eyes, just as the oculist gives vision by means of his lenses. Vinteuil did the same by revealing an unknown universe of the audible world. Bergotte does the same in the realm of literature. And La Berma helps the narrator to understand the essence and nature of dramatic art in its highest manifestations. These four artists represent pre-eminence in their respective artistic domains. To borrow a metaphor from Proust's fa-vorite poet, Baudelaire, each one is a beacon: "C'est un phare allumé sur mille citadelles" [It is a beacon lit on a thousand citadels], dominating the approaches to the narrator's discovery of the nature of art, and his own mis-sion as an artist.

Perhaps we can learn something of Proust's intentions concerning these four characters if we compare them with earlier manifestations of the same types of characters in Proust's first novel, *Jean Santeuil*. There are some marked similarities between certain figures of the two novels, but there are also some distinct differences, which may prove even more sig-nificant. Let us first consider the parallel cases.

It will at once be apparent that Proust, when he wrote his first novel, had not yet conceived his fictional characters of the great composer or the great actress. It seems more than a coincidence that Sarah Bernhardt is mentioned several times, for she seems to have contributed much as an original model for La Berma in *Swann*.[8] It is curious that no important role in the early novel is attributed to a composer, since music had such impor-tance for Proust. To be sure, it is already associated in *Jean Santeuil* with the themes of love and memory, just as it will be in *Du coté de chez Swann*, where the *petite phrase* becomes the musical motif or "national anthem" of Swann's love for Odette. In the early novel, Proust identifies Saint-Saëns as the composer of the "petite phrase" (III, 225).

The closest parallels existing between characters of the two novels are the prototypes of an artist and of a writer. I mention them together because they seem to have undergone an odd crisscross mutation in passing from the early novel to the later one. We know that Proust has taken as his model for the writer C. the American painter Alexander Harrison, whom he had met in circumstances similar to those described in *Jean Santeuil*, in his hotel dining room at Beg-meil. He will use the same incident in *A l'ombre des jeunes filles en fleurs*. But there, the celebrity whom the narrator and his friend Saint-Loup meet in the dining room at Balbec has reverted to his original profession as a painter: Elstir. Conversely, in the early novel, there is a painter, but Proust calls him by the name which he will later give to his great writer: Bergotte. There are, in fact, portraits of several writers described with admiration in the early novel: in addition to C., there is Sylvain Bastelle, M. de Traves, and even the Countess Gaspard de Réveillon, the thinly veiled portrait of the poetess Countess de Noailles. If Proust had succeeded in finishing his novel, possibly he would have fused some of these sketches to make a single writer by the process of amalgamation that he was to use so frequently in his later work.

Now we come to the characters in *Jean Santeuil* who appear to belong to the same category of idealized portraits, but differ significantly from those of the later novel. The difference is that, although they are treated somewhat in the manner of the later "beacons," they are *not* artists. Perhaps most surprising of all is Couzon, the socialist leader (also called Craveil), for whom Proust's model was Jaurès.[9] Jean describes him as a great statesman and orator, the champion of justice and humanity. We see him in action, in a moving session at the Chamber of Deputies that follows rather closely an actual incident. There is, of course, no such character as Couzon in Proust's later novel. Jean Santeuil also expresses admiration verging on enthusiasm for Frédéric d'Utraine, a noble esthete and art collector, a sort of nineteenth-century version of the *honnête homme*. Swann comes the nearest to resembling this character. But Swann is subjected to a more critical viewpoint, and is shown to expend his energies in frivolous pursuits, incapable even of finishing his study on Vermeer. Swann is the man Proust might have become had he lacked will power. Swann is the opposite of a "beacon," unless he be the kind that acts not as an example but as a warning of the shoals of dilletantism.

Finally, there is the philosophy professor Beulier (also called Daufoy). Proust modeled him, we know, after his esteemed lycée professor Darlu, about whom we are today fully informed, thanks to the research of Henri Bonnet.[10]

The inclusion of these characters in the early novel is not difficult to explain. The posthumous novel is a potpourri of sketches taken at random of persons or incidents that Proust had observed. But these particular characters were possibly inspired, at least to some extent, by Emerson and Carlyle. For we know that *Jean Santeuil* was begun at the very period when its author was steeped in the works of these philosophers. About a year before he began the novel, we find him discovering Emerson's *Essays*, which he read with rapture. It was no doubt in that same year that he read *Representative Men* (in translation, since Proust did not read English). Carlyle's *On Heroes (Culte des Héros)* was one of the books Proust had with him on his trip to Beg-Meil, where he began his novel in September 1895. It would be only reasonable to assume, therefore, that Emerson's and Carlyle's essays dealing with statesmen, philosophers and poets contributed an impetus to Proust in creating his own portraits of such figures. It is nevertheless worth pointing out one difference between the heroes of the English and American philosophers and those of the young French writer. For Proust's are not historic figures; all are contemporaries, presented as fictional characters in contact with the narrator Jean Santeuil.

The question remains: why has Proust eliminated these heroes from the empyrean of his later novel? If the radical statesman were the only one missing, we might attribute his omission to disillusionment of the author about political life and its leaders. Such an interpretation would, however, leave unexplained the elimination of Beulier, the philosophy professor. Perhaps Proust had lost his admiration for Jaurès, but we have no reason to suppose the same is true for Darlu. The explanation is quite simple. The heroes of *Le Temps perdu* had of necessity to be artists. The sacrifice of the others was required for esthetic reasons bearing on the unity and artistic economy of the novel. And it is this difference between the early and the later novel that points to the meaning of the "beacons." The unfinished early novel helps us to discern their underlying significance. Proust, in transforming the elements of that work into his definitive novel, has rejected the idealized portraits of men who were not artists in order to show that art alone can lead the narrator to the goal of his quest. Only the "beacons" can light his path and show the way to a greater happiness. At first he had failed to see or understand their message. He had sought happiness in his love for Gilberte, in his friendship for Saint-Loup, in his infatuation for the Duchess de Guermantes, in his deeper but jealous love for Albertine. Each time he had found disillusionment; neither love nor friendship gave him lasting satisfaction. But a higher, more exhilarating joy than these could give him he found in the art of the masters. This joy then he would seek, by creating his own work of art, after the example of his beacons, Elstir, Vinteuil and the others. Thanks to them, he finds his true vocation.

The novel's conclusion has a deep mystical tonality. The novelist setting out to recapture his past is almost a modern transposition of the mediaeval knight in quest of the holy grail. Such passages are marked by an unmistakable religious sentiment, in which Proust consciously and consistently uses terms borrowed from the vocabulary of Catholicism. He manages to convey, in such instances, a profound, reverent sense of the beauty and mystery of the universe, as in the descriptions of the hawthorn bushes, the apple trees in blossom, the scent of lilacs after a storm, the many seascapes and effects of sunlight on land and water.

The narrator, at the end of the novel, achieves a new dimension in his relationship with the four artists he admires. Until then, they have towered above him and all the other characters of the novel. But once their example has illuminated him and guided him, and he finds his true vocation, he is transformed, and assumes a new role. The *dénouement* suggests that he will take his place alongside these beacons, these creative artists. Thus he is worthy of being the novel's protagonist. For he himself becomes a beacon who will guide others, and shine, like a new star, in the night.

Notes

1. Letter to Emile Henriot. *Bulletin* de l'Association des Amis de Marcel Proust, no. 4 (1954), p. 5.

2. Elie-Joseph Bois, *Le Temps* (13 November 1913); cf. Robert Dreyfus, *Souvenirs sur Marcel Proust* (Paris, 1926), pp. 187 ff.; also in *The Creative Vision. Modern European Writers On Their Art,* ed. Haskell M. Block and Herman Salinger (New York and London, 1960), p. 68.

3. *Correspondance générale* de Marcel Proust, I (Paris, 1930), 167, letter CLXIII.

4. *Almanach Hachette* (Paris, 1928), p. 110: The critic speaks of "la série de ses romans autobiographiques" and states: Il y a cependant en lui [Proust] quelque chose d'inachevé, car il lui a manqué, au seuil de ce monde moral dont il s'est fait l'explorateur, une volonté plus ferme et une répugnance moins grande à l'effort."

5. Book catalogue of P. Berès, 1938, no. 1, item 103.

6. Quoted in Proust's preface to his translation of Ruskin, *Sésame et les lys* (Paris, 1906); see note on p. 36 of the 1926 edition.

7. Proust et J. Rivière, *Correspondance* (Paris, 1955), pp. 2–3.

8. *Jean Santeuil* (Paris, 1962); I, 210: II, 291; III, 36–37, 197.

9. See my identification of Proust's model as Jean Jaurès, "Proust's portrait of Jaurès in Jean Santeuil," *French Studies*, Oxford, XV (October 1961), 338–349.

10. *Alphonse Darlu maître de philosophie de Marcel Proust* (Paris, 1961).

Proust's Alchemy   Victor E. Graham*

Many comparisons have been used to describe the structure of *A la Recherche du temps perdu*. The novel is sometimes said to be like a great symphony or an opera. In this case, *Du Côté de chez Swann* stands as the introduction or overture, in which all the thematic material is presented. Later movements or acts utilize this material, often in surprising ways, picking up what seemed to be only an incidental fragment in the prelude, to develop it into a complete section. Among these, we find the *Molto vivace Presto* of *A l'Ombre des jeunes filles en fleurs,* the *Adagio molto e cantabile* of *Le Côté de Guermantes,* the *Allegro assai* of *Sodome et Gomorrhe* and the grandiose finale of *Le Temps retrouvé,* a sort of *Ode to Joy* with its

*From *Modern Language Review* 60 (1965):197–206. Reprinted by kind permission of the author and of the editor of the journal. Quotations from *A la recherche du temps perdu* come from the Kilmartin translation. All other translations are the work of the editor of this collection.

triumphant recapitulation, repudiating old age and death and finding in man's inner world the key to all enigmas. Alternatively, these same sections may be regarded as separate operas from a sort of vast trilogy[1] linked together by the characters and stylistic treatment. Proust, of course, admired Wagner tremendously and the rich texture of his novel with the complexities of its recurrent themes has often been compared to the Wagnerian *leit motif* technique.

The structure of *A la Recherche du temps perdu* has also been called architectural. *Du Côté de chez Swann* here is similar to the porch of a great cathedral which indicates clearly but on a minor scale the style and size of the whole structure. As one moves inside and down the centre aisle, the different sub-sections are like the immense pillars and arches which, linked together, support the vaulting of the superstructure up to the choir, the altar and the soaring spire which, in turn, counterbalance the porch with its bold towers.

Proust himself liked to speak of his novel as being similar in conception to the *rosace* or rose-window sometimes found in the great west wall or the transept of Gothic cathedrals. From a distance, one sees the simple circular aperture crossed by stone, supports whose interwoven tracery suggests a rose—a symbol, incidentally, of special significance to Proust. On looking closer, one can observe how each section is linked rhythmically to the next. As the eye moves from unit to unit, we finally find ourselves back where we started, but for Proust, at any rate, this was not to be regarded as merely a cycle, even though he tells us that in the first fever of his inspiration, he wrote at the same time the opening pages of *Du Côté de chez Swann* and the very end of *Le Temps retrouvé*.

What all these comparisons try to show, of course, is the symmetry, the unity, the subservience of elaborate detail to purpose, the grandeur and the simplicity of the whole novel. Each is useful in its own way, but there is yet another comparison which can be evoked to emphasize the sequential nature of the novel as it builds up to the stunning climax of *Le Temps retrouvé*—a climax which the very existence of the novel presupposed and which gives meaning to all that has gone before, revealing in a single flash the truth that has been the ultimate goal.

From one important point of view, *A la Recherche du temps perdu* is simply the story of how Proust came to write his novel, and in his long search for a *raison d'être* the author might be said to be a sort of alchemist pursuing the quest for the philosopher's stone, which has the power of transmuting base elements into higher forms, but which brings with it the elixir which cures ills and circumscribes time and death. The years of diligent but unsuccessful experimentation, the tedious and often frustrating sequence of steps in the process are all to be found in the novel up to the sudden discovery of the mysterious power. There is even the desperate haste to transcribe the process for other initiates before death strikes (xv, 216).[2] Like his predecessors, the alchemists of old, Proust is convinced that he has found the secret which others failed to comprehend. Like theirs, his description of the process can only really be understood by other devotees; the general public is divided into two camps—the gullible and the scoffers.

In the popular mind, alchemy is most often thought of as a sort of quackery—the preoccupation with turning base metals into gold, with demonstrations usually employing some form of deceit. All the tricks of this sort of alchemist's trade are described by Chaucer and Ben Jonson. The actual origin of the study of alchemy like the word itself, is shrouded in mystery. "Al" is the Arabic particle "the" and "chem" is thought to come either directly from the very ancient Egyptian "khem" or "khamé" which means "black earth" and is later used as a name for Egypt, or from a Greek derivative. The earliest alchemists were expatriates, Jews or Egyptians who wrote in Greek, but led nomadic existences as they sought protection to practise their secret arts.

Here too, we can note a superficial analogy with Proust. By reputation, at least, he is lightly spoken of as a sort of hypochondriac, an asthmatic half-Jew bundled up in overcoats and scarves, isolated from the world in a cork-lined room where he dabbled in the occult, sleeping all day and writing at night about sodomy, sadism and decadent French society. This is a part of the Proust legend which will continue to be propagated, no matter how little it has to do with Proust, the writer.

Basically, of course, alchemy is a philosophy of life, and there is just as much difference between the genuine alchemist and a fake one as there is between the real Proust and the legend. Alchemy is the search for the realization of order in the universe, the harmonizing of the mysteries of Creation and of life. Its purpose is to reveal the simplicity of natural order, to perfect all things in their kind, to imitate and indeed to surpass nature. From the unification of nature into a single scheme comes the ability to transmute elements but this was a result, not the prime purpose. The true alchemists were learned scholars who spent a lifetime studying and experimenting in quest of ultimate truth, a truth whose physical proof lay in the discovery of the philosopher's stone. The consecration to science which characterized the true alchemists is also the dominant trait in Proust's character. We may deplore his eccentricities, his hypochondria and his snobbishness, but we must admire his devotion to his craft. It is not far from the truth to think of him as a dedicated alchemist isolated from society while he purifies and transmutes the base elements of experience and observation into the essence which became the gleaming gold of his art.

For all the alchemists, there were just four elements—earth, air, fire and water. Each of these elements were distinguished by a combination of two of the characteristics: hot, cold, moist, and dry. More complicated bodies were a combination of some or all of the four elements in different proportions along with a fifth component—the *quinta essentia* which constituted its unique distinguishing characteristic. Transmutation was postulated by the substitution of one characteristic for another, but in order to reproduce or transmute compounds, the alchemist had first to discover and isolate the quintessence. This was done in a long process involving various stages characterized by the slow, steady application of heat, during which different colours appeared in sequence, resulting in the end in the production of the red philosopher's stone and gold.

Of the four elements, the most important from the point of view of the alchemist were water and fire. They were the most dramatic and they epitomized most clearly exact opposites. That is why the discovery of alcohol—the water that would burn—seemed so important to them.

From the literary point of view, the psychological significance of these two elements in particular has continued to influence poets and writers, even though chemically the concepts have long since been outdated. In French literature, of course, there are fascinating studies on the symbolism of these sources of inspiration by Gaston Bachelard, the first *L'Eau et les rêves*, and the second *La Psychanalyse du feu*.[3]

One of the fundamental aspects of Proust's style is his use of metaphor or images. He believed that beauty or truth can only be expressed obliquely and this is why he used clusters of images or strings of morphemes to focus on the truth by a sort of "stylistic convergence."[4] In an early essay, he had accused Flaubert of being deficient in images.[5] Elsewhere, he criticizes Balzac for consistently using images that are discordant, ["which explain instead of suggesting, which are not subordinate to any goal of beauty or harmony"].[6] Proust believed that ["the metaphor alone can give a kind of eternity to style"],[7] and he felt that his own unique gift as a writer lay in the ability so highly praised by Aristotle ["to discover a profound link between two ideas, two sensations . . . to feel between two impressions, between two ideas, a very subtle harmony which others do not feel"].[8] In other words, Proust sought to penetrate to the essence of experiences and ideas in order to transmute them. Among the important sub-sections in *A la Recherche du temps perdu*, the first—*Du Côté de chez Swann*—is permeated with water imagery, while the one which counter-balances it—*Le Côté de Guermantes*—is incandescent with imagery drawn from light and fire.

In the narrator's youth, when his family used to visit relatives at the small village of Combray, the two paths which they used to take for walks seemed to him diametrically opposed. The first is "Swann's Way"—the shorter path which led to Méséglise by way of Swann's estate, where he and his wife Odette lived in the summer with their daughter Gilberte. Marcel is quite familiar with Swann who often visits him and his parents and grandparents, but he is not at first aware of Swann's prestige in the world of society—his membership in the Jockey Club and his intimacy with the social élite of Paris. For Marcel's family, Swann is a perfectly ordinary bourgeois who has married a woman of the demi-monde and therefore ostracized himself from society.

The longer walk leading past the Guermantes estate is quite different.

Marcel has never met the Duchesse de Guermantes but he is obsessed by her—her descent from Geneviève of Brabant and Louis XI, her chateau, her social connections and her appearance. She seems far above Swann and ordinary mortals, and his great ambition in life is to see and then to meet this fabulous creature.

In the underlying pattern of imagery associated with Combray and Swann's Way, Proust draws heavily on images having to do with water.[9] The spring blossoms which he admires are compared to sea foam (I, 185) or little boats (I, 189). They are said to be as fresh as water drops (I, 193), and the breeze bearing their perfume is like breakers crashing at his feet (I, 198). Fresh air and fine days are like cool water, and the sky with its clouds is similar to the sea with its sportive sharks or dogfish (I, 223). One could go on enumerating similar comparisons, churches like cliffs (II, 227) or sea shells (I, 94); lighted houses at night like boats floating on the dark water (I, 206); people sitting at their doors like seaweed or shells festooning a river bank (I, 125) and soldiers passing through the streets on horseback like a furious current scarcely contained by its channel (I, 124). It is specially significant that the little madeleine cake which, when dipped in tea and tasted by the narrator, calls up the whole train of reminiscences about Combray, is shaped like a shell (I, 65), and lest it be thought that attaching any importance to this is altogether ridiculous, we should note that in the sketch of this episode in Proust's early work *Contre Sainte Beuve*, it is not a madeleine at all which evokes the experience, but a bit of toast.

As every reader knows, Proust himself was very much interested in philology. In *A la Recherche du temps perdu*, the narrator is always directing questions about the etymologies of place names first to the curate at Combray and, later, to Brichot, the professor from the Sorbonne. The fact that these two are so often in disagreement and that contemporary philologists have found much to criticize in what they believe to be Proust's own notions about philology is an interesting commentary on one of Proust's favourite ideas—the relativity of knowledge.[10]

At any rate, Proust undoubtedly uses the etymologies of certain proper names as not-too-obscure private symbols. Combray, for example, means a confluence or the meeting of rivers. It is the spot from which the two paths diverge, the bourgeois Swann's Way and the noble Guermantes way. It is also the point of juncture of the narrator's past and the present. Ultimately the past and the present join, as do Swann's Way and the Guermantes way (XIII, 310, 328). The narrator is just as surprised as the alchemists were at the union of fire and water. Swann's widow becomes the last mistress of the Duc de Guermantes and Swann's daughter, Gilberte, marries the aristocratic St Loup, the nephew of the Duke and Duchess of Guermantes. Their daughter, in turn, symbolizes the double union of the two ways and of the narrator's past and the present. It was at Combray that the narrator had first desired to express himself by means of the written word, and it is in memories of Combray that he finally experiences the activating stimulus which at last sets him to writing.

The special significance of the name Combray is clearly indicated by Proust in the final volume of his work where he gives keys to so many of the enigmas of the earlier sections. In speaking of the successive changes in social position which any one individual experiences, he says: ["I could see that this was a social phenomenon less rare than I had at first supposed and that from the single *fountain-basin* of Combray in which I had been born there were in fact quite a number of *jets of water* which had risen, in symmetry with myself, above the liquid mass which had fed them" (*RTPK* 3:1015)] (XV, 134).[11] On the next page, in referring to the career and life of a family friend from Combray in relation to his own, he goes on to say that ["Legrandin's life seemed to bear absolutely no resemblance to my own, the two seemed to have followed widely divergent paths, and in this respect I was like a stream which from the bottom of its own deep valley does not see another stream which proceeds in a different direction and yet, in spite of the great loops in its course, ends up as a tributary of the same river" (*RTPK* 3:1015)] (XV, 135).

When we turn to the Guermantes way, we find plenty of evidence to suggest that Proust, in his choice of imagery, was thinking in terms of the contrasting alchemical element, fire. To begin with, since the walk in this direction at Combray was much longer than the one to Méséglise, it could only be undertaken (as the narrator himself says) on days that were extremely hot and dry (I, 223). These are, in fact, the alchemical properties of fire.

For Proust, names are of fundamental importance for they designate people and places, and the imagination builds around the name, which is developed or modified according to the changing nature of the person or place it represents.[12] The name, from that point of view, is in fact the *essence* of the person designated. The principal name which Proust projected upon the screen of his readers' imagination was that of Guermantes since all of his principal characters become in the course of the story related to that family through ties of blood, marriage, or friendship. And it is the *name* of Guermantes, the family name, which Proust expends his artistic fervour most lavishly in making alive. There is a mystery in the name itself, Proust felt, and a great name almost creates the people who bear it.[13]

Proust constantly associates the name Guermantes with the colours of flame—red, yellow and orange. It is said to have golden syllables (XV, 181), like sunlight (VII, 32), autumn woods (VII, 39), or a yellow tower (VI, 14). It has about it the emanation of mysterious rays (XIII, 193), and it is described at times as orange and brilliant (VI, 35), at others as amaranth, a deep red or reddish purple (VI, 15). Its final syllable—*antes* is also said to be orange or amaranth in colour (I, 231–2, (VII, 38).

Flame, burning, fire and lightning are extensively used in figures connected with Guermantes personalities. For example, the Jupiterian duke, who is like the gold statue by Phidias (VII, 131), is frequently angry at the Duchess, and under the circumstances he is said to be hurling thunderbolts (XV, 199). We see him in his rage, [his eyes ablaze with anger and astonishment, his crinkly hair seeming to emerge from a crater (*RTPK* 2:708)] (IX, 109). The Duchess is especially fond of red or flame coloured clothes and her skin, surprisingly enough, is the same colour. (VI, 33, 42, 74, VIII, 244; IX, 82; XI, 39, 45; XV, 82). Before the narrator had even met her, he used to imagine her taking him around the garden of her estate pointing out unknown red and purple flowers and naming them for him (I, 233).

Let us quote Proust himself to prove that he was used to thinking synaesthetically about names and works of fiction. Again in *Contre Sainte Beuve*, in speaking of Gérard de Nerval's *Sylvie*, he says: ["The color of *Sylvie* is a crimson color, the color of a crimson rose made of crimson or purplish velvet, and has nothing to do with the watercolor tones of their temperate France. At every moment there is a touch of red, shooting matches, red scarves, etc. And this name which is itself crimsoned by its two Is—Sylvie, the true daughter of Fire."][14]

When we consider such a subtle analysis, surely it is a little too obvious to propose that Proust's ideas on the colour of the Guermantes names were probably suggested to him by the analogy of *Guermantes* and *amaranthe*, the reddish-purple flower whose colour the name reflects.[15] The amaranth stands for immortality and this is a connotation which Proust wants associated with the name Guermantes (VI, 15) but the pattern of imagery is much more profound than that.

In some of Proust's letters we find him asking friends for information on the etymology of the name *Guermantes*.[16] No answers to these letters have been found, but it is most probable, on the analogy of Combray, that Proust would have liked the etymology to be associated with heat and flame. He tells us that its syllables are *Guerm* and *–antes* instead of *Guer–* and *–mantes* as one would normally expect. He also says that the name is of Germanic origin. One possible origin of the root *Germ* or *Guerm* is a celtic form of the Indo-European *ghwerm* which gives Greek *thermos*, English *warm* and so forth. There is nothing to indicate that Proust was acquainted with this bit of information, but there is ample evidence to underline the dichotomy between Swann's Way with its water imagery and the Guermantes Way with its fire. The vast tableaux of Society with their amazing complexity of detail and the virtuosity displayed in characterizations, disconcerting as they all are, are merely incidental to the ultimate quest and when the narrator equates fire and water, he achieves in fact the transmutation which he had been seeking. He discovers his own particular vocation through the philosopher's stone which he has at last found through the involuntary memory and the ability, by means of art, to recreate the past which exists in the inner world, the only real world we can ever know.

Let us turn now to the question of gold and the quest for the philosopher's stone. Many of the individual characters in *A la Recherche du temps perdu* are searching for a *raison d'être*. The Baron Charlus seeks it in physical pleasure. The painter Elstir and the writer Bergotte seek it in artistic creation, whereas Swann, like the narrator whom he resembles in so many ways, is torn between the two. Swann has his attraction to Odette de Crécy but he also has his unfinished study on the Dutch painter Vermeer. He never completes this monograph but his attraction to Odette compensates for it, since he sees in her resemblances to paintings (IV, 25). She becomes, in effect, his creation, which means that he loves, not her, but the mental image which he has made of her.

For the narrator, the physical attraction is Albertine and, to a lesser degree, Gilberte, Mademoiselle de Stermaria and all the other *jeunes filles* who at one stage or another obsessed his imagination. Madame de Guermantes represents all that is desirable in the world of society. At the same time, the narrator's principal aim is to write a novel, and the only real joy he finds is in creative effort. He declares that his elation at writing as a youth the description of the three steeples at Martinville was one of the great moments of his life.

In *A la Recherche du temps perdu* we can isolate various quests which the narrator pursues consciously or not in his search for a meaning to life. These are all closely associated with imagery drawn from gold, the higher metal resulting from the transmutation of baser forms through the long, steady application of fire or heat. Marcel's first love is nature, and on the walks at Combray he seeks truth in nature. One scarcely needs to mention the many elaborate descriptions of trees, flowers, birds, and fish in *Du Côté de chez Swann*. Through them all runs the elusive glint of the gold which represents the ideal being sought. Light is gold (II, 78), and the effect of the sun on rocks (I, 240) or wet surfaces (VI, 71; XI, 11, 13; XV, 159), a wall (V, 229), leaves (I, 198; XI, 11) or snow (II, 241) is to transform them into gold. Fine days are like precious gold (II, 240, 241, 244, 251, 275; V, 229–30; VI, 107), and when the curtains in his room are drawn back to reveal outside a hot, midsummer day, the narrator is reminded of a precious golden mummy (V, 230). The narrator tells us, significantly, that if he were on his deathbed and a warm ray of sunshine penetrated the room, a part of his personality would respond to it and rejoice (XI, 13). The golden sun has the power to rejuvenate him (XI, 11), and in the significant aesthetic experience of the three steeples, the towers themselves are said to be gold (I, 245) along with the notes of the striking bells (I, 122, 225; XI, 101). Behind the golden sun on the rock (I, 240) and the three steeples (I, 242–3), there is some message which the narrator cannot quite seize. He continues to love nature but he realizes that he cannot find final truth in it.

On Marcel's youthful walks at Méséglise, he once saw Gilberte Swann and was attracted to her. Later on he got to know her in Paris and he used to play with her and her friends at the Champs Elysées. Gilberte was his first innocent love and again a gleam of gold runs through the references to her. Her hair and skin are golden (III, 170) and her eyes are like gold or fire (II, 247–8). Her team in the Champs Elysées is also gold (II, 244) and Marcel eagerly covets a place on it. The Swann home where he has his first experiences in the world of society is like gold (III, 125, 141, 209) or Klingsor's magic laboratory, a sort of alchemist's paradise.

Through the years the narrator is constantly attracted to strange girls. They may be milk-maids, waitresses, passers-by whom he never meets, but the sight of them fills him for the moment with urgent desire. These girls are often compared to gold, flame or the sun (II, 279; IV, 71–2; V, 138, 184; XI, 172, 206; XIII, 86, 181, 332). One in particular whom he sees from a railway carriage is especially remarkable:

> [Above her tall figure, the complexion of her face was so burnished and so glowing that it was as if one were seeing her through a lighted window. She retraced her steps. I could not take my eyes from her face which grew larger as she approached, like a sun which it was somehow possible to stare at and which was coming nearer and nearer, letting itself be seen at close quarters, dazzling you with its blaze of red and gold. (*RTPK* 1:706–07)] (IV, 72)

In another comparison, water and fire are symbolically linked with a specific reference to alchemy which makes the image very significant:

> And yet the supposition that I might some day be the friend of one or other of these girls, that these eyes, whose incomprehensible gaze struck me from time to time and played unwittingly upon me like an effect of sunlight on a wall, might ever, by some miraculous alchemy, allow the idea of my existence, some affection for my person, to interpenetrate their ineffable particles, that I myself might some day take my place among them in the evolution of their course by the sea's edge—that supposition appeared to me to contain within it a contradiction. . . . (*RTPK* 1:853)] (V, 40)

This refers of course to the particular band of young girls whom the narrator met at Balbec, the sea-coast resort town where he visited twice. As a group, these girls are shining rays of light or [drops of gold, always dissimilar and always surpassing our expectation (*RTPK* 3:59)] (XI, 77). One of them, Andrée, has hands as gold as autumn leaves (V, 187); another, Gisèle, is all gold (V, 149), but most especially, Albertine, the great love of his life, is associated with gold (XII, 159). The light on the stairs signalling her arrival (IX, 166) and the light in her room (XII, 159) are gold. In the curious symbolic passage where the narrator falls desperately in love with her just after convincing himself that the attraction was transitory, we find this description:

> [I could not repress a sob when, with a gesture of oblation mechanically performed and symbolising, in my eyes, the bloody sacrifice which I was about to have to make of all joy, every morning, until the end of my life,

a solemn renewal, celebrated as each day dawned, of my daily grief and
of the blood from my wound, the golden egg of the sun, as though pro-
pelled by the rupture of equilibrium brought about at the moment of co-
agulation by a change of density, barbed with tongues of flame as in a
painting, burst through the curtain . . . whose mysterious frozen purple
it annihilated in a flood of light. (*RTPK* 2:1166)] (X, 334–5)

At Balbec, which is also said to be gold (IV, 93; VI, 98), the narrator
first met St Loup who was to become his great friend and the Open-Sesame
to the Guermantes clan. St Loup like all the rest of the family (VII, 42;
VIII, 72; XV, 143) has hair and skin of gold (IV, 159; VI, 73, 74; XIV, 82),
but he is the most notable: ["The colouring which he possessed in a greater
degree than any other Guermantes—that air of being merely the solidified
sunniness of a golden day" (*RTPK* 3:722)] (XIV, 15). Madame de Guermantes has the same colouring and even the hair on her arms, impalpable
as that of a Duchess should be, is ["as it were a perpetual golden mist"
(*RTPK* 2:388)] (VII, 244). In her voice ["there lingered . . . the rich and
lazy gold of a country sun" (*RTPK* 2:210)] (VII, 33. Cf. XII, 211). Knowing
Proust's interest in names, one can be certain that the choice of her Christian name—which is *Ori*ane (cf. VIII, 119) was no accident.

The narrator does not find the truth he was seeking in social relations
with Mme de Guermantes any more than he did in love or friendship. He
does not find it in travel either. He had always wanted to visit Italy and
especially Florence and Venice, cities of gold (II, 227, 235; XII, 240–I,
245). When he finally does see Venice, it charms him but, like everything
else, it does not bring him the complete satisfaction which he sought. It is
only after the narrator has finally renounced all desire to write and reconciled himself to mediocrity that he accidentally discovers the touchstone he
had been seeking.

Throughout his life, the narrator had been interested in the expression
of beauty through art (cf. I, 118). The great actress, La Berma, whose soul
he described as a central ray or flame (VI, 58) used her golden voice to
recreate dramatic masterpieces (III, 19) which, like other aesthetic experiences, the narrator in his youth completely failed to understand. The
painter, Elstir, and the writer, Bergotte who himself is gold (I, 138) transmute reality as it reaches their senses into a strange form which is representative of their inner worlds (V, 87–8, 90–2; XIV, 93). Their genius operates at high temperatures which have the power to dissociate and re-group
atoms in completely new ways (V, 118). It is the catalyst or transforming
power. Bergotte is even spoken of as an alchemist, since he transforms into
the gold of his art, the cheap gold he uses to pay girls who provide the
experiences which motivate his artistic powers (XI, 227). For Bergotte, art
is more important than life, or perhaps we should say Art *is* life. When he
is very ill, he goes to see a painting by Vermeer, despite the fact that it
may be the death of him. This is actually the case, but Bergotte dies revel-
ling in the truth presented to him by the contemplation of an exquisitely

painted bit of yellow-gold wall in the painting he has gone to see (XI 231–2). This truth is like the narrator's golden sun on the rock (I, 240) or the three gold steeples (I, 242–3) but it is presented to us through art, the only transmutation which we are able to assimilate.

The reagents necessary for the narrator's own discovery of the touchstone of his art were the experiences of the involuntary memory. After a long period of illness, he briefly returned to the haunts he used to frequent at a reception at the home of the Princesse de Guermantes, he found that certain physical stimuli—the feel of an uneven paving stone beneath his feet (XIV, 200; XV, 7, 8), the sound of a spoon on a plate (XV, 9, 10), the touch of a starched serviette on his lips (XV, 10), the sight of the cover of a familiar novel (XV, 28, 29), all evoked whole periods of his past because of the analogy of other stimuli long since forgotten. The catalyst or activating agent was the performance at the reception of an unfamiliar work by his favourite composer, Vinteuil. The narrator had always felt that music gets nearer to the truth than words do (XII, 215–16) and the septet by Vinteuil seemed to synthesize all the experiences of involuntary memory which had just happened to him (XV, 7). When he saw how strange new worlds could be created in a familiar idiom, he realized that he had within himself all the base elements ready to be mixed (XV, 216) or distilled into the higher form of art (cf. XII, 69). These elements are not subject to time; they are dependent only on their creator. Proust found that none of his quests were fruitless, but that in order to profit from them, they had to have died. The theme of death and resurrection is fundamental to alchemy; from the blackened and disintegrated base elements spring the higher elements which culminate in the red philosopher's stone and the golden seeds of truth.

It is only after death has touched the narrator in an infinite number of ways that the past can be resurrected through art. Many individuals dear to him are dead—Albertine, St Loup, his beloved grandmother, Swann, Bergotte, La Berma. Those who are still living are scarcely recognizable. Like metal in an acid bath, their qualities have changed with the passage of time (IX, 246). Even the narrator himself is a different person and all the former selves he used to be can only be resuscitated through the involuntary memory (cf. IV, 89–90; XV, 217). This is the golden treasure (XI, 11), the only reality (XI, 29).

Art alone lives. It is: ["the most real of all things, the most austere school of life, the true last judgment" (RTPK 3:194)] (XV, 23). The miraculous red stone which rises from the blackened ashes is Vinteuil's septet. In it, brilliant with purple and red (XII, 60, 65, 216; XV, 21), a joyous theme struggles with a melancholy one. This optimistic theme is a violent crimson and it tints the sky, ["as dawn does, with a mysterious hope" (RTPK 2:252)] (XII, 60). It literally tears the air: [". . . as vivid as the scarlet tint in which the opening bars had been bathed, something like a mystical cock-crow, the ineffable but ear-piercing call of eternal morning" (*RTPK* 3:252)] (XII, 60).

This vibrant, ecstatic theme, compared also to a scarlet angel blowing carmine notes on its trumpet (XII, 72–3) is bound to triumph over its sombre counterpart. To it at last the gates of Paradise open. Alchemy has triumphed and the golden seeds are everywhere—in nature, in love and in society—in the whole life, in short. The stone and the elixir are there for all to share. It only remains to transmute the base mass by recording the steps necessary for their production.

Notes

1. The novel was originally planned as a trilogy. Cf. Albert Feuillerat, *Comment Marcel Proust a composé son roman*, Yale Romanic Studies VII, Yale University Press, New Haven, 1934, pp. 14–15.

2. All references to *A la Recherche du temps perdu* are to the Gallimard edition of the *Nouvelle Revue Française* in 15 volumes. Roman numerals refer to volume numbers.

3. Gaston Bachelard, *L'Eau et les rêves, Essai sur l'imagination de la matière*, Librairie José Corti, Paris, 1942.

La Psychanalyse du feu, Collection Psychologie 7, Gallimard, Paris, 1949. Cf. Charles Bruneau, "L'Image dans notre langue littéraire" in *Mélanges de linguistique offerts à Albert Dauzat*, Editions d'Artrey, Paris, 1951, p. 65.

4. The term is borrowed from Yvette Louria, *La Convergence stylistique chez Proust*, Droz, Genève, 1957.

5. "A Propos du Style' de Flaubert," *Chroniques*, pp. 193–4.

6. *Contre Sainte Beuve, suivi de nouveaux mélanges, préface* de Bernard de Fallois, Gallimard, Paris, 1953, p. 56.

7. "A Propos du 'Style' de Flaubert," *Chroniques*, p. 193.

8. *Contre Sainte Beuve*, pp. 301–2. Cf. xi, 13 and Pierre Trahard, *L'Art de Marcel Proust*, Dervy, Paris, 1953, p. 56.

9. For a fuller treatment of this topic, see Victor E. Graham, "Water Imagery and Symbolism in Proust," *Romanic Review*, L (1959), 118–28.

10. See Milton Hindus, *The Proustian Vision*, New York, Columbia University Press, 1954, p. 98, and Léon Pierre-Quint, *Le Comique et le mystère chez. Proust*, Editions du Sagittaire, Paris, 1928, p. 55.

11. The italics are added.

12. See J. Vendryes, "Marcel Proust et les noms propres," in *Choix d'études linguistiques et celtiques*, Paris, 1953, pp. 80–8 or *Mélanges Huguet*, pp. 119–127.

13. Milton Hindus, op. cit. p. 189.

14. Op. cit. p. 168.

15. See S. Ullmann, *Style in the French Novel*, Cambridge University Press, 1957, p. 200.

16. See *Correspondance Générale*, Plon, 1932, Tome III, pp. 301–3 (letter to Martin-Chauffier) and E. de Clermont-Tonnerre, *Robert de Montesquiou et Marcel Proust*, Flammarion, 1925, p. 234.

Albertine: Characterization
through Image and Symbol

Nicholas Kostis*

In *A la recherche du temps perdu* Marcel Proust often portrays Albertine through imagery perceived by the narrator, Marcel. The loved object, Albertine, is predominantly a projection of Marcel's desires. The images through which he sees her communicate his emotional experience—happiness, jealousy, passion, suffering, and indifference—with Albertine. Springing from the depths of his consciousness, they are outpourings of lyricism. Consequently, the mood which sustains them cannot last for a long period of time. When these images, which are interspersed throughout the novel, are isolated and then juxtaposed, they form a lyrical poem.

Speaking to Albertine about Vinteuil, Marcel says:

> ce qui est senti par nous de la vie, ne l'étant pas sous forme d'idées, sa traduction littéraire, c'est-à-dire intellectuelle, en rend compte, l'explique, l'analyse, mais ne le recompose pas comme la musique où les sons semblent prendre l'inflexion de l'être, reproduire cette pointe intérieure et extrême des sensations qui est la partie qui nous donne cette ivresse spécifique que nous retrouvons de temps en temps et que, quand nous disons: "Quel beau temps! quel beau soleil!" nous ne faisons nullement connaître au prochain, en qui le même soleil et le même temps éveillent des vibrations toutes différentes. . . . il n'est pas possible qu'une sculpture, une musique qui donne une émotion qu'on sent plus élevée, plus pure, plus vraie, ne corresponde pas à une certaine réalité spirituelle, ou la vie n'aurait aucun sens. . . . Ces phrases-types, que vous commencez à reconnaître comme moi, ma petite Albertine, les mêmes dans la sonate, dans le septuor, dans les autres oeuvres, ce serait, par exemple, si vous voulez, chez Barbey d'Aurevilly, une réalité cachée, révélée par une trace matérielle.[1]

These typical phrases, which are the material traces of a hidden reality, may be compared to Proust's repetitive imagery, also subjective in origin. The author's use of imagery in reference to Albertine may be likened to a composer's use of sound to convey his emotions. By assigning a value to each image and then combining the images structurally, Proust elaborates a metaphoric structure much as the composer manipulates sounds harmonically to produce, through a gradual unfolding, a musical structure. For the critical reader to recapitulate the process by which the artistic effect is produced, he must examine the text and establish the underlying pattern of associated imagery. The purpose of this essay is (1) to interpret the value of the particular images of Albertine, (2) to find the relationship

*Reprinted by permission of the Modern Language Association of America from *PMLA* 84 (1969):125–35, and also by kind permission of the author. © 1969 by the Modern Language Association of America. By special request, this article has been left unchanged. Translations of its quotations from Proust appear in the notes; they are taken from the Kilmartin translation of *A la recherche de temps perdu*. The author's emendations to the translated quotations have been included in parentheses).

between them, and (3) to show how they constitute in their ensemble a structure which reveals (a) Marcel's perception of Albertine and hence Albertine as a character, and (b) his love for her and its evolution.

Proust draws many of his images of Albertine from painting, sculpture, and animals, but the most striking and numerous images fall into three major groups: the flower, the sea, and the bird. Although I have classified the imagery according to these three categories, the images from the different groups are often interrelated. It is, therefore, not always possible to discuss one group without mentioning imagery from another group.

ROSE IMAGERY

Albertine and the other members of the little band, as they appear in *A l'ombre des jeunes filles en fleurs,* are conceived not as individuals with clearly delineated psychologies but as the collective mass and subjective reality of Marcel's experience. Like flowers, these girls arouse his senses: "Je regardais les joues d'Albertine pendant qu'elle me parlait et je me demandais quel parfum, quel goût elles pouvaient avoir: ce jour-là elle était non pas fraîche, mais lisse, d'un rose uni, violacé, crémeux, comme certaines roses qui ont un vernis de cire. J'étais passionné pour elles comme on l'est parfois pour une espèce de fleurs" (I, 888).[2] As flowers are in a state of metamorphosis, Albertine's face constantly changes color. Marcel is concerned with translating every nuance of his sensual delight in the company of these adolescents whose moral and intellectual lives are beyond his knowledge. "De sorte qu'essayer de me lier avec Albertine m'apparaissait comme une mise en contact avec l'inconnu sinon avec l'impossible, comme un exercice . . . aussi passionnant qu'élever des abeilles ou que cultiver des rosiers" (I, 881–882).[3] Thus, when we first meet Albertine, she is indistinguishable from the other girls. As Marcel separates her from the others, their qualities will be assimilated in her.

Marcel is introduced by one girl to another: "Et remontant de corolle en corolle dans cette chaîne de fleurs, le plaisir d'en connaître une différente me faisait retourner vers celle à qui je la devais, avec une reconnaissance mêlée d'autant de désir que mon espoir nouveau" (I, 891).[4] Although he feels irresistibly drawn to Albertine from the start, Marcel does not immediately turn all his thoughts to her, but allows his desire to wander from one girl to the next. Having been accepted by the little band, he makes his way among its members in the same way a gardener constructs paths around roses (I, 904–905). As he accompanies them on excursions to neighboring farms or mountain cliffs, he discovers he loves them individually and collectively, without exclusion, each one becoming almost a substitute for the other. After Albertine, with whom he decided to fall in love, repulses his efforts to kiss her, he finds himself once more in love with all of them: "Entre ces jeunes filles, tiges de roses dont le principal charme était de se détacher sur la mer, régnait la même indivision qu'au temps où je ne les connaissais pas et où l'apparition de n'importe laquelle me causait tant d'é-motion en m'annonçant que la petite bande n'était pas loin" (I, 944).[5]

White hawthorns, which are associated with church, Easter, and early childhood, symbolize purity. Red or pink hawthorns and, by extension, all red or pink flowers, indicate sensuality, and appear in the story for the first time just before the incident of Gilberte's concupiscent look. It is signifi-cant that Marcel associates Albertine almost exclusively with various shades of rose. Shaking her hand, for example, offers him "une douceur sensuelle qui était comme en harmonie avec la coloration rose, légèrement mauve, de sa peau" (I, 919).[6] Marcel later admits that it was sexual desire that had distributed "si largement et si minutieusement la couleur et le parfum sur les surfaces carnées de ces jeunes filles" (I, 950).[7] Yet the tone throughout A l'ombre des jeunes filles en fleurs is that of love kept platonic, and Mar-cel's relations with Albertine and her friends are almost entirely free from direct contact of fingers and lips. Their mere presence serves as a stimulus to his imagination and senses: "[les sens] donnent à ces filles la même con-sistance mielleuse qu'ils font quand ils butinent dans une roseraie, ou dans une vigne dont ils mangent des yeux les grappes" (I, 893).[8]

In A l'ombre des jeunes filles en fleurs Proust wants to depict the eva-nescence of sensations experienced in the presence of beauty. The happi-ness Marcel derives from the small band's company is that of an aesthete with a heightened sensitivity and intuitive faculty which allow him to ob-serve with delight those subtleties in others the average person fails to see. These girls, pursued by him under a blue, sunny sky and against a back-drop of blue sea, are representative of the fragrance and sensory loveliness of youth: "il n'était pas possible de trouver réunies des espèces plus rares que celles de ces jeunes fleurs qui interrompaient en ce moment devant moi la ligne du flot de leur haie légère, pareille à un bosquet de roses de Pennsylvanie" (I, 798).[9]

Marcel becomes saturated with the beauty radiated by these creatures. Yet he cannot help discerning in them slight signs of the physical traits which will characterize the mature woman: "Hélas! dans la fleur la plus fraîche on peut distinguer les points imperceptibles qui pour l'esprit averti dessinent déjà ce qui sera, par la dessication ou la fructification des chairs aujourd'hui en fleur, la forme immuable et déjà prédestinée de la graine" (I, 891).[10] The flower as a symbol of fleeting youth seems somewhat banal: "Comme sur un plant où les fleurs mûrissent à des époques différentes, je les avais vues, en de vieilles dames, sur cette plage de Balbec, ces dures graines, ces mous tubercules, que mes amies seraient un jour. Mais qu'im-portait? en ce moment, c'était la saison des fleurs" (I, 892).[11]

When a more mature Albertine visits Marcel in his Paris flat several years after that first summer at Balbec, he observes that his visitor has de-veloped mentally and morally as well as physically. Nevertheless, he con-tinues to associate her with the image of the pink flower: "Il suffisait qu'on me dise qu'elle était à Paris et qu'elle était passée chez moi pour que je la revisse comme une rose au bord de la mer" (II, 351).[12] He further evokes the flower to emphasize the multitudinous tints of her flesh. When Françoise unexpectedly enters the room with a lamp, its light brings into focus on Albertine's face "des surfaces si brillamment, si uniformément colorées, si résistantes et si lisses, qu'on aurait pu les comparer aux carnations soutenues de certaines fleurs" (II, 360).[13]

Yet the idyllically sensuous phase of Marcel's love for Albertine is about to end, in part because of his sudden awareness of the physical defects of a girl who is no longer an adolescent. His disillusionment is reflected in the changed image: "quand elle était non plus balancée par mon imagination devant l'horizon marin, mais immobile auprès de moi, elle me semblait souvent une bien pauvre rose devant laquelle j'aurais bien voulu fermer les yeux pour ne pas voir tel défaut des pétales et pour croire que je respirais sur la plage" (II, 351–352).[14] The flower image is no longer evoked as often as before for yet another reason. By kissing Albertine's cheeks, Marcel thinks he will know at last the fragrance of the rose that blooms in them (II, 364). It is inevitable that he will be disappointed upon attaining what he has so long desired. Imagination operates only on what is absent; the object of Marcel's desires, like everything else in the Proustian world, turns into nothingness upon possession: "tout d'un coup, mes yeux cessèrent de voir, à son tour mon nez, s'écrasant, ne perçut plus aucune odeur, et sans connaître pour cela davantage le goût du rose désiré, j'appris, à ces détestables signes, qu'enfin j'étais en train d'embrasser la joue d'Albertine" (II, 365).[15]

The first of the two phases of Marcel's love for Albertine is now almost over. The hero has seen, pursued, and tasted of a woman who existed for him solely as a physical sensation of rose-colored flesh. Having been satisfied, his desire for her diminishes until the evening she telephones to tell him that she would rather not come to his apartment that night.

> En entendant ces mots d'excuse, prononcés comme si elle n'allait pas venir, je sentis qu'au désir de revoir la figure veloutée qui déjà à Balbec dirigeait toutes mes journées vers le moment où, devant la mer mauve de septembre, je serais auprès de cette fleur rose, tentait douloureusement de s'unir un élément bien différent. Ce terrible besoin d'un être, à Combray j'avais appris à le connaître au sujet de ma mère, et jusqu'à vouloir mourir si elle me faisait dire par Françoise q'elle ne pourrait pas monter. Cet effort de l'ancien sentiment pour se combiner et ne faire qu'un élément unique avec l'autre, plus récent, et qui, lui, n'avait pour voluptueux objet que la surface colorée, la rose carnation d'une fleur de plage, cet effort aboutit souvent à ne faire (au sens chimique) qu'un corps nouveau, qui peut ne durer que quelques instants. Ce soir-là, du moins, et pour longtemps encore, les deux éléments restèrent dissociés. (II, 733).[16]

This passage forebodes the nature Marcel's relationship with Albertine will assume. Her imminent death as a physical sensation of rose-colored flesh is forcefully suggested in this same scene: Marcel crushes a carnation in his buttonhole by turning away from Françoise as she attempts to remove it (II, 729).

The image of the flower is a constant source of literary inspiration to Proust during the happier phase of Marcel's relationship with Albertine, that is, until Marcel becomes aware of her deceptiveness and special proclivity during his second stay at Balbec. Since he now finds a psycho-erotic and aesthetic gratification with all the members of the small band, he is no longer in love with Albertine and hardly ever sends for her. His attitude changes abruptly one day in the casino at Incarville when Cottard, while watching Albertine and Andrée waltz with their breasts touching, observes that the two girls are probably lesbians. Marcel's jealousy aroused, he beings to persecute Albertine with questions and sarcasm.

Although Albertine's sexuality was undetermined during Marcel's first stay at Balbec, it is possible that she and her friends were already practicing Sapphists disguised as "jeunes filles en fleurs." Marcel now begins to wonder if the obstinacy with which she refused to give up an outing or some other pleasure during the summer he met her did not have as an ulterior motive the secret pursuit of illicit sensual pleasure. The implication is that her Sapphism already existed during his idyllic romance with the small band. The flower now offers two levels of interpretation, the aesthetic and psychological: it becomes a symbol of Albertine's secret vice after having represented the volatile beauty of her adolescence.

Proust equates the rose with a mysterious irritant when Marcel undergoes a strong urge to remain with Albertine upon hearing her laugh—a laugh which immediately evokes "les roses carnations, les parois parfumées contre lesquelles il semblait qu'il vînt de se frotter et dont, âcre, sensuel et révélateur comme une odeur de géranium, il semblait transporter avec lui quelques particules presque pondérables, irritantes et secrètes" (II, 795).[17] His suspicions calmed, Marcel enters upon a serene though voluptuous relationship with Albertine, taking long drives with her into the country or lying next to her on a moonlit beach. So intoxicated is he by contact with her that he feels her presence even when she is no longer with him: "je ne me sentais pas plus seul dans la voiture que si, avant de la quitter, elle y eût laissé des fleurs" (II, 1017).[18] The substitution of flowers for Albertine further indicates that the image is not an ornamentation separable from his conception of her but rather an organic part of his vision of the woman he loves.

The qualities of the small band are eventually transferred into a single rose—Albertine—which Marcel picks and takes away from Balbec (III, 68). But after he has made Albertine a captive in his Paris apartment, the rose no longer arouses a vision and sensation of adolescent innocence. One day he returns with some branches of syringa given him by Mme de Guermantes and surprises Andrée and Albertine having relations in the latter's bedroom. To stall for time, the two women pretend they hate the odor of syringas; after Albertine's death, however, Andrée confesses to him that they really loved the odor of these flowers (III, 55, 600–601). Once again Proust relates the flower to Albertine's secret vice. Marcel admits that the drives he takes with his prisoner do not give him the same calm and joy as those beautiful excursions at Balbec. He describes the latter retrospectively as "se détachant en beaux massifs de fleurs sur le reste de la vie d'Albertine comme sur un ciel vide devant lequel on rêve doucement, sans pensée" (III, 106).[19] At Balbec he took into account only the hours she spent with him; he was not on the lookout, as he is now, for a betrayal. The flower comparison is no longer that of infinite well-being but of tortured doubt before the mystery of her sexuality. Temporary appeasement and happiness for Marcel occur only when the conscious mind of his captive is absent, as in the famous scene when Albertine asleep reminds him of a long flowering stem (III, 69).

Since, on the psychological level, the image of the flower suggests only physical aggravation in the hero, Proust must turn to another image to convey the mental agony Albertine awakens in Marcel. And Albertine, whom Marcel describes as "une jeune fille qui ne serait d'abord, sur l'horizon de la mer, qu'une fleur . . . mais une fleur pensante et dans l'esprit de qui je souhaitais si puérilement de tenir une grande place" (III, 501),[20] will become the living mystery and evocation of the sea.

SEA IMAGERY

Albertine, whom Marcel beholds for the first time on the beach at Balbec, will always be seen by his memory "silhouettée sur l'écran que lui fait, au fond, la mer" (I, 829).[21]

Proust gives aesthetic unity to his characterization of Albertine by relating aspects of her appearance to the sea. Her nose is like a little wave (I, 891), and her cheeks (I, 946) and eyes (III, 18) are fluid like the sea. Her breath reminds Marcel of the sound of waves (III, 69) and of the sea breeze (III, 70). And her hair is transformed into waves (III, 18–19).

The sea offers several levels of interpretation.[22] It is another illustration of the manner in which Marcel pursues an emotional dream and an aesthetic reality in the women he loves. It was his poetic idealization of Bergotte and Swann and the pleasure he felt when he perceived Gilberte standing behind a hedge of hawthorn which made him fall in love with her. In the same way, it was his belief in a road bordered with flowers and the enchantment of seeing Mme de Guermantes haloed with the aureole of the stained-glass window of Gilbert le Mauvais which made him fall in love with the duchess. And Marcel says of the members of the small band: "Mais quand, même ne le sachant pas, je pensais à elles, plus inconsciemment encore, elles, c'était pour moi les ondulations montueuses et bleues de la mer, le profil d'un défilé devant la mer. C'était la mer que j'espérais retrouver, si j'allais dans quelque ville où elles seraient. L'amour le plus exclusif pour une personne est toujours l'amour d'autre chose" (I, 833).[23] Many years after the death of his passion for Albertine, he reflects that it was the sea, against which he had originally beheld her, that contained the very essence of his love for her (III, 839).

The sea also symbolizes the mobility of Albertine's voice, attitude, and appearance, all of which change each time Marcel sees her. Her curious gaze, rude tone of voice, and slang give him the impression that she is the cruel, vulgar, pleasure-seeking mistress of some professional racing cyclist (I, 793). Later, at Elstir's party, he is introduced to a respectable young lady deprived of her curious gaze and with an unattractive flushed temple as the optical center around which her features are arranged. She employs the adverb "parfaitement" in place of "tout à fait" and thus indicates a degree of culture and civilization (I, 871, 873). Still later, he barely recognizes her when he is greeted on the beach by a girl who is completely unlike the one he met at Elstir's. Now she is coarse, ill-mannered, no longer characterized by an inflamed temple; with a drawling nasal enunciation she uses such expressions as "Quel temps . . . au fond l'été sans fin de Balbec est une vaste blague! (I, 876).[24]

Albertine never has time to solidify as Marcel views her passing from what might be called one fluid state to another. While this transformation is occurring, certain elements may be said to join together momentarily to create the successive images of Albertine. These are not permanent images but fleeting impressions, and the background of sea against which Marcel sees Albertine and the other girls corresponds to their changing appearance. As the elements of the sea decompose perpetually to give us the impression of seeing each day another sea, ever new, ever old, so does Albertine appear exciting and newly created each time Marcel gazes at her. This change in her is due not only to her adolescence, but also to the mercurial climates of his spiritual needs:

> Pour être exact, je devrais donner un nom différent à chacun des moi qui dans la suite pensa à Albertine; je devrais plus encore donner un nom différent à chacune de ces Albertines qui apparaissaient devant moi, jamais la même, comme—appelées simplement par moi, pour plus de commodité, la mer—ces mers qui se succédaient et devant lesquelles, autre nymphe, elle se détachait. Mais surtout . . . je devrais donner toujours son nom à la croyance qui, tel jour où je voyais Albertine, régnait sur mon âme, en faisait l'atmosphère, l'aspect des êtres, comme celui des mers, dépendant de ces nuées à peine visibles qui changent la couleur de chaque chose par leur concentration, leur mobilité, leur dissémination, leur fuite. (I, 947–948).[25]

Water imagery, a symbol of flux in Albertine's appearance, also becomes a sign of her moral and psychological mystery, as Proust gradually indicates. Marcel is disappointed upon discovering that the girl to whom he is finally introduced at Elstir's party is not the one he has been pursuing by the sea, one who is to a great extent the creation of his own imagination.

The latter is characterized by athletic prowess, unintellectuality, vulgar language, and willful disregard for the feelings of others. The charming ways, timidity, culture, and accessibility of the girl whose acquaintance Marcel makes stop the flight of his imagination. Upon his return from Elstir's, he declares: "En face de la médiocre et touchante Albertine à qui j'avais parlé, je voyais la mystérieuse Albertine en face de la mer" (I, 875).[26] Convinced that Albertine is chaste, he concludes: "Ainsi s'était dissipée toute la gracieuse mythologie océanique que j'avais composée les premiers jours" (I, 949).[27] Thus, Marcel distinguishes between two Albertines early in their relationship, and he prefers the agitated, sensual girl who leads an uncontrolled existence, the essence of whose life is so unlike his own. Yet Albertine still attracts him as a "jeune fille en fleurs" of respectable bourgeois origin, even though she has lost her halo of mystery, symbolized by the sea.

Grieved during his second stay at Balbec by his grandmother's death, Marcel remains alone in his hotel room and refuses to see Albertine until one day the sensuality and gaiety of the beach make him long for her presence. He makes the mistake of trying to forget her by looking at the sea through the window of his hotel room: "Et, une fois, ne pouvant plus résister à mon désir, au lieu de me recoucher, je m'habillai et partis chercher Albertine à Incarville" (II, 784).[28] The sea and Albertine have become substitutes for each other in Marcel's mind. When he learns that Mlle Vinteuil, a notorious lesbian, has practically raised her, the image of the sea is immediately eclipsed: "Derrière Albertine je ne voyais plus les montagnes bleues de la mer, mais la chambre de Montjouvain où elle tombait dans les bras de Mlle Vinteuil avec ce rire où elle faisait entendre comme le son inconnu de sa jouissance" (II, 1117).[29] That unknown, symbolized by the sea, has become more specifically the unknown of Sapphic love. In an earlier scene Proust prepared for the extension of the sea image to include Albertine's lesbianism. When Albertine, whom Marcel had been plying with countless questions about her motives, declared that she would drown herself by throwing herself into the sea, he replied: " 'Comme Sapho.' 'Encore une insulte de plus; vous n'avez pas seulement des doutes sur ce que je dis, mais sur ce que je fais.' 'Mais, mon petit, je ne mettais aucune intention, je vous le jure, vous savez que Sapho s'est précipitée dans la mer' " (II, 801–802).[30] Only in retrospect does the reader understand the intimation of a remark, seemingly harmless on first reading, made by Marcel during the first stages of his relationship with Albertine: "Certains jours, mince, le teint gris, l'air maussade, une transparence violette descendant obliquement au fond de ses yeux comme il arrive quelquefois pour la mer, elle semblait éprouver une tristesse d'exilée" (I, 946).[31]

As we have seen, it is when Marcel begins to suspect Albertine of being a lesbian that he falls desperately in love with her. Thereafter he is attracted to her whenever his jealous curiosity is aroused. He again finds charm in his prisoner, for example, when he regards her as the rude unknowable girl whom he first saw in front of the sea at Balbec (III, 67–68). Occasionally, when he is most indifferent to her, he remembers a moment on the beach when Albertine, not far from a woman with whom he is now certain she had relations, burst out laughing and looked at him in an insolent manner. Shame, jealousy, remembrance of his first desires and of the dazzling setting restore to Albertine her beauty and former value: "Albertine, tantôt sortie de ce milieu, possédée et sans grande valeur, tantôt replongée en lui, m'échappant dans un passé que je ne pourrais connaître, m'offensant auprès de la dame, de son amie, autant que l'éclaboussure de la vague ou l'étourdissement du soleil, Albertine remise sur la plage ou rentrée dans ma chambre. en une sorte d'amour amphibie" (III, 174). Again Marcel is drawn to Albertine when a masculine gesture of departure on her part restores to her "sa nouveauté première, son inconnu et jusqu'à son cadre. Je vis la mer derrière cette jeune fille que je n'avais jamais vue me saluer ainsi depuis que je n'étais plus au bord de la mer" (III, 193).[32]

When Marcel first saw Albertine by the sea at Balbec, he intuited that he would not possess her if he did not possess the mystery in her eyes (I, 794). Near the beginning of her captivity under his roof, he likens her eyes to the sea: "Ses longs yeux bleus—plus allongés—n'avaient pas gardé la même forme; ils avaient bien la même couleur, mais semblaient être passés à l'état liquide. Si bien que, quand elle les fermait, c'était comme quand avec des rideaux on empêche de voir la mer. C'est sans doute de cette partie d'elle-même que je me souvenais surtout, chaque nuit en la quittant" (III, 18).[33] The mystery of Albertine's sexual tastes will continue to elude him. She is no longer a woman but an unknowable being, "une mer que nous essayons ridiculement, comme Xerxès, de battre pour la punir de ce qu'elle a englouti" (III, 104).[34] Proust has already used the image of Xerxes punishing the sea in his depiction of Charlus, in order to show that there is beauty in an inexplicable, mad gesture (III, 47). It here serves a double moral purpose, for Albertine also belongs to the Cities of the Plain. Her slightest actions, most casual remarks, the intonation of her voice, and her very silences become symbols to be deciphered by Marcel. The hopelessness and fatality of the situation become clear to him as he compares his caressing her to handling a stone which contains the salt of oceans immemorial; whereupon he declares; "je sentais que je touchais seulement l'enveloppe close d'un être qui par l'intérieur accédait à l'infini" (III, 386).[35]

Only while Albertine sleeps does she cease to deceive Marcel by gathering within her all of her selves. At such moments the sea is calmed (III, 70–71). As he touches and kisses Albertine asleep, Marcel does not gain any knowledge of the countless selves which constitute her soul and which he has long desired to know. At best he is momentarily assured that this creature who constantly lies to him in her waking state cannot continue to escape from him. Albertine's sleep now becomes an exciting adventure upon which Marcel embarks:

Sa respiration peu à peu plus profonde soulevait régulièrement sa poitrine et, par-dessus elle, ses mains croisées, ses perles, déplacées d'une manière différente par le même mouvement, comme ces barques, ces chaînes d'amarre que fait osciller le mouvement du flot. Alors, sentant que son sommeil était dans son plein, que je ne me heurterais pas à des écueils de conscience recouverts maintenant par la pleine mer du sommeil profond, délibérément je sautais sans bruit sur le lit, je me couchais au long d'elle, je prenais sa taille d'un de mes bras, je posais mes lèvres sur sa joue et sur son coeur, puis, sur toutes les parties de son corps, ma seule main restée libre et qui était soulevée aussi, comme les perles, par la respiration de la dormeuse; moi-même, j'étais déplacé légèrement par son mouvement régulier: je m'étais embarqué sur le sommeil d'Albertine.

Parfois, il me faisait goûter un plaisir moins pur. (III, 72)[36]

In this passage purely carnal pleasure is made to appear almost incidental to Marcel's cerebral ecstasy. As he clasps her waist with one arm, places his lips first on her cheek and then on her heart, and his free hand on every part of her body, he begins at last to possess Albertine. This does not mean that he seduces her, for they never consummate their relationship.[37] Sexual pleasure, though not excluded from Marcel's attraction to Albertine, is really incidental to it. Throughout *La Prisonnière* Marcel's physical attraction to Albertine has become a kind of intellectualized erotic desire in which concupiscence is supplanted by an endless curiosity to know the past, present, and future existence of Albertine.[38] This desire is far less easily assuaged than that of seducing her. By touching every part of the surface of the sea, calm while she sleeps and containing within it every point in time and space that her conscious mind has ever occupied, he arrives at a kind of possession of her (III, 73). Appeased in the same way as lovers who have just consummated the sexual act, Marcel tastes a delicious calm as he continues to lie next to her.

The gradual disintegration of Marcel's love is conveyed through the sea imagery. So often an encumbrance to him while she was his prisoner, Albertine regains her value after her flight: "comme un coquillage auquel on ne fait plus attention quand on l'a toujours sur sa commode, une fois qu'on s'en est séparé pour le donner ou l'ayant perdu et qu'on pense à lui, ce qu'on ne faisait plus, elle me rappelait toute la beauté joyeuse des montagnes bleues de la mer" (III, 453).[39] When he learns of her accident, the shock and sorrow he experiences push jealous thoughts out of his mind and only fond memories of her haunt him: "L'élan de ces souvenirs si tendres, venant se briser contre l'idée qu'elle était morte, m'oppressait par l'entrechoc de flux si contrariés que je ne pouvais rester immobile" (III, 482).[40] Marcel realizes eventually that his love had for its object less an objective being than an inner creation of his own sensibility which he linked with the sea. It was not Albertine at all whom he loved, for his love was greater than she, "l'enveloppant, ne la connaissant pas, comme une marée autour d'un mince brisant" (III, 503).[41] As the reality of her death presses in on his consciousness, he chooses to equate her death with the sea: "L'idée qu'Albertine était morte, cette idée qui, les premiers temps, venait battre si furieusement en moi l'idée qu'elle était vivante que j'étais obligé de me sauver devant elle comme les enfants à l'arrivée de la vague, cette idée de sa mort, à la faveur même de ces assauts incessants, avait fini par conquérir en moi la place qu'y occupait récemment encore l'idée de sa vie" (III, 534).[42] Marcel once again likens the sea to his suspicions, which are slower in leaving him than his fond memories of her: "Comme sur une plage où la marée descend irrégulièrement, j'étais assailli par la morsure de tel de mes soupçons quand déjà l'image de sa douce présence était retirée trop loin de moi pour pouvoir m'apporter son remède" (III, 535).[43] Involuntary memory, which at first evoked happy images of Albertine, gradually awakens painful memories of her guilt. Even his jealous despair at Albertine's guilt disappears as the final process of oblivion sets in: "De même que . . . la présence d'Albertine [avait perdu la signification] . . . des vallonnements bleus de la mer . . . de même l'idée douloureuse de la culpabilité d'Albertine serait renvoyée hors de moi par l'habitude" (III, 536).[44]

BIRD IMAGERY

As with the sea imagery, Proust enhances the poetic value of his portrayal of Albertine by comparing her to a bird. The young girls' speech reminds Marcel of the chirping of birds; and their voices will change, for he observes in their twitterings notes women do not possess (I, 908). He likens certain expressions Mme de Bontemps taught Albertine to the piping of the parent goldfinches which serves as a model for their newly hatched offspring (II, 356–357). The footsteps of Marcel's prisoner are similar to those of a little woodcock (III, 78); the charming, unconscious words she utters upon waking are like bird pipings (III, 115); and her curling hair, when she is seated at the pianola and turns to ask what she is to play next, resembles a wing (III, 303).

Marcel describes the small band upon its first entrance into the novel as "débarquée on ne sait d'où, une bande de mouettes qui exécute à pas comptés sur la plage—les retardataires rattrapant les autres en voletant—une promenade dont le but semble aussi obscur aux baigneurs qu'elles ne parissent pas voir, que clairement déterminé pour leur esprit d'oiseaux" (I, 788).[45] With this comparison of the young girls to birds in flight begins what is to be a constant and versatile image associated with Albertine. These birds, whose movements the bathers do not understand, are of an unknown origin. A few pages later, Proust reintroduces the image of the bird: "Elles firent quelques pas encore, puis s'arrêtèrent un moment au milieu du chemin sans s'occuper d'arrêter la circulation des passants, en un agrégat de forme irrégulière, compact, insolite et piaillant, comme un con-

ciliabule d'oiseaux qui s'assemblent au moment de s'envoler; puis elles re-
prirent leur lente promenade le long de la digue, au-dessus de la mer" (I,
792).[46] The amorphousness of the flock further indicates its elusiveness. The
girls are compared to birds that gather on the ground at the moment of
flight but do not fly away, preferring to resume their leisurely walk along
the shore. The mobility and mystery of these birds will eventually symbolize the fugacity of Albertine's ambiguous sexual life. The author tempo-
rarily abandons the bird imagery, just as he abandons the sea imagery, in
order to associate the small band almost exclusively with the flower image.

Proust reintroduces the image of the bird in flight near the end of *A
l'ombre des jeunes filles en fleurs,* when the girls at the close of summer
are dispersed "non pas toutes ensemble, comme les hirondelles, mais dans
la même semaine" (I, 950).[47] The author purposely casts a shadow of mystery over Albertine's departure: "Albertine s'en alla la première, brusque-
ment, sans qu'aucune de ses amies eût pu comprendre, ni alors, ni plus
tard, pourquoi elle était rentrée tout à coup à Paris, où ni travaux, ni distractions ne la rappelaient" (I, 950).[48] Was this sudden flight a reaction to
instinct, a necessary movement, like the migration of birds?

As seen above, Marcel's love for the adolescent Albertine is symbolized primarily by the flower. When this love dies, it is replaced by another
love, inspired by jealousy and symbolized not only by the sea but also by
the bird. This change is indicated by the transformation of the flower,
which has already been equated with Albertine's aberrant love, into a bird,
in a passage concerned with Mme de Cambremer's visit to the sea wall:
" 'Oh! elles s'envolent, s'écria Albertine en me montrant les mouettes qui,
se débarrassant pour un instant de leur incognito de fleurs, montaient
toutes ensemble vers le soleil. . . . Je les aime beaucoup, j'en voyais à Amsterdam, dit Albertine. Elles sentent la mer, elles viennent la humer même
à travers les pierres des rues' " (II, 814).[49] Albertine, like the sea gulls, occasionally casts aside her "incognito de fleurs," as during the dancing incident in the casino and again when Marcel catches Albertine secretly staring
at two other lesbians in a mirror in the same casino. It is not the sea gulls,
however, that represent her special proclivity, but the sea, the symbolism
of which has already been discussed: as the sea gulls are attracted to places
which smell of salt air, homosexuals are drawn to the habitats of their fel-
lows.

Albertine's love of birds and the very fact that she observes them in
flight may be interpreted as foreboding her eventual flight from Marcel's
apartment. The bird imagery, in association with the flower and sea imagery, has a more profound significance than this. The flower accidentally
grows by the sea, whereas the sea gull is a creature of the sea. Once Albertine ceases to be a "jeune fille en fleurs," she becomes an "incognito de
fleurs" that desires the sea. For the flower to reach the sea, it must transform itself into a bird. Whenever Albertine yields to her Sapphic sensibil-

ity, she abandons her "incognito de fleurs" and assumes the form of a bird, thus allowing Marcel a momentary perception and insight, even though the bird soon reverts to its aspect of flower.

He finally decides to bring the matter of lesbianism before Albertine. At the start of the conversation, he observes: "je la conduisis jusqu'à ma porte. Celle-ci en s'ouvrant fit refluer la lumière rose qui remplissait la chambre et changeait la mousseline blanche des rideaux tendus sur le soir en lampas aurore. J'allai jusqu'à la fenêtre; les mouettes étaient posées de nouveau sur les flots; mais maintenant elles étaient roses. Je le fis remarquer à Albertine" (II, 828).[50] The gulls have resumed their "incognito de fleurs" just as Albertine, after the incident in the casino when she followed her sexual tastes, takes back hers. The transformation of the room and gulls into red is symbolic of sexuality, and prepares the reader for the image that follows. After pretending to Albertine that he is in love with Andrée, Marcel pauses before approaching the real issue at stake:

> Je m'interrompis pour regarder et montrer à Albertine un grand oiseau solitaire et hâtif qui, loin devant nous, fouettant l'air du battement régulier de ses ailes, passait à toute vitesse au-dessus de la plage tachée çà et là de reflets pareils à de petits morceaux de papier rouge déchirés et la traversait dans toute sa longueur, sans ralentir son allure, sans détourner son attention, sans devier de son chemin, comme un émissaire qui va porter bien loin un message urgent et capital. (II, 830–831)[51]

This image indicates that Albertine has renounced her "incognito de fleurs," for the "petits morceaux de papier rouge déchirés" correspond to petals which have fallen on the beach. At the same time the red reflections suffuse the image with an atmosphere of awakened sexuality. The speed, suggested by the flight of the bird, corresponds to Albertine's elusiveness whenever Marcel attempts to grasp her nature mentally: "Entre vos mains mêmes, ces êtres-là sont des êtres de fuite. Pour comprendre les émotions qu'ils donnent et que d'autres êtres, même plus beaux, ne donnent pas, il faut calculer qu'ils sont non pas immobiles, mais en mouvement, et ajouter à leur personne un signe correspondant à ce qu'en [sic] physique est le signe qui signifie vitesse" (III, 92).[52] Albertine's physical attractiveness is subordinated to her hidden life. This explains why Marcel falls in love with and imprisons a girl whom after her death he will remember as having been very stout, masculine, and unattractive (III, 643). For if the bird is identified with an elusive being, its symbolic wings are a projection of the narrator's attitude:

> A ces êtres-là, à ces êtres de fuite, leur nature, notre inquiétude attach- ent des ailes. Et même auprès de nous, leur regard semble nous dire qu'ils vont s'envoler. La preuve de cette beauté, surpassant la beauté, qu'ajoutent les ailes, est que bien souvent pour nous un même être est successivement sans ailes et ailé. Que nous craignions de le perdre, nous

oublions tous les autres. Sûrs de le garder, nous le comparons à ces autres qu'aussitôt nous lui préférons. (III, 93).[53]

The bird is no longer red after Marcel places it in a cage, because Albertine is not able to frequent other lesbians: "Une fois captif chez moi
l'oiseau que j'avais vu un soir marcher à pas comptés sur la digue, entouré
de la congrégation des autres jeunes filles pareilles à des mouettes venues
on ne sait d'où, Albertine avait perdu toutes ses couleurs, avec toutes les
chances qu'avaient les autres de l'avoir à eux" (III, 173).[54] By capturing her,
Marcel has immobilized her and made her a physical, immediate being ac-
cessible as a present sensation to his experience. But all present sensations
pass into nothingness in the Proustian world, and Albertine ceases to interest her captor: "Parce que le vent de la mer ne gonflait plus ses vêtements,
parce que, surtout, je lui avais coupé les ailes, elle avait cessé d'être une
Victoire, elle était une pesante esclave dont j'aurais voulu me débarrasser"
(III, 371).[55]

Although Albertine has lost her colors, she is still a "oiseau mystérieux." The cage of Marcel's apartment holds her in a deceptive way only,
since the object of his desires is not her physical being, symbolized by the
bird, but the sea to which the bird flies. By imprisoning the bird, Marcel
has not captured its mystery. To do this, he would have to capture the sea
as well. Because he is not sure whether Albertine is or is not a lesbian, he
has not solved the mystery of her sexual tendencies. She is a lesbian who
has abandoned the sea until one day the sea breeze calls her again: "Lâchée
de nouveau, ayant quitté le cage d'où, chez moi, je restais des jours entiers
sans la faire venir dans ma chambre, elle avait repris pour moi toute sa valeur, elle était redevenue celle que tout le monde suivait, l'oiseau merveil-
leux des premiers jours" (III, 472–473).[56]

Proust emphasizes Marcel's failure to possess Albertine by showing, as
he has already done with the image of the sea, that the hero never possesses what is in her eyes. While Albertine was free, her eyes shone like
the transparent wings of a sky-blue butterfly (I, 946). In the scene when
Marcel watches her sleep, he compares her eyebrows to a halcyon's downy
nest (III, 72). At first glance this image only implies the peace of sleep for
Albertine and the calm of possession for Marcel. The halcyon is a fabulous
bird of good omen that builds its nest on a calm sea. Albertine's eyebrows
and the globes of her eyelids correspond to the bird's nest and the sea. The
sea of Lesbos being calm, the bird alights on it to build its nest. Albertine
is no longer "un être de fuite." It would seem that Marcel is once again
leading with his captive the halcyon existence of Balbec. The eyelid, however, covers the eye; the two are not identical. Marcel has not penetrated
the essence behind Albertine's eyes by capturing her. His possession is il-
lusory and Albertine captured is still elusive; only while she sleeps does
she cease to be deceptive. Shortly before her flight, he compares her eyes
to the mauve, silken wings of a butterfly placed under glass (III, 383). Dur-

ing Albertine's captivity under his roof her eyes have merely become more resistant to his effort to penetrate their mystery.

After her escape, life becomes unbearable for Marcel. Unlike Manon Lescaut, of whom he thinks after her flight:

> 'Hélas, l'oiseau qui fuit ce qu'il croit l'esclavage,
>   Le plus souvent la nuit
> D'un vol désespéré revient battre au vitrage,'

(III, 452)[57]

Albertine does not return except in the form of a bird of prey to devour Marcel. While Andrée, whom he feels was Albertine's secret ally, speaks to him, Marcel reflects: "tandis que l'espace que j'avais pu concéder encore à l'innocence d'Albertine se rétrécissait de plus en plus, il me semblait m'apercevoir que malgré mes efforts, je gardais l'aspect figé d'un animal autour duquel un cercle progressivement resserré est lentement décrit par l'oiseau fascinateur, qui ne se presse pas parce qu'il est sûr d'atteindre quand il le voudra la victime qui ne lui échappera plus" (III, 548).[58] By going high in the sky and making itself visible, the bird of prey reveals the existence of other birds. In the same way Marcel imagines that Andrée will reveal to him the mystery of Albertine's sexual tastes.

Albertine is wearing her Fortuny gown with its design of oriental birds and the Grand Canal when Marcel kisses her shortly before her escape. "Je l'embrassai alors une seconde fois, serrant contre mon coeur l'azur miroitant et doré du Grand Canal et les oiseaux accouplés, symboles de mort et de résurrection" (III, 399).[59] The idea of copulating birds alludes to the sexual practices which Albertine will resume after her flight; the death, to her death shortly after she escapes; and the resurrection to the past recaptured. Albertine will die and be resurrected through Marcel's memory. When he attempts to kiss her, she instinctively draws away like animals who feel death. He asks her to take off her Fortuny gown: "je n'ose pas vous approcher pour ne pas froisser cette belle étoffe et il y a entre nous ces oiseaux fatidiques" (III, 400).[60] But Albertine refuses to remove her dress: she is determined to return to the sea of Lesbos.

She now sits on Marcel's bed and they continue their conversation. "Tout d'un coup nous entendîmes la cadence régulière d'un appel plaintif. C'étaient les pigeons qui commençaient à roucouler. 'Cela prouve qu'il fait déjà jour,' dit Albertine; et le sourcil presque froncé, comme si elle manquait en vivant chez moi les plaisirs de la belle saison: 'Le printemps est commencé pour que les pigeons soient revenus' " (III, 400).[61] Just as the pigeon wants to escape and fly away with the arrival of fine weather, Albertine desires to go back to the sea of Lesbos now that spring has returned. The same night on which these events take place, Marcel hears her open her window violently. Although she knows this is forbidden because the night air is harmful to him, she disobeys his orders. This ominous sign becomes for him "un présage plus mystérieux et plus funèbre qu'un cri de chouette" (III, 402).[62] After Albertine's flight, Françoise discovers two rings she has left behind. In answer to her master's statement that one ring came from Albertine's aunt and the other was bought by Albertine, the servant reawakens his suspicions about her infidelity. She points out to him that the same eagle's head is carved on both rings and that the same person must have given Albertine both of them (III, 462–463). The eagle, one of the strongest birds of prey, becomes symbolic of Albertine's successful escape from her captivity.

In order to come and live with Marcel, Albertine, who loves the sea (II, 1114) and yachting (II, 1123), had given up the idea of going on a cruise with Mlle Vinteuil and her friend (II, 1114; III, 10). Her sacrifice symbolized the abandonment of her sexual pursuits, of going to the sea of Lesbos. After her flight, he attempts to lure her back by writing to offer her the yacht she desired. He suggests in the same letter that she could go cruising while he, not well enough to accompany her, would wait for her at the port. "Le yacht était déjà presque prêt, il s'appelle, selon votre désir exprimé à Balbec, le 'Cygne'" (III, 455).[63] By giving Albertine a swan yacht, Marcel is telling her that she may cruise the sea of Lesbos, and he will not interfere. After her death, he suddenly remembers how she blushed when he mentioned her shower-wrap. Anxious to confirm his suspicions and resolve the mystery of her sexuality, he sends Aimé to Balbec, to the sea, for answers to the enigma which for so long has been the source of his intermittent anguish. In a letter to Marcel, Aimé reveals that Albertine had liaisons with other women in the baths (III, 515–516). From further information obtained from Aimé, he at last seems to penetrate the mystery of Albertine's lesbianism as he imagines her bathing with other women. The setting is a secluded spot on the bank of the Loire where Albertine used to meet a certain laundress and her friends at dawn. Here Marcel envisages them lying about in the nude on the grass while drying, playing, caressing, and pushing each other into the water. The image of these nude female bodies reminds him of a painting by Elstir. In this painting, one of the girls is raising her thigh in such a way that it makes the same swan's neck curve with the angle of the knee that was made by the droop of Albertine's thigh when she was lying by his side on the bed (II, 190).

> Me souvenant de ce qu'elle était sur mon lit, je croyais voir sa cuisse recourbée, je la voyais, c'était un col de cygne, il cherchait la bouche de l'autre jeune fille. Alors je ne voyais même plus une cuisse, mais le col hardi d'un cygne, comme celui qui dans une étude frémissante cherche la bouche d'une Léda qu'on voit dans toute la palpitation spécifique du plaisir féminin, parce qu'il n'y a qu'un cygne, qu'elle semble plus seule. . . . Dans cette étude le plaisir, au lieu d'aller vers la femme qu l'inspire et qui est absente, remplacée par un cygne inerte, se concentre dans celle qui le ressent. (III, 528).[64]

With the swan-Leda image, symbolic of sexual desire and nudity, the culmination of the symbolism of Albertine's lesbianism is reached. The circle
is completed: the sea gull has returned to its mysterious point of origin.

Many years after Albertine's death when Marcel, grown old, has
nearly stopped thinking of his past love for her, he chooses to remember
her as he saw her originally on the beach of Balbec "foulant le sable ce
premier soir, indifférente à tous, et marine, comme une mouette" (III,
848).[65]

Introduced by Marcel soon after he first sees Albertine, the images of
the rose, sea, and bird form a system of correspondences. The beach flower
is transformed into a sea gull whose natural habitat is the sea. Albertine, at
first a constantly changing surface (the flower), becomes an elusive being
(the bird) who fascinates Marcel because of the mystery of her sexual inversion (the sea). Marcel evokes the image of the flower to suggest the exterior
multiplicity of Albertine. The vastness and vagueness of the sea convey his
overwhelming failure to dominate her inner flux. The image of the bird is
that of the imprisoned Albertine; it also indicates that her role is one of
flight. Herein lies the truth of her immense power over Marcel. The unknown, symbolized by the sea, would cease to attract him if Albertine were
not in flight, since immobility on her part would allow him to possess her.
Whenever this happens, the sea disappears and he finds himself confronted
by a commonplace girl whose presence prevents him from seeking other
conquests.

Marcel realizes that in his devotion to Albertine her role is insignificant insofar as it does not pertain to her flight. Hence she is not a loved
person who exists independently of that love; rather, she is a projection, a
vision of that love. She is conceived not as a "real" human being in the
naturalistic sense, but as a complex structure of images emerging from
Marcel's longing to possess an entity within himself. Albertine's personality, which remains an enigma for Marcel and the reader, is never eluci-
dated. It is for this reason that, in spite of appearing in the novel more than
any other character with the exception of the narrator himself, she never
emerges with clearly delineated contours.

The constantly recurring images of the flower, sea, and bird become
central to an understanding of Marcel's perception of Albertine and hence
Albertine as a character. As seen through these images, she is characterized
by constant change on both the physical and psychological levels. With
each succeeding image, she asserts her presence while at the same time
escaping Marcel's grasp. When he does succeed in immobilizing her, as
when he kisses her or when he is assured that she is not deceiving him,
the experience is transformed into nothingness. Because of the intimacy
and duration of Marcel's relationship with this "grande déesse du Temps"
(II, 387),[66] his failure to possess her becomes symbolic of Proust's belief in
the impermeability of everything in time and space.[67] The imagery con-

cerning Albertine, therefore, offers a clear demonstration of the Proustian conception of the human condition, and takes its place within the framework of the entire novel. Recognizing the insignificance of Albertine as an objective being, the hero does not admit defeat but turns at last and looks within himself to discover what he ultimately sought in her, the essence of his own being.

Notes

1. Marcel Proust, *A la recherche du temps perdu*, III, 374–375. Henceforth, all references in parentheses will be to the three-volume Pléiade edition of this work and will include only the volume and page numbers. [what we feel about life not being felt in the form of ideas, its literary, that is to say intellectual expression describes it, explains it, analyses it, but does not recompose it as does music, in which the sounds seem to follow the very movement of our being, to reproduce that extreme inner point of our sensations which is the part that gives us that peculiar exhilaration which we experience from time to time and which, when we say "What a fine day! What glorious sunshine!" we do not in the least communicate to others, in whom the same sun and the same weather evoke quite different vibrations . . . It is inconceivable that a piece of sculpture or a piece of music which gives us an emotion that we feel to be more exalted, more pure, more true, does not correspond to some definite spiritual reality, or life would be meaningless . . . These key-phrases, which you are beginning to recognise as I do, my little Albertine, the same in the sonata, in the septet, in the other works, would be, say for instance in Barbey d'Aurevilly, a hidden reality revealed by a physical sign. . . . (*RTPK* 3:381–82)].

2. [I gazed at Albertine's cheeks as she spoke, and asked myself what might be the perfume, the taste of them: that day she was not fresh and cool but smooth, with a uniform pinkness, violet-tinted, creamy, like certain roses whose petals have a waxy gloss. I felt a passionate longing for them such as one feels sometimes for a particular flower (*RTPK* 1:949)].

3. [So that trying to make friends with Albertine seemed to me like entering into contact with the unknown, if not the impossible, an occupation . . . as absorbing as keeping bees or growing roses (*RTPK* 1:942)].

4. [And as I passed from corolla to corolla along this chain of flowers, the pleasure of knowing a different one would send me back to the one to whom I was indebted for it, with a gratitude mixed with as much desire as my new hope (*RTPK* 1:952)].

5. [Among these girls, rose-sprigs whose principal charm was that they were silhouetted against the sea, the same indivisibility prevailed as at the time when I did not know them, when the appearance of no matter which of them had caused me such violent emotion by heralding the fact that the little band was not far off (*RTPK* 1:1007)].

6. [had a sensual sweetness which was in keeping somehow with the pink, almost mauve colouring of her skin (*RTPK* 1:981)].

7. [so generously, so carefully, so minutely, colour and fragrance over the fleshly surfaces of these girls . . . (*RTPK* 1:1013)].

8. [(the senses) give to these girls the same honeyed consistency as they create when they go foraging in a rose-garden, or a vine whose clusters their eyes devour (*RTPK* 1:953–54)].

9. [it was not possible to find gathered together rarer specimens than these young flowers that at this moment before my eyes were breaking the line of the sea with their slender hedge, like a bower of Pennsylvania roses (*RTPK* 1:856)].

10. [Alas! in the freshest flower it is possible to discern those just perceptible signs which to the instructed mind already betray what will, by the desiccation or fructification of

the flesh that is to-day in bloom, be the ultimate form, immutable and already predestined, of the autumnal seed (*RTPK* 1:952)].

11. [As in a nursery plantation where the flowers mature at different seasons, I had seen them, in the form of old ladies, on this Balbec shore, those shrivelled seed-pods, those flabby tubers, which my new friends would one day be. But what matter? For the moment it was their flowering-time (*RTPK* 1:953)].

12. [It was enough that I should be told that she was in Paris and that she had called at my house for me to see her again like a rose flowering by the sea (*RTPK* 2:364)].

13. [surfaces so glowingly, so uniformly coloured, so firm and so smooth, that one might have compared them to the sustained flesh tints of certain flowers (*RTPK* 2:373)].

14. [when she was no longer swaying in my imagination before a horizon of sea, but motionless in a room beside me, she seemed to me often a very poor specimen of a rose, so much so that I wanted to shut my eyes in order not to observe this or that blemish of its petals, and to imagine instead that I was inhaling the salt air on the beach (*RTPK* 2:364)].

15. [suddenly my eyes ceased to see, then my nose, crushed by the collision, no longer perceived any odour, and, without thereby gaining any clearer idea of the taste of the rose of my desire, I learned, from these obnoxious signs, that at last I was in the act of kissing Albertine's cheek (*RTPK* 2:379)].

16. [As I listened to these words of excuse, uttered as though she did not intend to come, I felt that, with the longing to see again the velvet-soft face which in the past, at Balbec, used to direct all my days towards the moment when, by the mauve September sea, I should be beside that roseate flower, a very different element was painfully endeavouring to combine. This terrible need of a person was something I had learned to know at Combray in the case of my mother, to the point of wanting to die if she sent word to me by Françoise that she could not come upstairs. This effort on the part of the old feeling to combine and form a single element with the other, more recent, which had for its voluptuous object only the coloured surface, the flesh-pink bloom of a flower of the sea-shore, was one that often results simply in creating (in the chemical sense) a new body, which may last only a few moments. That evening, at any rate, and for long afterwards, the two elements remained apart (*RTPK* 2:759)].

17. [the flesh-pink, fragrant surfaces with which it seemed to have just been in contact and of which it seemed to carry with it, pungent, sensual and revealing as the scent of geraniums, a few almost tangible and mysteriously revealing particles (*RTPK* 2:823)].

18. [I felt no more alone in [the car] than if before leaving me she had strewn it with flowers (*RTPK* 2:1050].

19. [standing out like clustering flowers against the rest of Albertine's life as against an empty sky beneath which one muses pleasantly, without thinking (*RTPK* 3:101)].

20. [a girl who would at first be no more, against the horizon of the sea, than a flower . . . but a thinking flower in whose mind I was so childishly anxious to occupy a prominent place (*RTPK* 3:511)].

21. [silhouetted against the screen which the sea spreads out behind her (*RTPK* 1:888)].

22. In *The Imagery of Proust* (Oxford: Basil Blackwell, 1966), Victor E. Graham has attributed Proust's use of sea and water imagery to the author's conception of the world as being eternal and in constant flux, and to the poetic beauty of the sea. To prove his point, he gives many examples of sea imagery employed by Proust in his evocation of Albertine. Although Mr. Graham is not wrong as far as he goes, he offers no special importance for the sea imagery in reference to Albertine.

23. [But when, even without knowing it, I thought of them, they, more unconsciously still, were for me the mountainous blue undulations of the sea, the outline of a procession against the sea. It was the sea that I hoped to find, if I went to some town where they had gone. The most exclusive love for a person is always a love for something else. (*RTPK* 1:891)].

24. ["What weather! . . . really the perpetual summer of Balbec is all stuff and non-sense" (*RTPK* 1:937)].

25. [To be quite accurate, I ought to give a different name to each of the selves who subsequently thought about Albertine; I ought still more to give a different name to each of the Albertines who appeared before me, never the same, like those seas—called by me simply and for the sake of convenience "the sea"—that succeeded one another and against which, a nymph likewise, she was silhouetted. But above all . . . I ought always to give its name to the belief that reigned over my soul and created its atmosphere on any given day on which I saw Albertine, the appearance of people, like that of the sea, being dependent on those clouds, themselves barely visible, which change the colour of everything by their concentration, their mobility, their dissemination, their flight (*RTPK* 1:1010–11)].

26. [Confronted with the commonplace and touching Albertine to whom I had spoken that afternoon, I still saw the other mysterious Albertine outlined against the sea (*RTPK* 1:936)].

27. [Thus had there faded and vanished all the lovely oceanic mythology which I had composed in those first days (*RTPK* 1:1012)].

28. [And once, unable any longer to hold out against my desire, instead of going back to bed I put on my clothes and set off for Incarville to find Albertine (*RTPK* 2:812)].

29. [Behind Albertine I no longer saw the blue mountains of the sea, but the room at Montjouvain where she was falling into the arms of Mlle Vinteuil with that laugh in which she gave utterance as it were to the strange sound of her pleasure (*RTPK* 2:1154)].

30. ["Like Sappho." There you go, insulting me again. You suspect not only what I say but what I do." "But, my lamb, I didn't mean anything, I swear to you. You know Sappho flung herself into the sea" (*RTPK* 2:829–30)].

31. [On certain days, thin, with a grey complexion, a sullen air, a violet transparency slanting across her eyes such as we notice sometimes on the sea, she seemed to be feeling the sorrows of exile (*RTPK* 1:1009)].

32. [Albertine, now abstracted from that environment, possessed and of no great value, now plunged back into it, escaping from me into a past which I should never get to know, humiliating me before the lady who was her friend as much as the splashing of the waves or the dizzying heat of the sun,—Albertine restored to the beach or brought back again to my room, in a sort of amphibious love (*RTPK* 3:172)].

33. [Her blue, almond-shaped eyes—now even more elongated—had altered in appearance; they were indeed of the same colour, but seemed to have passed into a liquid state. So much so that, when she closed them, it was as though a pair of curtains had been drawn to shut out a view of the sea. It was no doubt this aspect of her person that I remembered most vividly each night on leaving her (*RTPK*, 3:10–11)].

34. [a sea which, like Xerxes, we scourge with rods in an absurd attempt to punish it for what it has engulfed (*RTPK* 3:100)].

35. [I felt that I was touching no more than the sealed envelope of a person who inwardly reached to infinity (*RTPK* 3:393)].

36. [Her breathing, as it became gradually deeper, made her breast rise and fall in a regular rhythm, and above it her folded hands and her pearls, displaced in a different way by the same movement, like boats and anchor chains set swaying by the movement of the tide. Then, feeling that the tide of her sleep was full, that I should not run aground on reefs of consciousness covered now by the high water of profound slumber, I would climb deliberately and noiselessly on to the bed, lie down by her side, clasp her waist in one arm, and place my lips upon her cheek and my free hand on her heart and then on every part of her body in turn, so that it too was raised, like the pearls, by the breathing of the sleeping girl; I myself was gently rocked by its regular motion: I had embarked upon the tide of Albertine's sleep.

Sometimes it afforded me a pleasure that was less pure (*RTPK* 3:66)].

37. See III, 97: "D'ailleurs, Albertine m'effrayait en me disant que j'avais raison . . . de dire que je n'étais pas son amant, puisque aussi bien, ajoutait-elle, 'c'est la vérité que vous ne l'êtes pas.' Je ne l'étais peut-être pas complètement en effet. . . ." [Albertine alarmed me further when she said that I was quite right to say . . . that I was not her lover, since "for that matter," she went on, "it's perfectly true that you aren't." I was not perhaps her lover in the full sense of the word. (*RTPK* 3:91)].

38. See III, 95: "elle me donnait des satisfactions charnelles, et puis elle était intelligente. Mais tout cela était une superfétation.Ce qui m'occupait l'esprit n'était pas ce qu'elle avait pu dire d'intelligent, mais tel mot qui éveillait chez moi un doute sur ses actes. . . ." [she did give me some carnal satisfaction, and moreover she was intelligent. But all this was supererogatory. What occupied my mind was not something intelligent that she might have said, but a chance remark that had aroused in me a doubt as to her actions. (*RTPK* 3:90)].

39. [like a sea-shell to which one ceases to pay any attention when it is always there on one's chest of drawers, and once one has parted with it, either by giving it away or by losing it, one begins to think about again, she recalled to me all the joyous beauty of the blue mountains of the sea. (*RTPK* 3:461)].

40. [The influx of these tender memories, breaking against the idea that Albertine was dead, oppressed me with such a clash of warring currents that I could not remain still (*RTPK* 3:492)].

41. [enveloping her, unconscious of her, like a tide swirling round a tiny rock (*RTPK* 3:513)].

42. [The idea that Albertine was dead, which at first used to contest so furiously with the idea that she was alive that I was obliged to run away from it as children run away from an oncoming wave, by the very force of its incessant onslaughts had ended by capturing the place in my mind that a short while before was still occupied by the idea of her life. (*RTPK* 3:544)].

43. [As upon a beach where the tide recedes unevenly, I would be assailed by the onrush of one of my suspicions when the image of her tender presence had already withdrawn too far from me to be able to bring me its remedial balm (*RTPK* 3:545)].

44. [Just as . . . Albertine's presence [had lost the significance] . . . of the blue undulations of the sea . . . similarly the painful knowledge of Albertine's guilt would be expelled from me by habit (*RTPK* 3:547)].

45. [a flock of gulls arriving from God knows where and performing with measured tread upon the sands—the dawdlers flapping their wings to catch up with the rest—a parade the purpose of which seems as obscure to the human bathers whom they do not appear to see as it is clearly determined in their own birdish minds (*RTPK* 1:846)].

46. [They walked on a little way, then stopped for a moment in the middle of the road, oblivious of the fact that they were impeding the passage of other people, in an agglomerate that was at once irregular in shape, compact, weird and shrill, like an assembly of birds before taking flight; then they resumed their leisurely stroll along the esplanade, against the background of the sea (*RTPK* 1:849–50)].

47. [not all at once, like the swallows, but all in the same week (*RTPK* 1:1013)].

48. [Albertine was the first to go, abruptly, without any of her friends understanding, then or afterwards, why she had returned suddenly to Paris whither neither her work nor any amusement summoned her (*RTPK* 1:1013)].

49. ["Oh! they're flying away," exclaimed Albertine, pointing to the gulls which, casting aside for a moment their flowery incognito, were rising in a body towards the sun . . . "I do love them: I saw some in Amsterdam," said Albertine. "They smell of the sea, they come and sniff the salt air even through the paving stones" (*RTPK* 2:842–43)].

50. [I escorted her to the door of my room. Opening it, I scattered the roseate light that was flooding the room and turning the white muslin of the curtains drawn for the night

to golden damask. I went across to the window; the gulls had settled again upon the waves; but this time they were pink. I drew Albertine's attention to them (*RTPK* 2:857)].

51. [I broke off to admire and point out to Albertine a great, solitary, speeding bird which, far out in front of us, lashing the air with the regular beat of its wings, flew at full speed over the beach, which was stained here and there with gleaming reflexions like little torn scraps of red paper, and crossed it from end to end without slackening its pace, without diverting its attention, without deviating from its path, like an envoy carrying far afield an urgent and vital message (*RTPK* 2:859–60)].

52. [Even when you hold them in your hands, such persons are fugitives. To understand the emotions which they arouse, and which others, even better-looking, do not, we must realize that they are not immobile but in motion, and add to their person a sign corresponding to that which in physics denotes speed (RTPK 3:86–87)].

53. [To such beings, such fugitive beings, their own nature and our anxiety fasten wings. And even when they are with us the look in their eyes seems to warn us that they are about to take flight. The proof of this beauty, surpassing beauty itself, that wings add is that often, for us, the same person is alternately winged and wingless. Afraid of losing her, we forgot all the others. Sure of keeping her, we compare her with those others whom at once we prefer to her (*RTPK* 3:88)].

54. [As soon as she was a captive in my house, the bird that I had seen one afternoon advancing with measured tread along the front, surrounded by a congregation of other girls like seagulls alighted from who knew where, Albertine had lost all her colours, together with all the opportunities that other people had of securing her for themselves (*RTPK* 3:170–71)].

55. [because the sea breeze no longer puffed out her skirts; because, above all, I had clipped her wings, and she had ceased to be a winged Victory and become a burdensome slave of whom I would have liked to rid myself (*RTPK* 3:378)].

56. [Set free once more, released from the cage in which, here at home, I used to leave her for days on end without letting her come to my room, Albertine had regained all her attraction in my eyes; she had become once more the girl whom everyone pursued, the marvellous bird of the earliest days (*RTPK* 3:481)].

57. [Alas, the bird which flees what it believes to be slavery/Most often at night/Returns to beat despairing wings against the window pane (Editor's translation of *RTP* 3:452)].

58. [while the space that I had still been able to concede to Albertine's innocence became smaller and smaller, it seemed to me that, despite my efforts, I presented the paralysed aspect of an animal round which a bird of prey is wheeling in steadily narrowing circles, unhurriedly because it is confident of being able to swoop on its helpless victim whenever it chooses (*RTPK* 3:558)].

59. [I kissed her then a second time, pressing to my heart the shimmering golden azure of the Grand Canal and the mating birds, symbols of death and resurrection (*RTPK* 3:406)].

60. ["I dare not approach you for fear of crumpling that fine stuff, and there are those fateful birds between us" (*RTPK* 3:407)].

61. [Suddenly we heard the regular rhythm of a plaintive call. It was the pigeons beginning to coo. "That proves that day has come already," said Albertine; and, her brows almost knitted, as though she missed, by living with me, the joys of the fine weather, "Spring has begun, if the pigeons have returned" (*RTPK* 3:407)].

62. [an omen more mysterious and more funereal than the hoot of an owl (*RTPK* 3:409)].

63. [The yacht was almost ready; it is named, after a wish that you expressed at Balbec, the *Swan* (*RTPK* 3:464)].

64. [Remembering Albertine as she lay on my bed, I seemed to see the curve of her thigh, I saw it as a swan's neck, seeking the other girl's mouth. Then I no longer even saw a thigh, but simply the bold neck of a swan, like the one that can be seen in a voluptuous

sketch seeking the mouth of a Leda who is rapt in the palpitating specificity of feminine pleasure, because there is no one else with her but a swan, and she seems more alone . . . In
this sketch, the pleasure, instead of reaching out to the woman who inspires it and who is
absent, replaced by an expressionless swan, is concentrated in her who feels it (*RTPK* 3:538)].

65. [making her progress along the sand that first evening, indifferent to everybody
around her, a marine creature, like a seagull (*RTPK* 3:878)].

66. [mighty goddess of Time (*RTPK* 3:393)] [Note: reference incorrect; II, 387 should
read III, 387.]

67. Carl John Black, Jr., has written a perceptive and original article called "Albertine
as an Allegorical Figure of Time"—*Romanic Review* LIV (Oct. 1963), 171–186. Mr. Black's
interpretation of Albertine as a "grande déesse du Temps" traces the intricacy and scope of
the heroine's metaphorical role both as a psychological and structural entity.

Proust's Marcel and Saint-Loup:
Inversion Reconsidered   Melvin Seiden*

In the first volume of his Proust biography, George Painter gives us
an amusing sketch of a "Guermantes hostess," the Comtesse Rosa de Fitz-
James, "a Jewess from Vienna, née Gutmann [whom] at first the Faubourg
was inclined to find . . . unacceptable; but her husband was so unkind and
unfaithful that they . . . took her to their hearts . . . She was said to keep
a secret weapon in her desk: a list of all the Jewish marriages in the noble
families of Europe."[1]

Marcel, narrator and hero of *Remembrance of Things Past*, shows us
how to play the Comtesse Rosa's sort of game with homosexuals. Inversion,
he tells us, is "a reprobate part of the human whole, but an important part,
suspected where it does not exist, flaunting itself, insolent and unpunished
where its existence is never guessed; numbering its adherents everywhere,
among the people, in the army, in the church, in the prison, on the throne:
living, in short, at least to a great extent, in a playful and perilous intimacy
with the men of the other race, provoking them, playing with them by
speaking of its vice as something alien to it. . . ."[2] If the invert plays "a
game that is rendered easy by the blindness or duplicity of the others, a
game that may be kept up for years until the day of the scandal," we may
find ourselves challenged to inquire into the credentials of this Marcel-
who-is-not-Proust, Marcel-who-is-not-a-Jew, Marcel-who-is not-a-homosex-
ual. What Marcel himself teaches us about the guises and disguises of homosexuality tempts us to scrutinize his identity with the same sleuthing
zeal, if not the malice, with which the Comtesse, "nicknamed . . . 'Rosa
Malheur' (after the woman animal-painter Rosa Bonheur)" must have fer-
reted out those Jewish marriages.[3]

Consider the comic paradigm found in the conversations between the

*From *Contemporary Literature* 10, no. 2 (Spring 1969):220–40. Reprinted by permission of
the journal.

Baron Charlus and Professor Brichot on the subject of the homosexual conspiracy. Brichot is impressed with Charlus' acumen. "Decidedly, Baron,"
he says, "should the Board of Studies ever think of founding a Chair of Homosexuality, I shall see that your name is the first to be submitted" (Cap.
II, 461).

We know, since Marcel reminds us of it, that Charlus can find a complicated kind of pleasure in talking about inversion. His talk about it is part
of his inversion. We do not know what kind of pleasure the foolish professor enjoys in discussing the subject. Can it be possible that Brichot is sly
enough to be ironical at Charlus' expense? If so, what a devious game Marcel—who is reporting the conversation—is playing! Brichot's remark is
funny if spoken in earnest, funnier still if we have reason to impugn the
otherwise unexceptionable and indeed comic heterosexuality of this literally (half-) blind pedant who is so fascinated by the subject of inversion.

Yet a critical reading that disintegrates the claims of the narrator to his
respectable status as a Christian and a heterosexual poses serious problems.
It is as a friendly but often critical and urbane Christian that Marcel discusses Swann as a Jew, the differences and similarities between Swann and
other Jews, and the effects upon Swann's status in the Faubourg Saint-Ger-
main aristocracy of the Dreyfus case. Whatever else we may say about Marcel's opinions about Jews, these are, indubitably, meant to be an outsider's;
whatever the differences between Marcel's criticisms of Jews like Bloch and
his family and the crudities of ordinary anti-Semitism, these represent an
intelligently independent, but nevertheless Christian, point of view.

Morphologically, so to speak, Marcel's status vis-à-vis homosexuals and
the grand theme of homosexuality is the same: he is the sensitive, perceptive outsider, the sympathetic heterosexual who comments on and interprets the life style of inversion with the psychic and moral distance of, let
us say, an Edgar Snow reporting on Red China. If we do not like what Mr.
Snow is saying, if we suspect that there is less distance than he admits to
between his values and those of the society he describes, we may accuse
him of being a "fellow traveler." Marcel's intimate and obsessive dealings
with inversion leave him open to the same sort of charge. How far, though,
are we willing to go in submitting Marcel to our inquisition in order to ver-
ify or disprove our suspicion that Marcel is a fellow traveler in the homosexual camp?

Like groined ribs radiating out of crossed Gothic arches, the love affairs of Swann (and Odette) and Marcel (and Albertine) support an immense
superstructure of incident and theme. Disintegrate Marcel's heterosexuality and do we not, inevitably, destroy Albertine's credibility as well? If we
expose Marcel as a homosexual, must we not re-transpose Albert-Albertine
back to "his" true male status? Once we disbelieve in Albertine as a
woman, must we not view with suspicion everything that Marcel says, re-
ports, professes to believe and to value? The mind boggles at the assumption that everything we know through the mediating consciousness of this

"unreliable narrator" is of questionable authority. In short it would appear that we risk destroying the integrity of the novel as a whole in disintegrating the ostensible realities of Marcel's character.

The dilemma we face is a familiar one. Our accepted, traditional view of Proust's novel, it would seem, cannot easily survive a reading that leads us to inferences that go far beyond or contradict those that are apparently intended by the novelist.[4] On the other hand, given the hints and clues, the invitations, and the critical, questioning intelligence of Marcel's mind as a model, we cannot reject this disintegrating approach simply because it may do its work of disintegration too thoroughly. In the province of science we correctly describe such a priori rejections as frightened obscurantism.

We who read Proust's novel are all of us Albertines imprisoned in Marcel's consciousness. We struggle to make sense of data furnished us by a narrator who stands in the dock of a courtroom in which he presides as judge and functions as stenographer as well. There is no single key with which to open the door onto new vistas. We cannot expect to achieve certitude or demonstrable knowledge in dealing with this difficult problem of interpreting what Marcel tells us about himself and others. Yet interpret we must, and if to interpret is to disintegrate, we must recognize the dangers and the responsibilities at the outset. If the Marcel-Albertine affair cannot survive the implications of our critical scrutiny, subsequent criticism will have to reexamine the problem of homosexual love *presented* as the love of a man for a woman, represented by a narrator-lover whose reasons for disguise and transposition are themselves the proper concern of criticism.

However, the Albertine affair is not the primary concern of the analysis that follows here (though of course it must be in any reading of *Remembrance of Things Past* which seeks to give an adequate account of the novel as a whole). Let us restrict our inquiry to the relationship between Marcel and his friend Robert de Saint-Loup, for in dealing with the strange business of Saint-Loup's emergence as a homosexual in *The Sweet Cheat Gone*, we will find ourselves confronting the issues that have been raised thus far in a particularly acute and clearly defined form. We accept the risks of disintegration if only because Saint-Loup has not yet been dealt with satisfactorily by those critics who accept Marcel's putative sexual status and accept the Saint-Loup-Marcel friendship in the terms given by Marcel.

Saint-Loup's descent into Sodom begins when Marcel overhears him speak "cruel machiavellian words" to a servant. "Now I had always regarded him as so good, so tender-hearted a person," Marcel observes, "that this speech had the same effect upon me as if he had been acting the part of Satan in a play: it could not be in his own name that he was speaking" (SCG, 75). But it is. Saint-Loup is engaged in a homosexual negotiation with the servant, we later discover, after the pimp Jupien enlightens Marcel as to Saint-Loup's new proclivities.[5] Almost phlegmatically, Marcel announces his discovery about Saint-Loup as "a true nephew of M. de Charlus": "I had heard that Gilberte [his wife] was unhappy, betrayed by Robert, but not in the fashion which everyone supposed, which perhaps she herself still supposed, which in any case she alleged" (*SCG*, 356).

Marcel becomes particularly concerned with dating the inception of his friend's homosexuality. "If Jupien traced back to a quite recent origin the fresh orientation, so divergent from their original course, that Robert's carnal desires had assumed, a conversation which I had with Aimé and which made me very miserable showed me that the head-waiter at Balbec traced this divergence, this inversion to a far earlier date" (*SCG*, 259). Marcel meditates deeply on Saint-Loup's inversion, but Proust refuses to show it to us, to render it, with dramatic and emotional vividness. To be sure, there is the memorable and richly ironical symbol of Robert's *croix de guerre*, lost in Jupien's male brothel. This powerful though undeveloped moment is an exception to what we may call Marcel's dramatic reticence. Since, however, the *croix de guerre* incident is placed in the context of the melodrama of Charlus' masochism, it can only have a subsidiary importance; it is a variation on the larger theme of personal, social, political, and national decay in the France of the First World War.

Marcel registers no shock in confronting Saint-Loup's inversion. Proust will not use this lurid development for lurid artistic ends. What comes close to shocking us is the development, shown in the last volume, in which homosexuality not only has not coarsened Robert's nature (as we may find it comfortable to believe is the inevitable consequence of "degeneracy"); on the contrary, Saint-Loup now possesses "a sort of delicacy of feeling" that makes him in some ways even more admirable than he had been in the old days. Nothing could be more invidious than the comparison Marcel makes between the braggart Bloch and the self-effacing Saint-Loup, between Bloch, who is hypocritically both anti-militaristic and patriotic for self-serving reasons, and the homosexual Saint-Loup, who is idealistically patriotic and yet not in any way a jingoist. Robert dies in the war:

> Robert had often said to me sadly long before the war, "My life? Oh, let's not talk about it; I'm a doomed man already." Was he alluding to the weakness he had thus far succeeded in hiding from the world, but of which he was himself aware and the seriousness of which perhaps he exaggerated, just as children who have intercourse for the first time or, even before that, seek solitary gratification, imagine that they are like a plant that scatters its pollen, only to die thereafter? (*PR*, 171)

It is startling to find that inversion is now a "weakness . . . the seriousness of which perhaps he exaggerated. . . ." It is no longer a demonic possession, a vice, an ineradicable stigma, an existential condition akin to a racial affiliation, a tragic blight, a force that twists personality into terrible convolutions as in the case of Charlus. When Marcel tells us that the "new and strange sensation of inversion has at first an almost terrifying force, which lessens as time goes on," we cannot help but recall, in contrast to the numb weariness of his wisdom here, the passionate sympathy of his earlier description of the "race" of inverts in *Cities of the Plain*:

> Race upon which a curse weighs and which must live amid falsehood and perjury, because it knows the world to regard as punishable and scandalous, as an inadmissible thing, that which constitutes for every human creature the greatest happiness in life; which must deny its God, since even Christians, when at the bar of justice they appear and are arraigned, must before Christ and in His Name defend themselves, as from a calumny, from the charge of what to them is life itself. . . . (*CP*, 20)

The image we have cited above of "a plant that scatters its pollen only to die thereafter" repeats but drastically alters a similar image, complex, ramified, and central to Marcel's great prose poem on inversion in *Cities of the Plain*. The latter is prompted by Marcel's witnessing, quite accidentally, a homosexual liaison between Charlus and Jupien which takes place in the Guermantes courtyard. In this courtyard the Duchess has exposed "with that insistence with which mothers 'bring out' their marriageable offspring" a certain "precious plant" so that it may be fertilized by pollen carried by a bee. That bee becomes in Marcel's imagination an "ambassador to the virgin who had so long been waiting for him to appear"; and this ambassador-virgin relationship is the source of the botanical metaphors, part serious and part burlesque, with which the seduction of Jupien by Charlus is described: Jupien "stuck out his behind, posed himself with the coquetry that the orchid might have adopted on the providential arrival of the bee." Marcel comments, "This scene was not, however, positively comic, it was stamped with strangeness, or if you like a naturalness, the beauty of which steadily increased" (*CP*, 6). The moral paradoxes discerned by Marcel grow out of the organicism of his metaphor: the naturalness of the unnatural, the fecundity of sterility, the beauty—not merely aesthetic but moral too—of behavior which Marcel does not deny is also ugly. Following "the providential arrival of the bee," Marcel observes, "I had not supposed he [Jupien] could appear so repellent."

The Marcel who explores homosexuality in *Cities of the Plain* is a naturalist excited by his discoveries; he stands high upon a peak in Darien; he looks down upon Sodom; he is delighted with his own intellectual prowess; like Coleridge's ideal poet, he is able to perceive correspondences among phenomena hitherto unyoked by less imaginative minds. But the Marcel who reflects upon Saint-Loup's homosexuality no longer has the fervor of a discoverer. How dry and merely knowing he is in explaining—debunking— children's masturbation fears in the analogy of the plant that "scatters its seed only to die." In *Cities of the Plain* he sees into the moral and psychological complexities of inversion; here, he sees through the highly charged drama of guilt to the prosaic reality of mere habituation. He might have gone on to say, "Even the most evil and inhuman of men, if he persists in his ways, must come to seem quite ordinary to himself."

Reflecting on the tactics of Saint-Loup's homosexual infidelities, Marcel observes, "Homosexuals would be the best husbands in the world if they did not make a show of being in love with other women" (*SCG*, 364). As epigram or psychology, this may be admirable, but its equable tone is representative of the dispassionate meditations occasioned by Marcel's discovery of his friend's new sexual status. Though he claims to be, Marcel does not convince us that he is miserable about the fate of his friend Robert. The main, almost pathological source of his misery is in the supposed lesbianism and infidelity of his dead mistress Albertine. Like Porfiry tracking Raskolnikov—but how can we tell the detective from the criminal?—Marcel pursues the truth about Albertine back into the insoluble ambiguities of her already irrecoverable past, interviewing those who had known her and had dealings with her separate from his own. Even Saint-Loup is questioned for whatever light he can throw upon the character and behavior of Albertine. Indeed, Marcel's discovery about Saint-Loup is made in the course of uncovering information about Albertine. That Saint-Loup has become an invert is established beyond doubt, but the lurid, shadowy, second- and third-hand glimpses afforded Marcel of Albertine's inversion remain maddeningly inconclusive.

Marcel torments himself with a sordid, posthumous jealousy. It is another turn of the screw whereby Marcel the jailer is truly the captive, his prisoner, Albertine, having escaped him by dying; while the certitude he so ardently desires eludes him and knowledge confounds knowledge. Marcel's heterosexuality (whether genuine or spurious) allows him to assume a certain cool, distanced objectivity in pursuing his examination of male inversion. Marcel in search of the true identity of the dead Albertine is barely in control of himself. In trying Albertine in her grave, Marcel stands condemned in a self-portrait of profaning the dead, and in so doing, of diminishing his own humanity. His behavior is analogous to that of the lesbian Mlle. Vinteuil's ritual outrage when she allows her lover to spit on the photograph of her father.[6]

But of course the man who is showing us this—the compulsive snooper watched by the perceptive observer, both of whom are himself—understands that the Marcel he protrays is pathological. That is why Marcel is not a moral monster in the Albertine affair. He strips away his own pretenses, just as he tears the masks from the faces of the high and mighty who constitute society and parade their follies in those grand, joyless parties which dominate the *Remembrance*. It is to Marcel, to this man about whom we know so immensely and wearyingly much and who is yet faceless and as enigmatic as Hamlet—it is to Marcel and not to Proust that we attribute what Marcel says, thinks, and does. It is Marcel who needs to confess to the compulsions he describes in his postmortem examination of Albertine's character and sexual nature.

The Sodom and Gomorrah section which opens *Cities of the Plain* bears the subtitle: "Introducing the men-women, descendants of the inhabitants of Sodom who were spared by the fire from heaven." Insofar as Marcel considers inversion from a strictly sexual or physical point of view (and it is for him a relatively minor consideration), he describes the male invert as a man-woman, a feminine man. The man-woman loves the virility he lacks when it is found in another. Graphically (and again with a botanical image) Marcel points out "with what stratagems, what agility, what obstinacy as of a climbing plant the unconscious but visible woman in him seeks the masculine organ (*CP*, 30). (Apparently it is this notion of the man-woman that explains Marcel's dislike of the term "homosexual" and his preference for the word "invert.")[7]

Now Aristophanes, in *The Symposium*, describes a love that is truly one of *homo*-sexuality. Aristophanic homosexuality, as sketched in his serio-comic myth, is (for want of a better word) physiologically the opposite of Marcel's account of inversion.[8] There were once, Aristophanes says, three breeds of round, symmetrical beings: one, homogeneously male; the other, heterogeneous, part male and part female; and the third, homogeneously female. Having displeased Zeus, these creatures were split in two by a divine thunderbolt hurled in anger. Ever after the severed halves have gone in search of their missing parts—in search, that is, of their original unity. A bifurcated, once homogeneously male half seeks, quite naturally, its male complement. Heterosexual love is the consequence of a male half having been split off from its female complement. Thus for Aristophanes the male homosexual is not less virile than a heterosexual lover; he is more virile; he will not be content with anything less than his totally male former self. The homosexual lover is, we might say, all-male, and he demonstrates this fact in his inability to respond in a woman to the femaleness that is alien to his original nature. The not unserious moral of Aristophanes' sexual fable is that "happiness for our race lies in fulfilling the behests of Love, and each finding for himself the mate who properly belongs to him; in a word, in returning to our original condition."[9]

The Aristophanes myth not only ennobles homosexuality; it provides its sexual impulse with an intellectual motive, at least by implication. The quest for wholeness is a search for the Self—and why not, then, for an understanding of the Self? If that something less than a Self lacks, in the real world of fragmented men, the crucial half it must possess before it can become a fully integrated Self, the union between these incomplete halves is, it would appear, more than an erotic gratification. It is a means of achieving identity and thus self-knowledge. Aristophanes is Plato's device for reminding us, through parody, of Oedipus' holy pilgrimage. Gaining at last a true Self, Oedipus opens himself to an understanding not only of his own personality, but of the world around him.

Proust must have been familiar with *The Symposium;* nevertheless, he rejects the serious implications of Aristophanes' sexual characterology.[10] Marcel is contemptuous of the apologist for inversion who would appeal to the practices of the Greeks to justify his proclivities. Greek homosexuality,

Marcel reminds us, was conventional. In our time, "what survives is the neurotic kind, which we conceal from other people and disguise to ourselves" (*Cap.*, 280). The modern invert is a victim, a pariah, a Jew among hostile Christians in the secrecy of his despised affiliation. However, there is a "moral enhancement" in his submission to his neurosis.

What Marcel does not say yet seems to understand is that this moral enhancement is related to the heightened consciousness, the exacerbated intelligence that characterizes homosexuality in its Aristophanic implications and in the painful last phase of Saint-Loup's career. Granted (though it is only a half-truth) that homosexuality turns Charlus into a moral freak; yet it is not exaggeration to say that in becoming an invert Saint-Loup becomes an intellectual. If he is morally coarsened, he is also intellectually refined by his homosexuality. But the distinction between the moral and the intellectual is ours, not Marcel's, and it is inadequate insofar as we recognize that out of the tensions generated by Saint-Loup's homosexuality there springs an enhancement that is indeed moral. Proust would have relished the paradoxical wisdom of Yeats' Crazy Jane. . . .

Charlus' violence and fake virility suggest a homosexuality which, as explained in the etiology of Marcel's "treatise" on inversion, seeks in others what it is not and has not in itself. But Saint-Loup, who never loses his self-respect and dignity, seems very much the Aristophanic homosexual whose love is a search for Self, a reclamation of what is properly his. Marcel too is a seeker, a questioner, a theorist no less than an observer, an intellectual who does not hesitate to leap from the fragmentary evidence of his senses, emotions, and unwilled recollections to the generalization that confidently asserts, "This is the law that governs such phenomena." Marcel is surely the most extraordinary polymath ever to have imposed the power of his intelligence upon a work presenting itself as a novel. That power has fictive, aesthetic ends to serve, to be sure; but as a power, as sheer intelligence, it inevitably reminds us of the presence of the author; it is, after all, *his* intelligence; and so the tenuous distinction between Marcel and Proust is constantly being stretched to the breaking point by the immense authority of this intelligence which belongs to Proust and is, as it were, lent to Marcel.[11] Yet Marcel constantly reminds us of the limitations of intelligence, the blindness of thought, the "sterile lucidity" of intellect. Analysis is a fifth column used to subvert itself. Marcel's borrowed intelligence, like the mythic serpent *uroboros*, symbolic of perfection that is round and self-contained, bites its own tail.

We begin to suspect, then, that there is a profound connection—a secret affiliation—between what is almost a hypertrophy of intelligence in Marcel and the ubiquity of inversion in what, in a real sense, is meant to be *his* novel. If, more than any other human activity, love puts the inquiring mind to the test, the more complex and contradictory rhythms of illicit love pose an even greater challenge to the novelist who would understand human nature in all its variety. The Aristophanic homosexual uses his condition as a cognitive instrument, and Marcel uses Saint-Loup's homosexuality to gain a deeper insight into the mysteries of the human condition.

The strategies of the novel do not permit Marcel to love Saint-Loup carnally. Proust the moralist, who condemns his own unacknowledged inversion, must have an alter ego who is free of this vice. It is not only or primarily the golden lad Robert de Saint-Loup en Braye ("whose skin was as fair and his hair as golden as if they had absorbed all the rays of the sun") who is being punished. Saint-Loup's punishment—decreed by Marcel—is also self-punishment. Proust cannot or will not overtly punish himself by corrupting his hero-narrator with inversion. But Marcel, also a moralist and a novelist, can punish himself by transferring to his dear friend the burden of his own unconfessed guilt. Marcel, we suppose, lacerates himself in assigning a homosexual fate to Robert; this is the price he pays for what he knows and we know is the beautiful and morally enhancing love he bears for Saint-Loup—which is precisely what Aristophanes claims homosexual love really is: not a vice but a privilege and not a neurosis but a noble choice. Who can say whether it is the moralist or the liar or both in Marcel that will not allow him to assent to the claims made by Aristophanes? It is clear, though, that Marcel's position is a lonely and ambiguous one, suspended as it is between the two worlds of unequivocal sexuality, the "normal" and the perverted, the healthy and the neurotic, the open and the covert, with all its sneaking, guilt-ridden duplicities.[12]

Edmund Wilson points out that Proust "was preoccupied with morality . . . for all his Parisian sophistication, there remains in him much of the capacity for apocalyptic moral indignation of the classical Jewish prophet."[13] Yet there can also be found in Proust—directly in Marcel—a philosophical scepticism that cannot easily be reconciled with the certitudes of the moralist. If he is a Jeremiah, the Marcel who is as "superstitiously devoted to [books like Saint-Simon's *Mémoires*] as to the women I loved . . ." writes also as a social historian. In this role as observer of the rise, flowering, and decay of society, Marcel asks dispassionate psychological and philosophical questions for which there can be no traditional moral answers. Jeremiah cries out: "Smell the stench of corruption!" Saint-Simon assembles "data" so abundant, so richly varied and contradictory, that we are led to ask: How can we presume to say that inversion (or any other sexual phenomenon) has a moral nature? Indeed, in a hundred different ways Marcel is led by his experience to ask: Can the phenomenological world be said to have any nature at all except that of transience, of birth, change, and death? Marcel is caught up in the dilemma of being unable to square all that he knows about the varieties of human behavior and predilection with the emotional, perhaps aesthetic conviction that certain acts or conditions of humanity are by nature ugly or beautiful, healthy or perverted.

The pseudo-moralist finds it easy to judge others, impossible to condemn himself. For a genuine moralist like Marcel the difficulty is that he cannot contemplate the absurdities of his own character with the same enlightened tolerance he brings to his scrutiny of vanity fair. If we recognize Saint-Loup as a projection of what Marcel values most in himself, we can see in Robert's sodomy Marcel's way of confronting the moralist with the sceptic's questions. Do you dare sit in judgment of your friend's "decline"? Can you make any moral sense of what has happened to him? We imagine Marcel putting these questions to himself. They are, we suppose, *about* himself. Saint-Loup, who shares Marcel's intelligence, sensitivity, love of art, susceptibility to passion and self-criticism, is the mirror in which Marcel sees himself.

Trying to understand Saint-Loup's emergence as an invert, we cannot easily say what our feelings are or what they should be. From Marcel we have learned to respect Saint-Loup, to offer him a warm and on the whole uncritical affection. We may find ourselves resenting what has been "done" to Saint-Loup. Has he been sacrificed to the design of a rigid pattern wherein inversion, like treason, is discovered, all too predictably, in high places? Marcel is so avid to document the theme of lives "by Time's fell hand defaced" that we may wonder whether Saint-Loup is being victimized to point Marcel's didactic fable.

Our difficulty in accepting Saint-Loup as an invert is not due to any improbability in his change; it is perfectly credible. When first we meet him in the second volume of *Within a Budding Grove*—and this is many hundreds of pages before the disclosures of *The Sweet Cheat Gone*— Marcel drops hints which, with hindsight, can be seen as auguring Saint-Loup's inversion: "Dressed in clinging, almost white material such as I could never have believed that any man would have the audacity to wear, the thinness of which suggested no less vividly than the coolness of the dining room the heat and brightness of the glorious day outside, he was walking fast." Marcel is surely not unaware of the implications of his prose, and on the next page he remarks: "Because of his tone, of his impertinence befitting a young lion and especially of his astonishing good looks, some people thought him effeminate, though without attaching any stigma, for everyone knew how manly he was and that he was a passionate womaniser" (WBG, II, 3). No matter that we know Saint-Loup best as a reckless, romantic lover of "Rachel, when from the Lord" or that at the time of his conversion to homosexuality he is married to the glamorous Gilberte. The Don Juan may be a crypto-invert, Marcel explains in *Cities of the Plain*: womanizing and marriage may conceal a secret homosexual preference. Homosexuality, though "numbering its adherents everywhere," may not be suspected by the naive or uninitiated observer. Thus, though we are prepared for, indoctrinated to believe, that a Saint-Loup can be what he seems above all not to be, when we actually discover that he is a member of that "race upon which a curse weighs," it is painful to accept the emotional reality of this almost deterministic change.

With Charlus, Marcel convinces us that his inversion is his nature in the sense in which a drug addict has been defined as a man who is and feels himself to be normal only when under the influence of drugs. Charlus' homosexuality is the source of his demonic energy; if it is a tragic blight, so are the virtues of Tragedy's great heroes; and if we call it a perversion, that is to express about the Baron de Charlus a merely prudential social judgment that tells us nothing about the essentials of his character. Charlus defines himself, he sets the terms for our acceptance or rejection of his personality and values, he owes nothing to Marcel even though Marcel's words have given him existence. But Saint-Loup is critically implicated in the life and sensibility of Marcel. Marcel and Robert define themselves in terms of the other. Thus Marcel's efforts to dazzle us with the paradox of the invert's "moral enhancement" do not quite answer to the question of why Saint-Loup had to become a homosexual. Though as an invert Saint-Loup's "disposition was as affable and charming as his uncle's was suspicious and jealous, and he had remained as rosy-checked and charming as at Balbec" (PR, 70), we feel that Saint-Loup's case is one of perversion, a violation of the authenticity with which he has been endowed.[14]

We must consider an important episode in Marcel's relationship with Saint-Loup in order to take the full measure of the interplay between what is devious and what is candid, between concealment and confession, in Marcel's vast enterprise of self-characterization. During his visit to Saint-Loup's military camp in Doncières (the first volume of The Guermantes Way), Marcel experiences—somewhat vicariously, yet not altogether as a semi-invalid and a spectator—the soldier's life. He watches Robert drill in the field, he takes his meals with him, has long talks with him, meets and enjoys the company of the other soldiers. He is delighted with military life, which is made even more glamorous by Saint-Loup's presence. He is allowed to sleep in Robert's room, presumably in Robert's bed—a rare privilege for a civilian and an outsider; his joy is charged with the magic of the illicit. Doncières is an idyll of comradely love, of shared virility. But Marcel must return to the insomniacal prison of his hotel room, to sleep in his own bed, and to recapitulate the many nights he has known of sleeplessness in strange beds in new places.

Yet even while Marcel is suffused with the joy of military camaraderie, he is betraying his friend. It is, to be sure, a venial treachery: Marcel is using Robert, quite consciously cultivating him so as to procure from him an introduction to the Duchess of Guermantes. The romance that Marcel's imagination attached to the Duchess—the magic of her name, power, and position; the roots of the family in history; time, that is, as creator rather than destroyer—is even more potent than that other romance of arms and men. Saint-Loup is willing to help Marcel enter the society of the Guermantes, but Marcel knows himself to be mean and calculating in his dealings with his friend: "perhaps I wanted to flatter his self-esteem; perhaps also I was sincere, the sole touchstone of merit seeming to me to be the extent to which a friend could be useful in respect of the one thing that seemed to me to have any importance, namely my love [of Mme. de Guermantes]" (*GW*, I, 132).

Somewhat later, after a discussion of military strategy, we are teased with some Proustian (or Marcelian) strategy more subtle than the maneuvers being discussed by the soldiers: " 'I am jealous, furious,' Saint-Loup attacked me, half smiling, half in earnest, alluding to the interminable conversation aside which I had been having with his friends. 'Is it because you find him more intelligent than me? Well, I suppose he's everything now and no one else is to have a look in!' Men who are enormously in love with women, who live in the society of woman-lovers, allow themselves pleasantries on which others, who would see less innocence in them, would never venture" (*GW*, I, 155). We should note the following: it is not until the next volume, *Cities of the Plain*, that Marcel presents his disquisition on homosexuality; and it is not until the penultimate volume, *The Sweet Cheat Gone*, that Saint-Loup's inversion emerges distinctly. At this point, then, Marcel seems to be asking us to accept the "innocence" of Saint-Loup's "pleasantries."

Saint-Loup has no real cause for jealousy; Marcel, however, knows himself to be guilty of treachery in that other matter of the coveted introduction to the Duchess of Guermantes. May we not assume that it is because of Marcel's awareness of genuine betrayal (of a love that is, to be sure, innocent enough in its overt manifestations) that his mind turns to thoughts of the sexual identity game? Marcel's remark (quoted above) "clears" Saint-Loup of the suspicion of homosexuality, but the exculpation is double-edged; for it may, like Iago's "I dare be sworn I think that he is honest," raise precisely the doubt that it pretends to banish. Moreover, quite deliberately, it would appear, Marcel casts doubt upon his own "normalcy" by questioning Saint-Loup's.

Subsequently, Proust has Saint-Loup accuse Marcel of treachery; but the charge, absurdly, is that Marcel "had made a dastardly attempt to have relations with Rachel" (*GW*, II, 52). Not only do we not believe that Saint-Loup could have been foolish enough to have believed Rachel's accusation; the other, the covert purpose of the charge—to reinforce the credibility of Marcel as a woman-lover—is subverted. Marcel's erotic "normalcy," believable though it may be in the lyrical fantasies of "les jeunes filles en fleurs" and in the Albertine affair, is too tenuous, too much a compound of other things, to support the suspicion of gross lechery. (His supposed lusting after Mlle. de Stermaria and the maid of the Baroness Putbus are no more convincing.) At any rate, Marcel and Saint-Loup patch up the quarrel and Marcel observes cynically that "it is probable that Robert continued to believe in the truth of this allegation, but he had ceased to be in love with her [Rachel], which meant that its truth or falsehood had become a matter of complete indifference to him, and our friendship alone remained" (*GW*, II, 52).

We see, then, that the important charge—that Marcel has used Saint-Loup and valued his love for the Duchess of Guermantes more highly than his love for Saint-Loup—is never made by Saint-Loup. Marcel, we might say, will not allow him to make it. If we postulate not innocent friendship but the homosexual ardor which is so strongly suggested but never identified, in the Doncières episode and elsewhere, Rachel's—but also Marcel's—trumped-up story is mere camouflage, an Aesopian fable, as it were, alluding to Marcel's infidelity to Saint-Loup. Moreover, Robert's not quite credible jealousy suggests another transposition: that of Marcel, that is, of a homosexual whose lover, more than being unfaithful to him, has betrayed their "race" by loving a woman. In short, Marcel's jealousy is analogous to that of a wife who discovers that her husband is having an affair with another man.[15] But of course the jealousy we postulate of Marcel, transposed to Saint-Loup, must be concealed lest Albertine's credibility be impaired and she become the Albert which Marcel dare not allow her to be.

In arranging a homosexual fate for Saint-Loup, Marcel punishes himself; it is an act of confession and purgation. Without this hypothesis we can only infer a crypto-invert who hides his vice behind a smokescreen of talk about the disguised homosexuality of others, just as, it has been pointed out by Maurice Samuel, Marcel masks his identity as a Jew behind the opinions of an anti-Semite.[16] Samuel's brilliant essay recognizes the moral problem, but attempts to exonerate Marcel on both counts: "Marcel is and wants us to know that he is a homosexual. He is, and apparently does not want us to know that he is Jewish." Samuel understands the profound implications in the more than metaphorical connection between homosexuals and Jews insisted on by Marcel. Both are pariahs, both live bifurcated lives as aliens in the upper world peopled by the majority (Christians and lovers of women) and as citizens in the nether world of their choice, to which they give their most meaningful assent.[17] He is exceptionally illuminating in discussing both of these "concealments" which are no less revelatory than concealing; but his argument is unconvincing when he claims that "Proust-Marcel is, in his relationship to his Jewishness, pathological and tragic."[18]

Like Samuel we would be pleased to absolve Marcel of the charge of dishonesty and moral cowardice; but if in some real—i.e., fictive—sense Marcel is a Jew (a questionable assumption), then his Jewishness, like Proust's, is compounded of snobbery and sleight of hand: now you see it, now you don't. And it does not make us think any better of Marcel or of Proust to be told by Samuel that "a compulsion neurosis of honesty" forces Marcel to reveal "the stigmata of the author."[19] In Proust's hostile portraits of Bloch and his family, Samuel recognizes the self-hatred of "a programmatically assimilating Jew."[20]

How disappointing, though, to find Samuel missing the main artistic point: which is that in dealing with Jews Proust clearly lacks the compassion, complexity of vision, and most important, the wisdom that mark his treatment of homosexuals as particularized individuals and of homosexuality as an idea that reverberates through the novel. Marcel's heterosexuality is a tactical device which permits him to transcend the conventionality of his mask. Marcel's anti-Semitism is essentially the philistinism of bourgeois complacency. Hearing Bloch or Marcel speak about other Jews, we are unable to believe in the separate existence of Marcel; we are listening to the voice of Marcel Proust; it is a voice scarcely mediated by art; in its lack of charity and in its vulgarity, that voice belongs to the man who speaks of homosexuals with brutal epithets.

It is of course the homosexual Charlus who possess the unrivaled authority of a tragic figure. The justice Marcel denies Bloch he grants Charlus, though it is more accurate to say that it never occurs to us to ask whether Marcel has been just to Charlus. Charlus' complex fate cannot be calculated by the moral arithmetic of punishment and reward. When at the end of the novel we see Charlus as a vegetable remnant of what he was, a rouged old pervert with spittle leaking out of the corners of his mouth, totally dependent now upon the services of the pimp Jupien, his devoted servant, we recognize in these ironies the phenomenon of tragic inevitability. We cannot say and we do not try to determine whether Charlus' final destiny is deserved or undeserved. Everything that has gone before, everything that Charlus has ever said or done convinces us that this is what such a man's life must come to finally.

The ethical and the aesthetic, then, meet, are mutually enriched, and achieve perfect consonance in a Charlus who, in the damnation of sodomy, is both uniquely himself and, universally, the type of the homosexual. He is indeed like King Lear in being, even more than an individual and a type, representative of a principle of life itself.[21]

We can now see more clearly the grounds of Marcel's duplicities. Since he cannot admit to his true sexual nature, he cannot confess to the special guilt of a homosexual who betrays his lover by loving a woman. So Robert is precisely Marcel's *Doppelgänger* insofar as his true status is that of an invert while his assumed role is that of a heterosexual. True, these sexual matters are not quite as simple as that: Robert's love for "Rachel, when from the Lord" is evidently genuine, and his inversion represents a development, in some sense a new condition of his erotic nature. Leaving aside the question of Proust's homosexuality, we suspect that the ultimate truth about Marcel reveals the same pattern: his love for Albertine and other women is also genuine, but the most profound reality of his sexual nature—revealed in the homosexual fate he has given Saint-Loup—is that he is the Aristophanic lover who seeks himself in other men. Saint-Loup is that bifurcated part of Marcel's Self which Marcel seeks, loves, and yet cannot admit *is* himself. If the objection to these speculations is that they proceed with circular logic, and that the unity of Saint-Loup and Marcel cannot be demonstrated, the reply must be that this is because the novel demands our assent to Marcel's heterosexuality.

This much, though, is clear: Saint-Loup as invert has less emotional coherence than he had had so long as we, in our innocence, took him to be what he seemed to be in the passion and virility of his stormy affair with Rachel. We cannot make sense of Saint-Loup solely in terms of his own personality and our reactions to it. Marcel, after all, is quite candid about the many deceits and manipulations that mark his dealings with others— with one notable exception. Never does he suggest that he is anything less than honest in presenting himself as a man rather than—in his terms—a man-woman. If Marcel's heterosexuality is a lie, then Saint-Loup is the sac- rifice Marcel offers to the truth. When Saint-Loup is made to descend into Sodom, when Marcel's ingenious theories about the tactics of homosexual concealment are proven correct, that descent by its own logic, which is Marcel's logic, necessarily implicates Marcel, forces him into the same pat- tern, blots and invalidates Marcel's heterosexual credentials.

We have not found it necessary to fall back upon biographical evidence to confirm Maurice Samuel's case for the homosexuality of Marcel. The cu- rious career of Robert de Saint-Loup supports that case. However, Samuel says, we must remember, that "Marcel is and *he wants us to know he is* a homosexual" (italics added). Samuel is surely too certain about Marcel's intentions, and perhaps unaware of the disintegrating effect of imputing so slippery a motive of revelation through concealment to the narrator who is our only guide through *Remembrance*. Does Marcel want us to know he is a homosexual? Such a question may be open to the theoretical objections that have been raised against those who speak of unconscious motives in the minds of Shakespeare's characters. Strictly speaking—as E. E. Stoll might say of Hamlet—Marcel does not have a mind, conscious or uncon- scious. But Proust does, and there are no theoretical embarrassments in emending Samuel's statement to read: "Marcel is and Proust wants us to know Marcel is a homosexual." The intentions of a novelist are real, and they can be found in the strategies that give a direction, shape, and mean- ing to the materials of his book.

Notes

1. George R. Painter, *Proust: The Early Years* (Boston, 1959), p. 198.

2. Marcel Proust, *Cities of the Plain* (New York, 1927), p. 24. All of my references to *Remembrance of Things Past* are to the seven-volume Modern Library edition (1927–32). For American readers this edition, I believe, is both more available and convenient than the two- volume Random House edition which uses the same translation by C. K. Scott Moncrieff and that of Frederick A. Blossom for the final volume, *The Past Recaptured*. My reading of Proust, with all the dangers attendant upon such an enterprise, has been exclusively in this English language text. The following abbreviations are used for the volumes of *Remembrance* cited after quotations: *Swann's Way:* SW; *Within a Budding Grove:* BG; *The Guermantes Way:* GW; *Cities of the Plain:* CP; *The Captive:* Cap; *The Sweet Cheat Gone:* SCG; *The Past Recaptured:* PR.

3. Painter, p. 198.

4. Leo Bersani, *Marcel Proust* (New York, 1965), p. 16: "If we look to Proust's life to understand *A la Recherche du temps perdu,* if we may consider the book as simply another arrangement of the events of that life, we may very well be tempted—and this has been done—to correct the work: Albertine is "really" a man, Marcel is "really" a snob . . ." See also Harry Levin, "Proust Gide, and the Sexes," PMLA, LXV (June 1950), 649, a reply to Justin O'Brien's article, "Albertine the Ambiguous: Notes on Proust's Transposition of Sexes" (see Note 15 below). Levin writes: "I respectfully submit that, when mere acquiescence in a novelist's own designation of the sex of his heroine is held to be erroneous, we have reached a confusing epoch in the history of criticism. A heavy burden of proof falls upon any critic who sets his word against the word of the writer he is discussing." See also Levin, *Gates of Horn* (New York, 1963), p. 414: "But to argue that we should read Albert, for Albertine, raises many more questions than it answers."

5. In GW, II, 133 ff., we find an unequivocal denial that Saint-Loup is a homosexual lodged in the context of an exceedingly equivocal passage which cues us to a later disclosure that he is: "But the Prince de Foix, who was rich already, belonged not only to this fashionable set of fifteen or so young men, but to a more exclusive and inseparable group of four which included Saint-Loup. These were never asked anywhere separately, they were known as the four *gigolos,* they were always to be seen riding together, in country houses their hostesses gave them communicating bedrooms, with the result that especially as they were all four extremely good looking, rumours were current as to the extent of their intimacy. I was in a position to give these the lie direct so far as Saint-Loup was concerned. But the curious thing is that if, later on, one was to learn that these rumors were true of all four, each of the quartet had been entirely in the dark as to the other three." We can make only a negative inference with reasonable certainty: a passage such as this cannot be cited as an indisputable identification of Saint-Loup as a homosexual.

6. Edmund, *Axel's Castle* (New York, 1931), pp. 175 ff., comments on the profound significance of this episode.

7. CP, 9. In a parenthesis, Marcel points out that his botanical comparison is "without the slightest scientific claim to establish a relation between certain laws and what is sometimes, most ineptly, termed homosexuality. . . ."

8. Plato, *The Symposium,* trans. W. Hamilton (London, 1951).

9. Ibid., p. 65.

10. Painter, pp. 140 ff., points out that young Proust founded with his friends and wrote for a literary magazine the title of which was *Le Banquet.* Painter makes no comment on the ironical resonance of this title as auguring things to come.

11. Bersani claims in the Introduction, p. 4: "The distinction between Proust and his narrator (or Marcel) has great importance and must be maintained in any discussion of the novel, for it is on the basis of this distinction that a whole world of imaginary characters and events could be *invented* as the novelistic framework for an *essai* of self analysis." Yet Bersani's subtle and not altogether clear discussion of "Marcel the character and Proust the author" (in pp. 186ff.) does not credit Marcel with the role of inventor: "But society offers so many parallels with Marcel's psychology that it becomes difficult for us to believe that he is merely an observer of the external world: he seems rather to be recording a *dream* of nature and society. The dream, however, is presumably Proust's and not Marcel's: the memories belong to the character Marcel, but the novel is Proust's invention. But to the extent that the world the narrator objectively remembers reflects his personality, we have the impression that he has created that world, and our belief in the distinction between Proust the author and Marcel the main character is necessarily weakened." Mr. Bersani, it seems, is not quite certain where he stands in this difficult matter of assigning authorial responsibility.

12. See *Letters of Marcel Proust,* ed. Mina Curtiss (New York, 1949). In Letter 148, to Louis de Robert, Proust defends the objectivity of his treatment of inversion: "I do not think . . . that I need fear the sympathy of sadists. . . . The commentary which, according to you,

gives me the appearance of a defense lawyer (and perhaps you are right, I mean in thinking that I appear to be, for actually I am in no way a special pleader) is exactly, alas, what may perhaps turn away from me not only the sensitive spirits, but also, and chiefly, the sadists. Nothing could be more disagreeable to the people who seek out cruelty than to say to them: "Yours is a perverted sensibility."

13. Wilson, p. 144.

14. Proust relies on Saint-Loup's family status as a Guermantes—as "a true nephew of M. de Charlus"—to help to account for the strain of inversion in his character. Remembering those grand, doomed families of Aeschylus and Sophocles, we might credit Proust with a modern use of Greek technique for achieving tragic inevitability. Yet the ambiguous emotional effect of Saint-Loup's inversion does not warrant a comparison of such weight and prestige. The blood connection seems too facile an explanation. From Marcel himself we have been taught to expect deeper and more satisfying notions of causality.

15. Justin O'Brien, "Albertine the Ambiguous: Notes on Proust's Transposition of Sexes," PMLA, LXIV (1949), 933–952, answers the charge of Harold March that "one is tempted to believe that in writing the story of Albertine Proust transposed the sex of the original, thereby destroying the chief cause for the jealousy which he illogically retained" (quoted by O'Brien, p. 944). O'Brien points out—in contradiction to March's contention that "with a homosexual the situation is reversed; he is more or less indifferent to heterosexual behavior in the loved one, and is jealous only of homosexuality"—that "the type of jealousy depends on the taste of the beloved . . . in endowing Albertine with Lesbian impulses Proust was acting quite intentionally and logically. In other words, if Albertine had been named Albert and Marcel had been homosexual, Marcel would have suffered intensely from Albert's relations with women. In order for the travesti, or transposition of sexes, to be consistent, Albertine had to be bisexual." The argument we make concerning Marcel and Saint-Loup is similar and indebted to Professor O'Brien's point.

16. Maurice Samuel, "The Concealments of Marcel," Commentary, XXIX (January 1960), 8–22.

17. Oddly, Samuel misses the ironical similarity between Marcel's account of the homosexual underground and the standard myth of the Jewish conspiracy in anti-Semitic demonology. The person who believes in both myths might combine them into a conspiratorial "They"—i.e., Homosexual Jews.

18. Samuel, p. 22.

19. Ibid.

20. Ibid., p. 19.

21. In PR, p. 182, M. de Charlus is compared to King Lear: "It may be that he had up till then dyed his hair and now had been ordered to avoid the fatigue involved, but it seemed rather as if his illness, acting like a chemical precipitant, had rendered glisteningly visible all the metal saturating the strands of his hair and beard, which flung it into the air in geysers of pure silver, giving to the dethroned, aged prince the Shakespearean majesty of King Lear."

Why Vinteuil's "Septet"?

Sybil de Souza*

Four years ago I concluded an article on the importance of music for Marcel Proust (see the "Bulletin" no. 19) by wondering if he might not have been influenced in his choice of a "septet" as Vinteuil's posthumous masterpiece by the piece of music by Ravel entitled: "Introduction and allegro for harp, string quartet, flute and clarinet." But I thought it unlikely that Proust might have heard this "septet," for he does not really talk about Ravel's music in *A la recherche du temps perdu*. The only exception is a satirical allusion to a piece of music that was said to be by Ravel and which an unknown young man wished to hear at the afternoon's entertainment given by the new Princesse de Guermantes, formerly well known under the name of Mme Verdurin. This young man had been told that the piece in question was as beautiful as Palestrina but difficult to understand—and he had failed to recognize the Kreutzer sonata! (*RTP*, 3:1025–1026). Let us recall the pleasure with which the Narrator tells the story of the trick the violinist Morel played when the younger Mme de Cambremer asked him to play *Fêtes* by Debussy (*RTP* 2:954). It was in La Raspelière, where the Verdurins were living: together with M. De Charlus, Morel had just performed Fauré's first sonata for violin and piano. In a "spirit of mischief," Morel had ended up playing a march by Meyerbeer which the entire audience, believing it to be by Debussy, had considered sublime. What disconcerts the reader who knows something about music is that Proust does not seem to know that *Fêtes* is a piece for orchestra forming part of a composition entitled *Nocturnes*. All the same, he must have known that the connection between Ravel and Palestrina was as distant as that between a nocturne by Debussy and a march by Meyerbeer.

I had, in any case, pointed out in this article in the "Bulletin" that in the *Contre Saint-Beuve* [i.e. the 1954 edition edited by Bernard de Fallois] Proust's aesthetic seemed directed towards painting rather than towards music; however, Proust must have come to achieve the same familiarity with music as with painting. And while he was more familiar with the technique of painting it is above all from the art of music that he comes to borrow the metaphors that in the end dominate his work. It is thanks to a lecture given in London in 1963 by M. Michel Butor and which has been published under the title *Les Œuvres d'art imaginaires chez Proust*[1] that I solved this riddle. M. Butor, while giving other explanations, thinks he has found the source of the "septet" in the image of the prism—an image with Proust uses in *La Prisonnière* and which he already outlines in *Contre*

*Reprinted from *Bulletin de la Société des Amis de Marcel Proust*, no. 23 (1973):1596–1608, by kind permission of M. Henri Bonnet. The abbreviation *RTP* has been substituted by the editor for the abbreviation used for *A la recherche du temps perdu* by the author. The translation of the author's text was made by the editor of this collection. Passages from *A la recherche du temps perdu* are given in the Kilmartin translation. All other translations are by the editor.

Sainte-Beuve. For in this work he speaks of a picture by Gustave Moreau which he calls "Le Chanteur persan"—a picture which is "forever immobilized through the prism . . . of its tender colors" but "has lost nothing of the fresh paleness of its shades of blue" (*C.S.-B.*, p. 396) [sic: p. 390—ed.]. Here the metaphor of the prism has not yet taken on the dimensions which it will attain in the mature work of Proust—the prism only serves to fix the image, while in *La Prisonnière* Marcel will tell Albertine that "great writers have done nothing but refract" through different contexts "one single beauty which they bring into the world" (*RTP* 3:375; *RTPK* 3:382). Just as the prism separates the colors of the spectrum, reducing them to their original elements, the work of art, by enabling its creator to draw his inner universe from within himself, refracts it. To quote Proust himself: "As the spectrum makes visible to us the composition of light, so the harmony of a Wagner, the colour of an Elstir, enable us to know that essential quality of another person's sensations" (*RTP* 3:159; *RTPK* 3:156).

Let us take note in passing that M. Butor thinks that the symbolism of the seven colors of the spectrum influenced Proust in the choice of a "septet" rather than a "sextet" as the final work of Vinteuil. Of particular interest is the comparison which Proust establishes between the way in which Vinteuil works and the method adopted by Elstir—"note by note, brush stroke by brush stroke"—for, if the work of art is a prism, the technique of the creator is one too, since it is by that that he succeeds in externalizing this universe. For Elstir this technique of the creator is one too, since it is by that that he succeeds in externalizing this universe. For Elstir this technique is based on the "reciprocal metaphor" by which he transforms the port of Carquethuit into a landscape where the boats in dock turn into houses taller than those of the little town, while the town itself takes on, for its part, a marine aspect. Even so, in Monet's painting, the Japanese bridge in his garden sometimes takes on the appearance of a solid structure, and sometimes that of the mass of leaves surrounding it.

The metaphor belongs to the domain of language; thus the language of a writer, his technique, is a prism for him too, because it allows him to reveal his universe to a reader. This is what will make Gide say, in *Paludes*, that there are as many ways of saying a thing as there are readers. Proust was his own reader to a greater extent than Gide, and painting was for him the "middle term" by which he moved from music to literature (Butor, op. cit., p. 13).

Proust says that it was thanks to his sonorities that Vinteuil was able to externalize his personal vision of the universe (*RTP* 3:258). It is also thanks to musical instruments that these sonorities came to be heard and appreciated. In *Jean Santeuil* it was one phrase of a piece played on the piano without any accompaniment which for Jean had the same evocative power which the little phrase of Vinteuil's sonata for violin and piano was to have for Swann when he heard the sonata played again in its entirety, at the Saint-Euverte evening reception. At this point already, the piano was no longer sufficient for Proust to create the music of Vinteuil, because there are "qualitative essences" which the piano is unable to express. Let us recall Verlaine: ". . . la nuance seule fiance / Le rêve au rêve et la flûte au cor." [Nuance alone betroths / Dream to dream and flute to horn.]

The piano is by itself unable to convey that particular nuance. For that all the instruments of the orchestra are necessary. As this taste for color in music grew in Proust and as this metaphor of the prism reached a more profound level in him, it was natural that he should have sought to express his ideas by having recourse to a more varied group of instruments—a "sextet" or a "septet."

But, in order to bring out some of the implications of this idea, I should like to get back to this melody from *Tristan and Isolde* (on which Proust comments for the first time in an article published in the *Figaro* in 1907: *Impressions de route en automobile*. [Sybil de Souza says "get back" because she commented on the melody played on a shepherd's pipe in this opera in her "L'Importance de la Musique pour Proust," *BSAMP* no. 19, 1969, 884–885—ed.] It is thanks to M. Henri Bonnet's book *Marcel Proust de 1907 à 1914*, that I am able to give the precise date of this article, because I had read it first of all in the volume *Pastiches et mélanges* published many years after *Swann*. It seems to me that we have in this the proof that Proust took an interest early in his career in the instruments of the orchestra (and more particularly in the woodwinds), for what the car horn announcing his return to his parents recalled to him was that it was not only to the "strident repetition . . . of two notes whose succession is sometimes produced by chance in the unorganized world of sounds," but also, "to the pipe of a poor shepherd, the growing intensity, the insatiable monotony of his meager song that Wagner . . . entrusted the most prodigious expectation of felicity that has ever filled the human soul." This melody from *Tristan,* played on a shepherd's pipe, that Proust must have heard played on an oboe with its alto sound, certainly struck him, and he came back to it in at least two of the volumes of *A la recherche du temps perdu*.

The first allusion which Proust makes in *La Recherche* to these two passages of *Tristan* is to be found in *Sodome et Gomorrhe* when Marcel is waiting for the telephone call which is to tell him if Albertine will come to spend the evening with him: "I was tortured by the incessant recurrence of my longing, ever more anxious . . . , for the sound of a call; . . . I suddenly heard, mechanical and sublime, like the fluttering scarf or the shepherd's pipe in *Tristan,* the top-like whirr of the telephone" (*RTP* 2:731; *RTPK* 2:757).

This motif of the fluttering scarf is yet again a motif played first by the flutes and then by the English horn, which Proust chooses as the first example of the felicity which Wagner evokes in *Tristan*. Here is the way Reynaldo Hahn describes his first scene of the second act of *Tristan*. "Night has fallen. While king Mark lingers at the hunt, Isolde waits for Tristan in the silent park . . . Brangaine, filled with remorse, tries in vain to calm this woman in love; the fanfares fade into the distance and the moment has come for her to call her beloved. How beautiful is this brief vision from the top of the terrace! Isolde waves her veil in the night. The flutes, the oboes, the clarinets trace on the dark background of the strings the white trail of the scarf" (*L'Oreille au guet*, p. 73). This "white trail" of the scarf is traced according to Proust by these two notes whose succession is sometimes produced by chance. In fact it is nothing more than a motif which derives its value from the dramatic situations in which it has been placed.

The second example Proust gives of the manifestation of felicity in *Tristan*—the tune of the shepherd's pipe—is developed at much greater length in *La Prisonnière* where it is connected with Marcel's reflections on the creation of a work of art. This tune appears in the third act of the opera. What is involved is in fact two tunes played by the shepherd, and the way in which Proust talks of them makes me think that he tended to run them together. The first, played by the shepherd at the beginning of act 3, is the only one to which such expressions as "the growing intensity" and "the insatiable monotony" of the "meager" shepherd's song really apply. In fact it is a chromatic tune, which explains its intensity; but it is also a sad tune which presages the death of Tristan, although in his eyes death is the synonym of happiness. When Isolde's ship is perceived the tune becomes joyful—the shepherd is now playing a dance tune which will shortly be dominated by the motif of the Liebestod. Thus it is of the first tune that Proust is speaking when he says in *La Prisonnière:* "Before the great orchestral movement that precedes the return of Isolde, it is the work itself which has attracted towards itself the half-forgotten air of a shepherd's pipe" (*RTP* 3:161; *RTPK* 3:158). Here Proust has fully grasped the situation, for it is this monotonous air, like a kind of recitative, which will finally dominate the orchestra and which, after having been played by the strings, will come back on the horn, then pass to the clarinet; the violins will then take it up before it disappears to make way for the kind of fanfare which precedes the dance tune announcing the arrival of Isolde—a tune the orchestra immediately takes over while, however, extending it very little. . . .

Proust's reasoning in *La Prisonnière* does not lose its value because he had run the two tunes of the shepherd into one, for here what is emphasized is the joy of the creator rather than the happiness of the lovers and what is involved is no longer an "expectation" of felicity. One might have wished that Proust had consulted the score of *Tristan* before writing this section of *La Prisonnière*—according to the text the narrator apparently consulted a short score for piano. But nothing can shake the perfect accuracy of Proust's reasoning in the passage which follows the one I have quoted above: "And, no doubt, just as the orchestra swells and surges at the approach of the ship, when it takes hold of these notes of the pipe, transforms them, imbues them with its own intoxication, breaks their rhythm, clarifies their tonality, accelerates their movement, expands their instrumentation, so no doubt Wagner himself was filled with joy when he discovered in his memory the shepherd's tune, incorporated it in his work, gave it its full wealth of meaning" (*RTP*, 3:161; *RTPK*, 3:158).

If Wagner experienced joy in creating this beginning of the 3rd act of *Tristan*, it is in part due to this memory. This idea reminds me of the conclusion of *Contre Sainte-Beuve:* "The most beautiful things we will write . . . are within us in an indistinct state, like the memory of a melody which charms us without our being able to distinguish its outline" (*C.S.-B.*, p. 312). Being able to distinguish the outline of the melody in order to go on to use it in one's work is, for the musician just as much as for the writer, "to feel the joy of reality regained. . . ."

In his choice of a septet rather than a sextet as the final composition of Vinteuil, M. Butor thinks that Proust was influenced, not only by this metaphor of the prism revealing the seven colors of the spectrum, but also by the multiplicity of the characters he had created and by their complexity. Without going as far as M. Butor in his taste for parallels, I am willing to suppose that this choice may have been dictated by his desire "to orchestrate" in some way certain aspects of his characters. The love of Marcel for Albertine is more complicated than that of Swann for Odette and the music associated with this love must necessarily be of a greater complexity. Perhaps, under the influence of the works of César Franck, Proust may have thought of creating a Vinteuil quartet which would be for Marcel and Albertine what the sonata had been for Swann and Odette. And a note glued to one of the rough drafts of the second volume of *A la recherche du temps perdu*—*A l'ombre des jeunes filles en fleurs*—talks about a piano quintet provisionally attributed to Franck, which would be played at the afternoon reception of the Princesse de Guermantes. But at the time when he was writing *La Prisonnière*, this quintet had already become a sextet, the last work of Vinteuil. And in the definitive edition this final work is the septet, which is played, not at the Guermantes afternoon reception but at the home of Mme Verdurin. However, in the manuscript of *La Prisonnière*, Proust alludes to the "quartet" of Vinteuil: "The resemblance between their cooing (that of the pigeons) and the crowing of the rooster was as profound and as obscure as, in the Vinteuil quartet, the resemblance between the scheme of the adagio and that of the conclusion" (*RTP* 3: notes, 1092). The details Proust gives us on the movements of the "quartet" do not coincide in any way with what he tells us about the septet, except at the end.

And when Marcel reflects on the materialist hypothesis according to which he had no basis for believing that certain phrases of Vinteuil's music were as profound as certain sensations he wonders: "And why then do we suppose to be specially profound those mysterious phrases which haunt certain quartets and this septet by Vinteuil?" (*RTP* 3:382 [sic: 381—ed.]; *RTPK* 3:388).[2] The text of the Gallimard [i.e. the first Gallimard—ed.] edition makes the passage much less explicit—"certain works" for "certain quartets." Then why did Proust give up "his" quartet? The reason can only be found in the complexity of his work. As the subject matter of his novel became more complex, he was obliged to recast its composition. If he had started off by intending to keep the "quintet," which became the "concert," then the "septet," for the end—the Guermantes afternoon reception—he must have changed his mind on realizing that it was necessary to "orchestrate" the loves of Marcel and Albertine. The "concert" to which Marcel alludes is certainly something different from a piano quintet. In fact Proust did name all the instruments of the septet although not at all in a precise manner; but we are aware from the very beginning that besides Morel, the violinist, there were also a harpist, a pianist and a cellist.

I have already drawn the reader's attention to the importance that the last quartet of Beethoven held for Proust; and he was certainly influenced by the cyclic composition of the quartets of Debussy and Franck. And he was perhaps sensitive to the resemblance between the finale of the latter's quartet and the finale of the "Ninth" (symphony) by Beethoven. Franck, like Beethoven, brings back in his finale all the themes of the other movements only to reject them, while however keeping, unlike Beethoven, the theme of the first movement as the principal theme of his finale. And it is from his quintet that he will borrow one of the important themes of his *Variations symphoniques*.[3] So if Proust rejected the idea of a piano quintet to represent Vinteuil's posthumous masterpiece, it was because he demanded from music something which an ensemble of that kind, with rather neutral tones, could not give him.

In his book *La Musica, il Tiempo, l'Eterno nella Recherche de [sic] Proust* (pp. 47–48) Luigi Magnani points out the similarities between the personalities of Franck and Vinteuil. Just as Debussy said of Franck that "Whenever he had found a beautiful harmony it was enough to fill him with joy for a day" (M. Croche: *Antidilettanti*, 1921, p. 151), in the same way Proust speaks of the joy which "certain sonorities" (*RTP* 3:254; *RTPK* 3:356) had brought to Vinteuil. But M. Magnani also informs me that for the German poet Hoffmann, the timbre of the basset horn (an instrument of the clarinet family) evoked the scent of red carnations. That reminds me of the fragrance of geraniums which seemed to Marcel to emanate from the Septet (*RTP* 3:375). And in its turn that makes me think of the description of Albertine's laugh: "And this laugh at once evoked the flesh-pink, fragrant surfaces with which it seemed to have just been in contact and of which it seemed to carry with it, pungent, sensual and revealing as the scent of geraniums, a few almost tangible and mysteriously revealing particles" (*RTP*, 2:795; *RTPK*, 2:823). This laugh of Albertine's had a sensual quality which was reflected in Vinteuil's music but not at all, or so it seems to me, in Franck's. Even his piano quintet could not convey the sensual quality which makes Marcel say that the Septet evoked for him "the perfumed silk of a geranium." It was therefore necessary to find the equivalent in music of Albertine's laugh, and for that neither the string quartet nor the piano quintet would suffice; what was necessary was a group in which there would also be wind instruments. And that reminds me that already, in *Du côté de chez Swann,* describing the marriage of Dr. Percepied's daughter which took place in the church of Combray, Proust had written ". . . the sun . . . shed a geranium glow over the red carpet . . . and covered its woolen texture with a nap of rosy velvet, a bloom of luminosity, that sort of tenderness, of solemn sweetness in the pomp of a joyful celebration, which characterize certain pages of *Lohengrin,* certain paintings by Carpaccio, and make us understand how Baudelaire was able to apply to the sound of the trumpet the epithet 'delicious' " (*RTP,* 1:78 [sic: 178—ed.] *RTPK* 1:194). In its sensual aspect it is rather to the music of Wagner that Vinteuil's septet corresponds. But the tenderness, the sweetness which are mingled with pomp in *Lohengrin* find their expression in the tunefulness of the clarinet rather than in the excessively blaring timbre of the trumpet.

It is not Marcel but rather M. de Charlus who tells us directly what the other instruments of the septet were. This gentleman explains to Mme Verdurin at the end of the concert that if the Comtesse Molé had attended the concert, everything would have been ruined and "the flute and the oboe would have suddenly lost their voices" while "not a note would have issued from the brass" (*RTP,* 3:276; *RTPK,* 3:278). I think that in using the expression "the brass" M. de Charlus was alluding to the horn. If we limit "the brass" to the presence of a solitary horn, we will have a "septet" in this passage—perhaps M. de Charlus is not paying full attention to what he is saying. To replace the clarinet as the singer of rejoicing in the finale of the septet, Proust could not have done better than entrust himself to the horn, that instrument whose sonorities are so deeply moving.

I also owe to M. Magnani the suggestion that, in the septet, Proust— therefore, naturally, Vinteuil—was influenced by the orchestration of Debussy whose work he had learned to appreciate, a little late, by listening to performances of *Pelléas et Mélisande* on the "théâtrophone" [i.e. live from the theatre, on the telephone—ed.]. In a letter to Reynaldo Hahn, which M. Philip Kolb dates February 21, 1911, Proust says that after having listened to "all Pelléas" he had had an "extremely agreeable impression" (*Lettres à Reynaldo Hahn,* p. 191 [sic. p. 199—ed.]). Hahn must have criticized severely this taste of Proust for *Pelléas,* because in the long letter of March 4 or 5 of this same year, Proust replies: "I keep on asking for *Pelléas* on the "théâtrophone" . . . The parts I like the best are those of music without words . . . for example when Pelléas emerges from underground with an "Ah! I breathe at last" modeled on *Fidelio,* there are a few lines which are truly soaked in the freshness of the sea and the smell of roses which the breeze carries to him. Of course there is nothing 'human' about it but it is delightfully poetic even though it is . . . what I should most detest if I were really fond of music, that is to say nothing more than a fleeting 'notation' instead of those passages in which Wagner expectorates everything he contains . . . on a subject" (ibid., p. 202). Here Proust seems to admire not only Debussy's orchestration but also the economy of the means he uses to create an impression. There is no reason at all why one should not "be really fond of music" and at the same time like these "fleeting notations" which create the atmosphere of a passage. Proust knew that perfectly well, but he chose to spare Hahn's feelings because the latter did not like Debussy. Besides, he made use of his impressions of this music in the passage from *Sodome et Gomorrhe* in which Marcel compliments the dowager on the flowers in her property of Féterne:

> "It's true, we have a great many roses," she told me, "our rose garden is almost too near the house . . . It's nicer on the terrace at la Raspelière where the breeze wafts the scent of roses, but not so headily."
> I turned to her daughter-in-law: "It's just like *Pelléas*," I said to her, to gratify her taste for the modern, "that scent of roses wafted up to the terraces. It's so strong in the score that, as I suffer from hay-fever and rose-fever, it sets me sneezing every time I listen to that scene!"
> "What a marvelous thing *Pelléas* is," cried the younger Mme de Cambremer, "I'm mad about it." (*RTP*, 2:813; *RTPK*, 2:841–42)

Already, in his *Marcel Proust*, George Painter had noted the resemblance between the "programme" of the first movement of Debussy's *La Mer*—"From dawn to noon on the sea"—and the description, which Proust gives in *La Prisonnière*, of the Septet, where the song that pierces through the pink light of dawn is followed by the lurching joy of bells pealing at noon. In the same way, according to Painter, this movement by Debussy ends on a noonday carillon of trumpets and cymbals (*Marcel Proust, A biography*, vol. 2, p. 246). But for the narrator this song will become a call which will turn to certainty when the Mantegna archangel "sounding a trumpet" proclaims his joy. Here I must mention an important previously unpublished passage which was published by Henri Bonnet in the *Figaro* of February 1 1971. Henri Bonnet gives the article in which he analyzes this passage the title *Esquisse pour une Prisonnière*; for volume 6 of the *Recherche* was not yet written in 1915, which was the time when Proust wrote this note concerning Vinteuil's quartet, and he had not, according to Henri Bonnet, as yet made the most of "the extraordinary enrichment which he had derived from his experience with Agostinelli." We must not forget that the latter would be one of the "keys" of the character Albertine, already imagined but not yet completely developed by Proust. I have just suggested in this article that it was in part the complexity of Marcel's and Albertine's relationship that would lead him to replace Vinteuil's sonata by the "quartet" which would later become a sextet, before taking on its final form, that of a septet. But Henri Bonnet's commentary made me understand the "architectural" role of the Septet in the *Recherche*. For Proust it is above all a source of inspiration which will encourage him to develop more deeply in his impressions the essence common to the present and the past. Thus its role was over before the experiences which Proust relates in *Le Temps retrouvé*—"the exposition of the aesthetic by the refreshment table" as the unpublished passage puts it. And Proust understood that by causing the Septet to be played at the Verdurin reception, he would have marvelous success in preparing the revelation of *Le Temps retrouvé*. In the note in question he compares the lurching joy at the end of the quartet, which evokes bells in full peal, to the joy that should have been aroused in the narrator by the sight of waves in the sunshine at Balbec and he concludes as follows: "Is it not inevitable that our minds should work in such a way that we never perceive the pure savor of anything except when it is evoked by something else; and, in fact, I had never perceived the sweetness of the hazy morning sea as I did in the white stone angel of a fresco by Elstir where it was so pale and misty." This sentence brings me back to the metaphor of the prism and proves that it is also due to the art of Elstir that Proust was able to endow the final work of Vinteuil—the Septet—with a richness of colorings and sonorities which had been lacking in the quartet as in the sonata.

Proust changed his mind several times concerning his imaginary music in the course of writing the *Recherche*. Since he was very fond of the quartets of Debussy and Franck as well as those of Beethoven, he had contemplated first of all creating a "quartet" by Vinteuil. But to correspond to the complexity of his novel, which was constantly increasing, he looked for a less homogenous musical form. So he thought of the piano quartet of which Franck had provided him with a model. But already the coloring of this ensemble no longer corresponded to what he wanted to express. His conception of love, the supra-terrestrial joy which he wanted this music to evoke required more intense colorings; it was then that he created the Vinteuil "concert"—whether a sextet or a septet mattered little to him, for if the musician has seven instruments, instead of six, at his command, he can put more variety into the color. As for the art of instrumentation, Proust did not know much about it; he probably did not know how to recognize the wind instruments by their timbre; but perhaps he knew that Saint-Saëns had written a septet (for trumpet, piano, double-bass and string quartet). In another letter to Reynoldo Hahn, still on the subject of Debussy, although this time the work in question is *Le Martyre de saint Sébastien*, he comments on "a beautiful, joyful instrument" that is heard after the death of the saint. A professional musician—or a better informed amateur—could have named the instrument. My personal belief is that this "beautiful joyful instrument" must have been a wind instrument—a trumpet or a clarinet—and that, to transform the mysterious call from the beginning of the septet into a victorious song worthy of some "Mantegna archangel sounding a trumpet," it was necessary to have it played by one or the other instrument or, failing that, by the horn.[4]

As he said himself, Proust was not really a musician and in his description of Vinteuil's septet he had not wished to convey an impression in a really definite way so much as he wished to recreate it with the sense of what was inexpressible or even transcendental about it. It was in this way that he was able to speak of the "glowing Septet." What he looked for above all in music was an inspiration for his own work—a work which would have its own leitmotifs—the reminiscences which would provide a basis for more extensive developments. And music also brought him the proof of the reality of art, the proof that something other existed than the nothingness he had found in love. As my old teacher, M. Emile Bouvier, says so appropriately, in the chapter of his *Cours moyen* in which he speaks of Proust: "One can refuse to mingle philosophy with the novel and find it sufficient to gather risky pleasures in a casual way on the surface of the tangible world. But one cannot deny Proust the merit of having made of his work a coherent monument, a system in which everything holds together, the guiding thought, the composition and the style."[5] This style, this technique is for the writer just as much as for the musician the means by which he refracts his personal universe.

Notes

1. *Les Œuvres d'Art Imaginaires chez Proust*. The Athlone Press, London, 1964.

2. In the Pléiade edition the first reference to the "Vinteuil quartet" becomes in the text on page 401 [sic: p. 400—editor's note] the "Vinteuil septet," while in the second case the Pléiade text says forthrightly "certain quartets and this concert" instead of "certain works and this septet" in the Gallimard edition. Compare the passage in *Le Temps retrouvé* where Proust speaks of "the Vinteuil composition for a concert" (*RTP* 3:877). [Kilmartin uses the term "septet" (*RTPK*, 3:910)—ed.].

3. In the same way Marcel will notice later on in Vinteuil's Septet a phrase of his "Variation religieuse pour orgue (Religious variation for organ) which he had failed to notice on first hearing the work; it is on hearing this phrase played on the pianola by Albertine that he will recognize its origin (*RTP* 3:374 [sic: 373—ed.]).

4. The beautiful, joyful instrument which sounds to me like a quartet of horns and trumpets playing in unison—makes me think that it was after becoming aware of the music of Debussy that Proust wanted to have some "brass" in his Septet. However, as was always the case, he remained true to his first enthusiasms, as this letter to Sidney Schiff, written in 1921, bears witness: "I was thinking of you . . . and by dint of saying Schiff, Schiff, my plaintive cry took on something of Tristan's cry while awaiting the Ship. (See S. Ullmann *Essays in Honour of T.B.W. Reid*, p. 233, Blackwell, 1972).

5. E. Bouvier, *Initiation a la Littérature d'aujourd'hui, Cours Moyen*, La Renaissance du Livre, p. 230, 1932.

Proust and the Aesthetic of Suffering
J. E. Rivers*

Les plus belles oeuvres des hommes sont obstinément douloureuses.
[The most beautiful works of men are obstinately painful.]
—Gide, L'Immoraliste

*From *Contemporary Literature* 18, no. 4 (Autumn 1977): 425–42. Reprinted by kind permission of the author and the journal. All quotations from *A la recherche du temps perdu* come from the Kilmartin translation. All other translations are by the editor.

In *Axel's Castle* Edmund Wilson suggests that "Proust is guilty of the mediaeval sin of *accidia,* that combination of slothfulness and gloom which Dante represented as an eternal submergence in mud." He goes on to state that *A la recherche du temps perdu,* "in spite of all its humor and beauty, is one of the gloomiest books ever written."[1] In a recent book on Proust, Roger Shattuck takes issue with this reading. Proust's vision, according to Shattuck, is essentially comic. Indeed, Shattuck insists, Proust's techniques have affinities with farce and slapstick; and his all-pervasive humor is of the sort that makes us "[laugh] aloud." Shattuck concludes that *A la recherche* is "a far cry from the gloomiest book ever written."[2]

Shattuck's analysis of the comic element in *A la recherche* is valuable and illuminating. But it implies that the presence of comedy in the novel dispels the Proustian gloom of which Wilson speaks. I do not think this is the case. *King Lear* has some magnificient comic moments; but it is nonetheless a tragedy, a vision of the terrible limitations of man's ability to understand and retaliate against the cosmic cruelties that beset him. The same is true of *A la recherche.* Proust's novel is, finally, tragic, even pessimistic, in tone. Like all great tragedy, it depicts ennoblement through suffering; but it also reaches a point at which the suffering it describes cannot be redeemed or transcended, a point at which suffering triumphs over art. In order to see how this is so, we shall have to consider the many-faceted role suffering plays in the novel.

Proust's equation of love and suffering is too well known to need much discussion here. He believes that we love only those who make us suffer; we love them because they make us suffer; and, when we cease to suffer, we cease to love. This pattern holds true of all the major love affairs in the novel—those of Swann and Odette, Charlus and Morel, Saint-Loup and Rachel, and the narrator and Albertine. Though Proust's love affairs sometimes have charming moments of happiness and tenderness, they all turn out badly; all of them gradually evolve into the same sort of ["reciprocal torture" (*RTPK* 3:105)] that the narrator detects in his affair with Albertine.[3] Indeed, *A la recherche* gives us such a heavy dose of cruelty, suffering, and general emotional misery that it often seems to suggest that the human condition is one of utter futility, that no matter what happiness we experience, it will soon be overtaken by some great and unforeseen unhappiness. When things are not going well with Odette, Swann tries to comfort himself with the thought that ["one is never as unhappy as one thinks" (*RTPK* 1:385)]. But the situation goes from bad to worse, and Swann soon has to admit that ["one is never as happy as one thinks" (*RTPK* 1:386)] (I, 354–55). Proust's dramatization of misfortune in love follows geometrical progressions. We can never say that we have known the greatest suffering it is possible to know; there is always a suffering even more terrible waiting to overwhelm us.

The vicious circle of suffering is in some ways relieved by the palliative, redemptive power of art. Like many other writers, Proust draws intimate connections among suffering, knowledge, and artistic inspiration and creation. Even the scenes of blatant sadism and physical aggression with which the novel is salted have an important aesthetic dimension. They transform into ritual the cruelty and suffering inherent in life and love and thus become, in a sense, works of art in their own right. The formalistic, theatrical aspects of the lesbian scene at Montjouvain are apparent. Mlle Vinteuil and her friend indulge in ["ritual profanations"] and exchange ["liturgical response(s)"] (*RTPK* 1:177)] (I, 162). The entire scene has the over-stylized gestures and declamations that one could expect to find ["behind the footlights of a Paris theatre" (*RTPK* 1:178)]. Indeed, the narrator concludes from his observation of the two lesbians that ["when we find in real life a desire for melodramatic effect, it is generally sadism that is responsible for it" (*RTPK* 1:178–79)] (I, 163). As the producer, director, and central character of this sadistic melodrama, Mlle Vinteuil is ["an artist in evil" (*RTPK* 1:179)] (I, 164). She is an artist because she has created, however unconsciously and in however rudimentary a fashion, a poetic and dramatic structure that reflects not only a truth about her own life but an essential aspect of the human condition. Her actions symbolically outline what the narrator calls ["the most terrible and lasting form of cruelty" (*RTPK* 1:180)] (I, 165).

In the same way, Charlus' masochistic degradation in Jupien's brothel takes on aesthetic, even mythic significance. Jupien's brothel, like the brothel in Genet's *Le Balcon*, is a prototheater where the destructive urges of mankind are staged in carefully planned scenarios of cruelty: ["This house is . . . worse than a madhouse, since the mad fancies of the lunatics who inhabit it are played out as actual, visible drama" (*RTPK* 3:862)] (III, 832). In this particular *mise en scène*, Charlus becomes a mythic figure, a Prometheus prostrating himself before the eternal vengefulness of the universe. He is ["chained to a bed like Prometheus to his rock" (*RTPK* 3:843)]; he is ["this consenting Prometheus (who) had had himself nailed by Force to the rock of Pure Matter" (*RTPK* 3:868)] (III, 815; 838). The allegorical capitalizations underscore the larger symbolism of the scene. This is not just a drama of the cruelty of man to man; it is a drama of the cruelty of Force to Matter, an illustration of the principle of annihilation that invests all the affairs of the world. Like Mlle Vinteuil, Charlus is an ["artist in evil"] who transforms his own psychological drives into a spectacle that, when observed and interpreted by the narrator, illustrates universal truths.

Charlus has, as Jupien [*sic*: the narrator—ed.] points out, one of the primary qualifications for becoming a novelist: his life has been one of unremitting pain, one long ["current of pain" (*RTPK* 3:860)]. The narrator agrees, stating that ["a slap in the face or a box on the ear helps to educate not only children but poets" (*RTPK* 3:860)] (III, 831). But Charlus' art, like Mlle Vinteuil's, remains the primitive art of private ritual. Neither character is able to achieve the sustained transformation of suffering into art that ultimately characterizes the narrator's artistic vision. The art of Charlus and

Mlle Vinteuil is limited by its ["crude . . . symbolism . . . lacking in subtlety" (*RTPK* 1:179)] (I, 163)—whipping scenes and profanations of family
portraits. As artist figures, they only scratch the surface of the aesthetic potential of cruelty and suffering. Their lives are, obviously, prototypes of the
narrator's eventual movement from suffering to art; but they offer only dim
foreshadowing of the complex aesthetic uses to which the narrator puts his
own contact with suffering.

There is an irony involved in the narrator's development as an artist.
Suffering, as we shall see, finally becomes aesthetically and philosophically
indispensable to him. Throughout most of the novel, however, the narrator
of *A la recherche* appears as one of the characters least suited for dealing
with the realities of cruelty and pain. He is squeamish and delicate and
usually tries to avoid suffering whenever it confronts him. As a young boy
he is repelled by the malicious teasings to which his great-aunt subjects his
grandmother, saying, ["I preferred not to see them" (*RTPK* 1:13)] (I, 12).
Later, when he witnesses Rachel's conspiracy to have a young singer hissed
off the stage, he tries to shove the incident out of his mind: ["I preferred
not to speak of this incident" (*RTPK* 2:177)](II, 174). When the Verdurins
attack Saniette in their salon, the narrator is not among the metaphorical
["group of cannibals" (*RTPK* 2:965)]; rather, he tries to change the subject
and steer the conversation along different lines (II, 934; 936). And when he
learns of the Verdurins' plans to put an end to Charlus' social prestige by
turning Morel against him, he comments that ["I had but one thought,
which was to leave the Verdurins' house before the execution of M. de
Charlus occurred" (*RTPK* 3:313)] (III, 309).

It is, of course, a natural human impulse to shun the painful side of
things, and this is a trait the narrator shares with most of the other characters of the novel. Among the most typical—and most mordant—Proustian
scenes are those where characters go to elaborate lengths to avoid any contact with suffering, to avoid even having to admit that suffering exists. In a
particularly famous episode, the Duchesse de Guermantes hastens away to
a dinner party, pretending that she is pressed for time, but really so that
she will not have to stay and listen to Swann's announcement of his fatal
illness and imminent death. Similarly, in the interest of preserving the illusion of constant gaiety and good fellowship, the mention of death is *verbo-
ten* in Mme Verdurin's salon (II, 896) After the narrator's grandmother suddenly falls ill on the Champs-Elysées, Professor E., a doctor who is also a
friend of the family, looks her over hastily, preoccupied with the thought
that his suit will not be ready in time for a dinner engagement that evening. Performing the most cursory examination, he tells the narrator
abruptly, ["your grandmother is doomed" (*RTPK* 2:318)], and dismisses
them. From behind the closed doors of the office the narrator can hear the
doctor thundering at his maid for forgetting to prepare his boutonniere, an
oversight that will cost the doctor another ten-minute delay before leaving
for dinner (II, 318).

As Proust's characters flee from suffering, they flee also from reality. In scenes such as those just discussed, Proust echoes the Pascalian concept of *divertissement,* the idea that people invent all manner of diversions and distractions in order to shield themselves from the terrors of the human condition. As long as the daily round of habitual actions continues, we can live as if there were no such things as suffering and death. Indeed, the natural willingness of Proust's characters to confront, and especially to undergo, the experience of suffering finds perhaps its strongest support in the force of habit, which dulls all sensations, and works especially well to soften painful or unpleasant ones. Samuel Beckett comments brilliantly on this aspect of *A la recherche* in his study of Proust: "Habit [in Proust] is a compromise effected between the individual and his environment, or between the individual and his own organic eccentricities, the guarantee of a dull inviolability, the lightning-conductor of his existence. . . . Breathing is habit. Life is habit. . . . The periods of transition that separate consecutive adaptations . . . represent the perilous zones in the life of the individual, dangerous, precarious, painful, mysterious and fertile, when for a moment the boredom of living is replaced by the suffering of being."[4] Beckett echoes this idea in his own work. Vladimir says in *Waiting for Godot:* "Was I sleeping, while the others suffered? . . . We have time to grow old. The air is full of our cries. . . . But habit is a great deadener."[5]

So habit, in Beckett and in Proust, is the greatest *divertissement* of all. It is an anodyne, an analgesic, something that seals us off from reality—which is suffering—while giving us the pleasant but deceptive illusion of living. It allows us to perform the morally and aesthetically obtuse act of sleeping while others suffer, and it allows us to evade the moral and aesthetic implications of the cruelty and suffering in our own lives. It is, for Proust, ["stupefying habit, which during the whole course of our life conceals from us almost the whole universe, and . . . substitutes for the most dangerous or intoxicating poisons of life something anodyne" (*RTPK* 3:554)] (III, 544).

For a long time, the narrator, like most of the other characters in the novel, depends on habit to cushion the shocks of life, to absorb and defuse the new and threatening experiences that are potential sources of knowledge and inspiration. When he is a young boy at Combray his father sometimes leads the family home from their walks by an unfamiliar route after darkness has fallen. The narrator finds that the resulting disorientation and rupture with habit make his surroundings appear in an entirely new perspective. It is as if the dull, familiar buildings of Combray had suddenly become exquisite works of art: ["In each of their gardens the moonlight, copying the art of Hubert Robert, scattered its broken staircases of white marble, its fountains, its iron gates temptingly ajar. Its beams had swept away the telegraph office. All that was left of it was a column, half shattered but preserving the beauty of a ruin which endures for all time" (*RTPK* 1:124)] (I, 114). But the magic vision suddenly becomes soporifically common when the family reaches the back gate of Tante Léonie's, for there the force of habit once again takes over: ["And from that instant I did not have to take another step; the ground moved forward under my feet in that garden where for so long my actions had ceased to require any control, or even attention, from my will. Habit had come to take me in her arms and carry me all the way up to my bed like a little child" (*RTPK* 1:124–25).] (I, 115).

Proust's ideas on habit bear a striking similarity to a theory put forward by the Russian Formalist critic Victor Shklovsky, who formulated his aesthetic conceptions at roughly the same time Proust was writing *A la recherche*. For Shklovsky, artists aim at a process he calls *ostraneniye*, a term variously translated as "defamiliarization" or "making strange." As Shklovsky puts it: "Habitualization devours works, clothes, furniture, one's wife, and the fear of war. 'If the whole complex lives of many people go on unconsciously, then such lives are as if they had never been' [from Tolstoy's *Diary*]. And art exists that one may recover the sensation of life; it exists to make one feel things, to make the stone *stony*. The purpose of art is to impart the sensation of things as they are perceived and not as they are known. The technique of art is to make objects 'unfamiliar,' to make forms difficult, to increase the difficulty and length of perception because the process of perception is an aesthetic end in itself and must be prolonged."[6]

In *A la recherche* suffering is an important means of achieving this defamiliarization: ["Art is not alone in imparting charm and mystery to the most insignificant things; pain is endowed with the same power to bring them into intimate relation with ourselves" (*RTPK* 3:503)] (III, 493). There is an instructive parallel in Hemingway's fiction. In *The Sun Also Rises* Jake Barnes makes his way back to his hotel after having been knocked out by the expert boxer Robert Cohn. His head is still throbbing with pain, and the result is that

> walking across the square to the hotel everything looked new and changed. I had never seen the trees before. I had never seen the flag-poles before, nor the front of the theatre. It was all different. I felt as I felt once coming home from an out-of-town football game. . . . I walked up the street from the station in the town I had lived in all my life and it was all new. . . . It was all strange. . . . I had been kicked in the head early in the game. It was like that crossing the square.[7]

What physical pain accomplishes in Heminway, psychological and spiritual pain can accomplish in Proust. Swann's suffering over Odette, for instance, detaches him from the world to such an extent that he is able to see his familiar social surroundings as if for the first time, with the eye of an artist. As he enters the Marquise de Saint-Euverte's, full of anguish over his relationship with Odette, he finds that ["the tendency he had always had to look for analogies between living people and the portraits in galleries reasserted itself here, but in a more positive and more general form; it was society as a whole, now that he was detached from it, which presented itself to him as a series of pictures" (*RTPK* 1:352)] (I, 323). And there follows the bravura passage in which Swann's imagination transforms the footmen of the marquise into a living frieze composed of an executioner from a Renaissance painting, a warrior painted by Mantegna, a sexton painted by Goya, and so on. Jake Barnes has been pummeled on the head; Swann has been wounded in the spirit. But in both cases the result is the same. The pain involved overcomes and reverses the anaesthetic—the *an-aesthetic*—force of habit and opens the mind to modes of perception that usually go untapped.

Suffering, of course, is not enough to make an artist, as we have already seen in the cases of Charlus and Mlle Vinteuil. Swann, too, undergoes an experience of suffering that at times gives him an artistic perspective on the world. But he never actually creates; he never writes novels, composes music, or paints great pictures. Why? Because, for Proust, art is more than simple inspiration, whether that inspiration comes through suffering, through involuntary memory, through art produced by others, or whatever. One can have an artistic vision and still not have the special combination of gifts that will make it possible to give that vision concrete form. Craft, as well as inspiration, is necessary; the intelligence, as well as the emotions, must come into play (cf. III, 1034; 901). Charlus suffers, but he does not write novels; and the reason is, quite simply, that he ["had no gift for it" (*RTPK* 3:861)] (III, 831).

Conversely, Elstir is able to paint great pictures without, as far as we can tell, any profound experience of suffering. His art is largely the product of a special metaphorical vision that allows him to create impressionistic effects by, for instance, blurring the demarcation between land and sea in seascapes. Where Elstir's metaphorical vision comes from is not clear. For Aristotle, however, a mastery of metaphor is an intuitive, inborn disposition, "the one thing that cannot be learned from others,"[8] and it is perhaps best to leave it at that. Elstir seems to have, a priori, without any question of further detachment through suffering or any other means, a privileged vision, a perspective on life that is different from that of others. Just as suffering does not automatically make an artist, so, too, the artist does not always have to suffer in order to create.

Very often, however, and especially in the case of the narrator, suffering plays an indispensable role in drawing out the artist's innate vision, expanding it, strengthening it, and giving it form and direction: ["The imagination, the reflective capacity may be admirable machines in themselves, but they may also be inert. Suffering sets them in motion" (*RTPK* 3:946; cf. 942)] (III, 908; cf. 905). And at another point the narrator comments that ["unhappiness develops the forces of the mind" (*RTPK* 3:943)] (III, 906). More than this, suffering can give the artist a sense of self, a grounding in reality, an ontological foothold from which to create. One of the primary sources of suffering in *A la recherche* is the sensation of the discontinuity of the self, what Pierre-Henri Simon calls ["this vertiginous feeling . . . of an 'I' which shatters into momentary shards and incommunicable states, totally closed to one another"].[9] Paradoxically, however, the very suffering attendant upon such experiences gives the artist a way of unifying his existence and creating, or re-creating, an identity. Suffering is an experiential continuum; it is the ache that remains after the initial disappointment, the anguish that endures after the illusion has vanished. As such, it offers us affective proof of the continuity of our selves. It creates for each of us our own version of that ["current of pain"], that stream of pain generated by the life of the Baron de Charlus. Human beings have, according to Proust, a ["terrible capacity for registering things"] that ["makes the pain somehow contemporaneous with all the epochs of our life in which we have suffered" (RTPK 3:431)] (III, 425). In other words, whenever we suffer as our past selves suffered, ["we are no longer ourselves but he" (RTPK 1:692)]. (I: 643).

Similar access to the past, with its proof of continuous self-hood, is available, of course, through memory, especially the celebrated involuntary memory, in which the past and present selves suddenly and inexplicably interpenetrate. But suffering, for Proust, outlives memory and is therefore sometimes an even more valuable tool for conducting that *recherche* into man's existence in time, to which the title of the novel alludes: ["Like the harm that I had done my grandmother, the harm that Albertine had done me was a last bond between her and myself which outlived memory even, for with the conservation of energy which belongs to everything which is physical, suffering has no need of the lessons of memory. Thus a man who has forgotten the glorious nights spent by moonlight in the woods, suffers still from the rheumatism which he then contracted" (RTPK 3:537)] (III, 526).

As this passage indicates, there is in *A la recherche* a kind of involuntary suffering which corresponds roughly to involuntary memory. Though they are not precisely the same phenomenon, they are closely related and sometimes work together. After Albertine's death, while the narrator is reading the papers, a chance combination of words reminds him suddenly of Buttes-Chaumont, the region of Paris that Albertine swore she never visited with Andrée but that the narrator has reason to suspect she did. His reaction to the word "Chaumont" is not really a memory in any mental sense. It is something more organic, a wrenching, visceral stab of pain that bypasses the mind and goes directly to the soul. Intelligence and memory take over only after he has felt the full force of the shock, and it is only then that he realizes why the word "Chaumont" can cause him such devastating pain (III, 543).

Similarly, the narrator suffers for a long time over Albertine's supposed lesbian activities with the young laundress in Touraine. And yet, as time passes, there are moments when he forgets about this period of Albertine's life and the suffering it brought him, moments when Albertine and the laundress slip from his mind altogether. At such moments Albertine and the self that loved her can be reconstructed only when an unexpected resurgence of suffering reestablishes the broken contact between mind and heart: ["At times the contact between my heart and my memory was interrupted. What Albertine had done with the laundry-girl was indicated to me now by quasi-algebraic abbreviations which no longer meant anything to me, but a hundred times an hour the interrupted current was restored, and my heart was pitilessly scorched by a fire from hell, while I saw Albertine, resurrected by my jealousy, really alive, stiffen beneath the caresses of the young laundry-girl" (*RTPK* 3:538–39)] (III, 528). Just as an old wound in the body, a wound whose origins we have entirely forgotten, can suddenly throb with pain for no apparent reason, so the scars of the soul can involuntarily reopen and re-create the sensation of past suffering. When this happens, we do more than remember the way we were; we live, we feel, we ache precisely as we did in the past.

The pain we feel in such moments is, the narrator says, like the prick of a needle that makes a muscle jump in a dying man no longer capable of thought (III, 537). But that involuntary jerk of pain is of inestimable value to the artist in search of an identity. It is a last vestige of selfhood, one that lives on after memory has died, the point past which the self cannot be further reduced without being lost altogether. So the narrator clings desperately to such experiences. He even goes so far as to try to induce them voluntarily in order to maintain his uncertain grip on the swiftly crumbling past: ["And, during long periods, these stimulations occurred to me so rarely that I was driven to seek for myself occasions for grief, for a pang of jealousy, in an attempt to re-establish contact with the past, to remember her better" (*RTPK* 3:548)] (III, 537). Love is an illusion, says the narrator; but the pain caused by love, he also says, is real (II, 182; cf. III, 151). At the beginning of *Le Temps retrouvé*, however, the narrator points out that, like everything else in this world, suffering also eventually fades away, and fades more completely, leaving less of a trace behind, than anything else— even beauty (III, 695). So, in order to re-create the past, in order to re-create an identity, in order to re-create beauty, the narrator must re-create his suffering. Proust could almost as easily have called his novel *A la recherche de la souffrance perdue*.

But why do the characters of *A la recherche* have to suffer so much in the first place? Part of the answer seems to be that they suffer because they are guilty. Proust, who was a great admirer of Dostoevsky, is fascinated by the calculus of crime and punishment. But rarely does he establish a simple, one-to-one equation—this suffering as punishment for that crime. It almost seems, as Milton Hindus has suggested, that Proust's characters suffer for original sin, that their guilt and punishment are inextricably entangled with the fallen nature of humanity as a whole. "A man unfortunate enough to fall into the net of a woman like Odette," Hindus writes, "must ask himself at some point—what did I ever do to deserve this? The answer

that Proust gives to this question is 'Plenty!' "[10] Indeed, Proust often seems
the lesbians and their sadistic rituals, when he listened to the story of
to create a symbolic hell-on-earth whose inhabitants, damned to the ["reciprocal torture"] of love, prey on each other in a relentless cycle in which
mutual punishment breeds mutual guilt and mutual guilt breeds more mutual punishment. It is not wholly an accident that Proust so often refers to
jealousy as a "démon" (e.g., III, 103) or compares it to a ["fire from hell"
(*RTPK* 3:539)] (III, 528) or speaks of it, in images drawn from classical
myths of the torments of the underworld, as ["[a torture] where the task
must be incessantly repeated, like that of the Danaides, or of Ixion" (*RTPK*
3:147–48)] (III, 151).

The idea that suffering occurs as punishment for some primal sin
emerges most clearly in the scene where Albertine reveals to the narrator
that she knows Mlle Vinteuil and her lesbian friend. As soon as she speaks,
the narrator begins to search his past for some transgression to which he
can attribute the terrible onslaught of suffering Albertine's revelation unleashes:

> [At the sound of these words, uttered as we were entering the station of
> Parville, so far from Combray and Montjouvain, so long after the death
> of Vinteuil, an image stirred in my heart, an image which I had kept in
> reserve for so many years that even if I had been able to guess, when I
> stored it up long ago, that it had a noxious power, I should have sup-
> posed that in the course of time it had entirely lost it; preserved alive in
> the depths of my being—like Orestes whose death the gods had pre-
> vented in order that, on the appointed day, he might return to his native
> land to avenge the murder of Agamemnon—as a punishment, as a retri-
> bution (who knows?) for my having allowed my grandmother to die; per-
> haps rising up suddenly from the dark depths in which it seemed forever
> buried, and striking like an Avenger, in order to inaugurate for me a new
> and terrible and only too well-merited existence, perhaps also to make
> dazzlingly clear to my eyes the fatal consequences which evil actions
> eternally engender, not only for those who have committed them but for
> those who have done no more, or thought that they were doing no more,
> than look on at a curious and entertaining spectacle, as I, alas, had done
> on that afternoon long ago at Montjouvain, concealed behind a bush
> where (as when I had complacently listened to the account of Swann's
> love affairs) I had perilously allowed to open up within me the fatal and
> inevitably painful road of knowledge. (*RTPK* 2:1152)] (II, 1114–15)

The intricate syntax of this remarkable passage reflects the extreme complexity of the moral position it outlines. The narrator clearly feels he has
done something to deserve his suffering; but, as he examines his past to
discover what that something might be, his search vacillates between the
personal and the archetypal. Perhaps he is being punished for neglecting
his grandmother during her fatal illness or perhaps for having spied on the
two lesbians. After all, he thinks, do not evil acts produce perpetual rever-
berations, tainting not only those who commit them but also those who do

nothing more than look upon them or hear about them? When he spied on Swann's ill-fated affair with Odette, his innocence was destroyed. He acquired a dangerous and deadly knowledge. And that knowledge—of sadism, of jealousy, of lesbianism—has been preserved in his mind all these years, waiting there to smite him for his transgression—like the avenger Orestes, who was spared by the gods so that he might exact vengeance for the murder of Agamemnon.

When the narrator asks, "What have I done to deserve this?" the answer is, indeed, "Plenty!" But Proust's imagery enlarges the concept of guilt to such an extent that, by the time we reach the end of this long, meandering piece of self-incrimination—a long sentence even for Proust— we find it impossible to distinguish the narrator's guilt from the guilt of humanity in general. Whether the metaphor is the curse that lies upon the house of Atreus or the curse that followed the partaking of the fruit of the Tree of Knowledge, what it really signifies is the flawed, imperfect status of humanity as Proust perceives it. We want to be happy and find that we are unhappy; we want to be moral and find that we are cruel; we want to avoid evil and find that we are inexorably drawn to it; we want to live and find that we can only suffer. It is a situation that cries out for a redeemer. In the *Oresteia* it is Athena; in the Bible it is Christ; and in *A la recherche*, in very special ways, it is Elstir, Bergotte, Vinteuil, and the narrator himself—the artist figures of the novel.

Much has been written about the redemptive power of art in Proust. In general, the case has been overstated. It is true, as Barbara Bucknall has shown, that Proust assigns to art the traditional functions of religion.[11] He does not appeal to God; he appeals only to the power and vision of the artist. The moments of greatest joy, the moments of self-transcendence, the moments when we are made to feel that death is perhaps not so greatly to be feared, are the moments in *A la recherche* when we are in the presence of great art.

Aside from the narrator, Vinteuil is the supreme artist in this respect. It is appropriate that Vinteuil's life, as we know it from "Combray," is filled with pain and that his art speaks profoundly of suffering. Once Swann has been prepared by the agony of his affair with Odette, he is able to perceive depths and meanings in Vinteuil's music that he has never noticed before. The music he hears at the Marquise de Saint-Euverte's reminds him of his moments of happiness with Odette; but it also communicates the knowledge that all happiness is fleeting and, along with this knowledge, a sublime sense of resignation. Swann realizes that only one who had suffered greatly could create a work such as this: ["Swann's thoughts were borne . . . on a wave of pity and tenderness towards Vinteuil, towards that unknown, exalted brother who must also have suffered so greatly. What could his life have been? From the depths of what well of sorrow could he have drawn that god-like strength, that unlimited power of creation?" (*RTPK* 1:379)] (I, 348). Vinteuil is a great artist partly because he is able to transmute his suffering into forms that are meaningful to others; his art takes suffering and places it *sub specie aeternitatis.*

When a great artist can speak in his art of his suffering, and other human beings can recognize in that statement something that is true of humanity in general, this is, in itself, an act of partial redemption for Proust. The spark of art leaps the gap of exile and solitude that, in everyday life, separates us from our fellowmen and threatens our experience with eternal solipsism. Listening to the Vinteuil sonata, Swann ["felt that he was no longer in exile and alone" (*RTPK* 1:378)] (I, 348). Other people treat Swann's suffering as a thing of little importance. Vinteuil, however, seems to understand the cataclysmic eruptions of the soul, the new visions of life, that were created by Swann's anguish over Odette. Listening to Vinteuil's music, Swann understands that the experience of suffering is ["something not, as all these people did, less serious than the events of everyday life, but, on the contrary, so far superior to it as to be alone worth while expressing" (*RTPK* 1:379)] (I, 348–49).

The art of the narrator, like the art of Vinteuil, assigns a position of supreme importance to human suffering. The theoretical sections of *Le Temps retrouvé* reiterate again and again the conviction that, without the profound experience of suffering he has known in life, the narrator could never create the novel he envisions. In a multitude of different ways Proust reaffirms the *pathei mathos,* the "through suffering, knowledge" of the Greeks.[12] ["A woman is of greater utility to our life if, instead of being an element of happiness in it, she is an instrument of suffering, and there is not a woman in the world the possession of whom is as precious as that of the truths which she reveals to us by causing us to suffer" (*RTPK* 3:506)] (III, 496). Suffering leads to the truth. It encourages introspective examination of our most deep-seated motives; and it causes us to scrutinize with passionate attention the lives and identities of those who make us suffer: ["How much further does anguish penetrate in psychology than psychology itself!" (*RTPK* 3:425)] (III, 419). The narrator who once avoided the spectacle of suffering at all costs now sees that it must function as one of the primary tools of creation. ["It almost seems"], he says, ["as though a writer's works, like the water in an artesian well, mount to a height which is in proportion to the depth to which suffering has penetrated his heart" (*RTPK* 3:946)] (III, 908). His life of suffering, he realizes, has been a long and arduous apprenticeship for an artistic vocation.

To an even greater extent than Vinteuil, the narrator becomes in his novel both the high priest and the sacrificial victim of suffering. Proust does not hesitate to make his narrator something of a Christ figure in this regard. In discussing the way he suffers over Albertine, the narrator speaks of himself as wearing a ["crown of thorns" (*RTPK* 2:795)]; later, in his grief over Albertine's death, he compares himself to a madman who thinks that "Jésus Christ c'est moi" (III, 540); and, when he experiences involuntary suffering triggered by the word "Chaumont," he is careful to point out that Chaumont, *Calvus mons*, has the same etymology as Golgotha, the place where Christ was crucified (III, 543). Moreover, we encounter throughout the novel the suggestion that the narrator's suffering recapitulates the suffering of the other major characters. The story of the Albertine affair is filled with indications of how the narrator at once repeats and surpasses the suffering of Swann over Odette (e.g., III, 498–99; cf. II, 1121). Similarly, when the narrator's mother is in mourning over the death of the grandmother, the narrator points out that ["I was one day to experience a grief as profound as that of my mother" (*RTPK* 2:796)] (II, 768)—anticipating, of course, his grief after the death of Albertine. There is even a suggestion toward the end of the novel that when the narrator has the attack that causes him to stumble three times on the stairs, he has been stricken with the same illness that caused his grandmother to die (III, 1038–39).

Passages such as these suggest that all the varieties of suffering described in the novel symbolically converge in the experience of the narrator—just as the passion of Christ supposedly recapitulated the sufferings of all humanity.[13] And clearly, the narrator regards his transformation of suffering into art not only as a recapitulation but as a kind of atonement as well. By dying into the suffering depicted in his book, he and his characters will be reborn in a higher form, as works of art whose truths will abide and enrich the lives of future generations: ["To me it seems more correct to say that the cruel law of art is that people die and we ourselves die after exhausting every form of suffering, so that over our heads may grow the grass not of oblivion but of eternal life, the vigorous and luxuriant growth of a true work of art, and so that thither, gaily and without a thought for those who lie sleeping beneath them, future generations may come to enjoy their déjeuner sur l'herbe" (*RTPK* 3:1095)] (III, 1038).

Many critics have assumed that the idea contained in this sentence—that through his creations the artist attains "vie éternelle"—represents Proust's last word on the redemptive power of art. Very often we are asked to believe that the narrator's discovery of his artistic vocation functions as a sort of *deus ex machina* that obliterates suffering, expunges guilt, and solves all the seemingly insoluble problems of life. Charlotte Haldane's analysis of the narrator's state of mind in *Le Temps retrouvé* can stand as a representative example. Speaking of the moments of involuntary memory that occur at the Guermantes matinée and fix the narrator's resolution to create a work of art, Haldane writes: "As the result of this transcendental experience he has at last made conscious contact with Eternity. . . . now he has found the will-power, the courage, the zest for living which until then he had so lamentably lacked. . . . All his doubts, hesitations, anxieties and frustrations have now disappeared, as the result of his one great moment of self-revelation, with its affectual sense of happiness amounting to ecstasy, strong enough to enable him to overcome all the misery of the past. . . . The fear of death . . . has now been replaced by a new and ardent desire to live."[14]

Haldane interprets Proust's final vision as one of unadulterated optimism, but she overlooks some of the most important features of the dénouement of *A la recherche*. To be sure, Proust surrounds the narrator's discovery of his artistic vocation with religious imagery, which suggests that salvation can be attained through art. But, as *Le Temps retrouvé* continues to develop, Proust qualifies this idea drastically. As has been the case throughout the novel, the narrator's moments of ecstasy and happiness prove to be the exception rather than the rule; and salvation through art turns out to be a very limited form of salvation indeed.

There is, of course, a certain joy and transcendence in the act of artistic creation, even when that creation proceeds from suffering: ["Ideas come to us as the successors to griefs, and griefs, at the moment when they change into ideas, lose some part of their power to injure our heart; the transformation itself, even, for an instant, releases suddenly a little joy" (RTPK 3:944)] (III, 906). We should notice, however, the important qualifiers in this statement: ["some part"] and ["for an instant"]. And the narrator goes on to make it quite plain that the power of art to redeem the human condition, to overcome and expiate guilt, is severely restricted. Writing a novel in which he recognizes and condemns the immorality of his conduct toward his grandmother, for instance, can never be sufficient expiation for the guilt he accumulated by neglecting her during her illness: ["My grandmother, whom with so little feeling I had seen agonise and die beside me! I longed that in expiation, *when my work should be finished,* I might, incurably stricken, suffer for long hours, abandoned by all, and then die!" *(RTPK* 3:939)] (III, 902, italics mine). In statements such as this, Proust recalls one of the most pessimistic of Kafka's pronouncements: "Art for the artist is only suffering through which he releases himself for further suffering."[15] The narrator is caught in a cruel paradox. He has to suffer in order to create. But creation, though it can lessen pain and guilt, can never put a definitive end to it. Proust's narrative is brutally open-ended and therefore brutally honest. It anticipates the guilt and suffering the artist will have to endure after his work is finished and over which the work of art, once completed and laid aside, will have no redemptive or palliative power.

Furthermore, if one has to suffer in order to create, then one comes to dread the idea of undertaking any creative work at all: ["And then the idea of the preliminary suffering becomes associated with the idea of work and one is afraid of each new literary undertaking because one thinks of the pain one will first have to endure in order to imagine it" *(RTPK* 3:947)] (III, 909). Art is the only recourse the narrator has. But, since art is suffering and suffering is art, this means that ["suffering is the best thing one can hope to encounter in life"]. If this is so, then life is obviously worth very little, and one can think ["without terror, and almost as a deliverance, of death" *(RTPK* 3:947)] (III, 909).

To further darken the tone of the final pages, the narrator becomes gravely ill soon after the discovery of his artistic vocation. And when this happens, he says, all joy, all enthusiasm, go out of his life. From this time forth he experiences no more happiness—not from social life, not from the hope for fame, not even from the progress of his work. He is little more than a ["half-dead man" (*RTPK* 3:1100)] (III, 1042)—a Christ figure who gets only halfway out of the tomb before it swallows him up again. He writes mechanically and compulsively, morbidly obsessed with the idea of his imminent death. There is no satisfaction in living, no satisfaction in creative work (III, 1042–43). Even the idea that art holds out hope for a certain type of immortality is clouded over at the end. One has, the narrator says, to accept the fact that one's books, like one's body, will one day cease to exist: ["In ten years he will be no more, and in a hundred years his books will be no more. To last eternally is no more the lot of books than of men." (not in *RTPK*—translated by ed.)] (III, 1043).

What, then, motivates the narrator to keep writing here at the end? It is partly, as Leo Bersani has suggested, the need to "unload himself of the oppressive weight of his past."[16] But there is something more involved as well. The more we are made to appreciate the tragic limitations of the narrator's undertaking, the more heroic that undertaking appears. Without art, life would be meaningless. With art there is a partial salvation—but only a partial one. The narrator's struggle is a struggle undertaken with the knowledge that it can never be totally successful. In the end suffering, death, and destruction will triumph, and the rest will be silence.

And yet the narrator does not give up. He perseveres against nearly overwhelming odds, and this gives the work a truly tragic and truly noble flavor. One canot help but be moved by the figure of the narrator, old, tired, and sick, stripped of all illusions, stripped of all happiness and hope, continuing to struggle, continuing to cling to the one thing—art—which, though he is aware of its limitations, will at least allow him to re-create some of both the beauty and the sorrow of the world. And to do one thing more, something that will, after all, prove the community of the human spirit: ["extract from our grief the generality that lies within it" (*RTPK* 3:939).] (III, 902).

Notes

1. *Axel's Castle* (New York: Charles Scribner's Sons, 1931), p. 164.

2. *Marcel Proust* (New York: Viking Press, 1974), pp. 72, 80, et passim.

3. Marcel Proust, *A la recherche du temps perdu*, ed. Pierre Clarac and André Ferré, 3 vols. (Paris: Gallimard, 1954), III, 109. Further parenthetical references in the text will be to this edition.

4. *Proust* (New York: Grove Press, 1931), pp. 7–8.

5. *Waiting for Godot* (New York: Grove Press, 1954), p. 58.

6. "Art as Technique," trans. Lee T. Lemon and Marion J. Reis, in *Russian Formalist Criticism: Four Essays* (Lincoln: Univ. of Nebraska Press, 1965), p. 12.

7. Ernest Hemingway, *The Sun Also Rises* (1926; rpt. New York: Charles Scribner's Sons, 1970), pp. 192–93.

8. Aristotle, *Poetics*, 1459a5. Translation mine.

9. *Témoins de l'homme: La condition humaine dans la littérature contemporaine*, 3rd ed. (1951; rpt. Paris: Librairie Armand Colin, 1955), p. 5.

10. "The Pattern of Proustian Love," *New Mexico Quarterly*, 21, No. 4 (Winter 1951), 395–96.

11. Barbara J. Bucknall, *The Religion of Art in Proust* (Urbana: Univ. of Illinois Press, 1969).

12. See Aèschylus, *Agamemnon*, 177. Translation mine.

13. This well-known idea is developed in detail in the theology of Irenaeus. See J. T. Nielsen, *Adam and Christ in the Theology of Irenaeus of Lyons* (Assen, Netherlands: Van Gorcum, 1968), pp. 11, 14, 58–59, et passim; and Gustaf Wingren, *Man and the Incarnation: A Study in the Biblical Theology of Irenaeus*, trans. Ross Mackenzie (Philadelphia: Muhlenberg Press, 1959), p. 47 et passim.

14. *Marcel Proust* (London: Arthur Barker, 1951), pp. 134–35.

15. Gustav Janouch, *Conversations with Kafka*, trans. Goronwy Rees (New York: New Directions, 1969), p. 28; quoted in Stanley Corngold, trans. and ed., *The Metamorphosis*, by Franz Kafka (New York: Bantam Books, 1972), p. xx.

16. *Marcel Proust: The Fictions of Life and Art* (New York: Oxford Univ. Press, 1965), p. 54.

Marcel Proust and Architecture: Some Thoughts on the Cathedral-Novel
J. Theodore Johnson, Jr.*

". . . the vast structure of recollection" (*RTP* 1:47; *RTPK* 1:51)

"In long books of this kind there are parts which there has been time only to sketch, parts which, because of the very amplitude of the architect's plan, will no doubt never be completed. How many great cathedrals remain unfinished!" (*RTP* 3:1033; *RTPK* 3:1089)

At the end of *A la recherche du temps perdu*, the Narrator, thinking of his labor on the translation of certain truths he had experienced in the course of his life and which he intended to put in a book, said that it would

*This article first appeared in the *BSAMP*, no. 25 (1975):16–34 and no. 26 (1976):247–66. Acknowledgment for permission to reprint is gratefully made to the editor of the *BSAMP*, M. Henri Bonnet. The translation of the author's text was made by the editor of this collection. Quotations from *A la recherche du temps perdu* come from the Kilmartin translation. Quotations from Ruskin are given in his own words. All other translations of quotations are by the editor.

be necessary to construct his book "like a church" (*RTP* 3:1032; *RTPK* 3:1089). This declaration has led to diverse hypotheses on the part of his commentators, and also to attempts to establish close connections between the different parts of a cathedral and this novel.[1] It is time to reconsider the question, and I propose to consider it under the following aspects: Proust and architecture, the concept of an architect-writer, and the concept of a cathedral-novel.

I. PROUST AND ARCHITECTURE

We know very little about Proust's evaluation of architecture before 1900, the year when Proust showed an exceptional interest in everything concerning architecture. Already around 1896, according to Robert de Billy, Proust began to be interested in Gothic architecture.[2] He took an interest in Ruskin from 1897 on. In 1899 he was busy with a little study on Ruskin and certain cathedrals; in a letter to Marie Nordlinger in February 1900, Proust said that he knew by heart *The Seven Lamps of Architecture, The Bible of Amiens, Val d'Arno, Lectures on Architecture and Painting* and *Praeterita* and that he was looking for texts on Chartres, Abbeville, Rheims, Rouen etc.[3] Immediately after, he went to Amiens and Rouen. In the spring he visited Saint Mark's in Venice and the Chapel of the Arena in Padua, then Amiens again and Abbeville; in 1902 he visited Chartres, Provins, Saint-Loup de Naud, Saint-Leu d'Esserent, Senlis, Laon, Coucy; in 1903 he visited Avallon, Vézelay and Dijon, and later he visited Norman churches during his trips to Cabourg: Caen, Dives, Lisieux, Evreux, Bayeux, among many others.[4] The texts to which Proust alludes most frequently are the nine volumes of the *Dictionnaire raisonné de l'architecture française du XIe au XVIe siècle* by Viollet-le Duc (1875) and two books which came out in 1898: *La Cathédrale* by Huysmans and *L'Art religieux du XIIIe siècle en France: Etude sur l'iconographie du Moyen Age et sur ses sources d'inspiration* by Emile Mâle.

In the end these visits and this reading led to the production of a great number of texts on the subjects of Ruskin, architecture, reading and aesthetics. Proust was to make use of these texts in the lengthy prefaces he wrote to his translations of *The Bible of Amiens* (1904) and *Sesame and Lilies* (1906). His excellent edition of *The Bible of Amiens* proved that Proust had a remarkable knowledge of Gothic architecture, from the point of view of architecture and iconography. This interest was also shown later on in his article, "La Mort des cathédrales: une conséquence du projet Briand pour la Séparation" (1904), the review of the translation of *The Stones of Venice* (1906) and the text, "Impressions de route en automobile" (1909); it is apparent in the amazing pastiche of Ruskin in 1909, particularly in the second part, in which Proust criticized a view of history based on aesthetics instead of facts; last of all it appeared in "L'Eglise de Village" (1912), which looks forward to the theme of churches in *A la recherche du temps perdu*.

He went on reading books on architecture after the period in his life which we call Ruskinian. We know that he consulted scientific works while he was writing his novel. In a letter in 1912 to Mme Gaston de Caillavet, Proust wrote: "If I have an impression I need precise terms in order to explain it. And I do not know them. So I leaf through books on botany, or books on architecture, or else fashion magazines" (*CG* 4:126).

His studies and his reading taught him to read a church like a book. So why not construct a book like a church? Certainly Proust could have found in his reading examples of similar attempts. In the *Art religieux du XIIIe siècle,* for instance Mâle says that Dante "raised his invisible cathedral 'cum pondere et mensura.' Together with St. Thomas he was the great architect of the thirteenth century."[5] We know the deep affinities that connect the work of Dante with that of Proust.[6] According to Huysmans, the royal portal of Chartres Cathedral is at one and the same time the portal and "the first chapter of the book, summing up in itself alone the whole edifice! All the same they do seem bizarre, these conclusions preceding the premises, this recapitulation placed at the beginning of the work, when they ought, in strict logic, to be at the apse, at the end."[7] Is it not possible to utter the same exclamation before "Combray," before what some people call the "Overture" and other "the Porch" which opens onto *A la recherche du temps perdu*? Chateaubriand constructs his *Mémoires d'Outre-Tombe* like a temple to death raised up in the light of his memories,[8] and he works at it with "the fervor of a son building a mausoleum for his mother," his building materials having already been rough-hewn and brought together in his previous studies (*MOT* 1:399). Proust refers to the passage on the song of the thrush as an example of involuntary memory (*RTP* 3:919; *RTPK* 3:958). He could also have referred to the following passage on the subject of conceiving a literary work in architectural terms: "The same thing has happened to me as happens to every man who undertakes to work on a large scale: first of all I have erected the buildings at either end, then, moving my scaffolding around, I have raised up the stones and cement of the intermediary constructions; it took several centuries to finish building the Gothic cathedrals. If heaven grants me life, the monument will be finished by the succession of my varying years! The architect, always remaining the same, will only be of a different age" (*MOT* 1:435). How close we are to the Proustian notion of the creative personality, aware and enduring, who constructs a work like a church (cf. the one at Combray) which will overcome and survive successive epochs. Finally Proust knew Victor Hugo's *Notre Dame de Paris* and its famous chapter "Ceci tuera cela" (This will kill that") in which Hugo announces, in a voice of thunder, that printing will replace architecture: "The great poem, the great building, the great work of humanity will no longer be built, it will be printed."[9]

We have no text which proves beyond doubt that Proust intended his novel from the very beginning to be "like a church." We know that Proust had some hesitations about the form his novel was to take and that after that he had hesitated to call it a novel. The 1913 interview with Elie-Joseph Bois defines the psychological structure of the novel, but does not allude in any way to an architectural structure. As soon as the first part came out and because of the criticisms that were leveled at it for its apparent lack of structure, Proust begins to talk about structure in his correspondence. For example, in a letter to André Gide, Proust comments on the converging episodes of *Les Caves du Vatican* and says that they are "arranged as in a rose window," which is, to his taste, "the most masterful kind of composition." As for his own novel, Proust says that, after having called on all his resources to compose it, he had gone on to "erase those traces of composition which were too obvious."[10] In fact Proust often speaks of the veiled but rigorous composition of his novel.[11] Sometimes he is more precise and speaks of its "rigorous architecture"; he says that the book is "composed and concentric" (*CG* 1:167), with an "architectonic line which is already sufficiently complex in itself" (*CG* 3:300).

Unambiguous allusions to a cathedral are found for the first time in the celebrated letter to Comte Jean de Gaigneron (at the beginning of August 1919), in which Proust writes: "Your intelligence goes to the heart of things so profoundly that you do not only read the printed book I published, but the unknown book I should have liked to write. And when you speak to me of cathedrals, I cannot fail to be deeply affected by an intuition which allows you to divine what I have never told anyone and what I am writing here for the first time: it is that I had intended to give each part of my book the title: *Porch I, The Stained Glass Windows of the Apse*, etc. in order to reply in advance to the stupid criticism leveled at me about the lack of construction in books whose sole merit, as I shall show you, lies in the solid coherence of the smallest parts. I immediately abandoned these architectural titles because I found them too pretentious but I am touched that you should have found them again by a kind of divinatory intelligence" (*Lettres retrouvées*, 131). A note in the Cahier 57 (21v°) alludes to Gaigneron, and Proust writes that when people say they have known something they are referring not to what they have known but to a rather intense inner impression. Is this note connected with the letter to Gaigneron in which he speaks of a cathedral-novel? It is very possible. In any case, what matters for Proust is giving his readers the *impression* of being in a cathedral, and, like Proust, we can dispense with these architectural titles which would run the risk of weakening this impression by a superfluous preciseness.

In a letter to François Mauriac in 1919, Proust wrote that he could not accede to the request of Francis Jammes who wanted him to suppress an episode (without a doubt the scene between the two girls at Montjouvain) which Jammes considered shocking: "I have constructed this work so carefully that this episode in the first volume provides the explanation of the jealousy of the young hero in the fourth and fifth volumes, so that if I had torn down the pillar with the obscene capital I would have made the whole vault collapse further on."[12] In a letter to Paul Souday on November 10,

1919 Proust says more or less the same thing, for the recollection of the scene between two girls "is the mainstay of volumes IV and V (because of the jealousy it inspires, etc.). If I had suppressed it I would not have changed much in the first volume; but on the other hand, because of the close connections between the parts, I would have made two volumes, of which it is the cornerstone, come tumbling down on the reader's head."[13] In a letter to Jacques Rivière, Proust speaks of his work in terms of a construction in which "there are solid parts and pillars, and in the space between two pillars I can give myself up to minutely detailed paintings."[14] All these comparisons between his work and a cathedral—porches, stained glass windows, capitals, cornerstones, vaults, solid surfaces, pillars and minutely detailed paintings—seem very precise and suggest a very solid architectonic structure. However, one must beware of these comparisons, which are, all things considered, external to the essential nature of the cathedral-novel, for, as we shall see further on, in the structure of his novel Proust attempts to capture the spirit of the cathedral and not to transpose the different parts of a Gothic structure into texts which would rigorously correspond to a plastic shape.

The numerous drawings with which Proust decorated his notebooks or his letters to Reynaldo Hahn prove that he had no real talent for drawing and particularly not for architecture. We are very far from the architectural drawings of Victor Hugo with his visions, from Thomas Hardy with his firsthand knowledge of architecture, or, finally, from Ruskin, who was an accomplished draftsman. Proust's best drawings were those he had traced directly from books, particularly *L'Art religieux du XIIIe siècle*. He managed more or less to draw the façade of Amiens, which is by far his best architectural drawing, but aside from vague thematic sketches, his pen was unable to portray an imaginary church.[15] On the other hand, he could *imagine* a whole series of pictures around a plastic theme, such as the presentation of the Virgin at the Temple (Hahn, 81–82), or he could invent a stained glass window with a single subject (Hahn, 74) or a stained glass window composed of eighteen scenes (Hahn, 194–96).

It is obvious that when Proust used the terms *architecture* and *architect* to speak of his novel and of his work as a writer, he used them as metaphors or as abstract concepts. Rather than try to explore the possible analogies between the different parts of a cathedral and the work of Proust, which would lead us in a wrong direction, it seems to me that we should concentrate on the two concepts that are central to Proust's work: the writer as architect and the cathedral-novel.

II. THE CONCEPT OF THE WRITER AS ARCHITECT

Let us turn to the second panel of our study, Proust's concept of the writer as architect. In *Le Temps retrouvé* we learn that the Narrator sometimes had to reply to an invitation before taking up once more his "labours as an architect" (*RTP* 3:1040; *RTPK* 3:1098).

The ethics of the artist and the work of the artist, what Baudelaire calls "the hygiene of the artist," preoccupied Proust a good deal during the years when he was drafting his first novel. The artist B . . . , in the text "Conversation" intended for *Les Plaisirs et les jours*, prefigures the fictitious artists—the novelists C . . . and Traves and the painter Bergotte of *Jean Santeuil*. If Proust roughed out important texts on painters—Chardin, Watteau, Rembrandt, Gustave Moreau and Monet—on the other hand he left us no comparable texts on architects. Since he knew Ruskin's *Seven Lamps of Architecture* "by heart", did Proust consider that he had nothing further to develop in this field? As it happens, a comparison of this book of Ruskin's with Proust's ideas on the writer as an artist shows that there are many parallels between them; for example the long sentence on the way in which the Narrator visualizes his novel and where we find the phrase "build it up like a church" (*RTP* 3:1032. *RTPK* 3:1098) is astonishingly close to the leading ideas in Ruskin's book. Let us not forget that this book belongs to the group of texts in which Ruskin, as an aesthete and a moralist, attempted to inspire anew in the English workman a love for his trade. Insufficient attention has been paid to the importance of this work for Proust. He quotes from or alludes to this book quite often during his "Ruskinian period," and it figures in Proust's correspondence after this period. In August 1907 Proust asked Reynaldo Hahn to send him *The Seven Lamps of Architecture* in one of the two editions of the work he owned (Hahn, 143). In a letter sent in August 1911 Proust compared this book of Ruskin's to Schopenhauer's *Metaphysics of Music* and claimed that they were, together with a text of Hahn's, very beautiful texts on art, the most beautiful he knew (Hahn, 212). Finally, in a letter written on January 31, 1917 we learn that Proust was looking for this book in the French translation to send it to Jacques Hébertot, to whom the letter was addressed.[16]

The seven "lamps" or the seven "spirits" of architecture which, according to Ruskin, should light every architect, are the Lamp of Sacrifice, the Lamp of Truth, the Lamp of Power, the Lamp of Beauty, the Lamp of Life, the Lamp of Memory, and the Lamp of Obedience. Setting on one side the Building and its Construction, Ruskin defines Architecture as follows: "Architecture is the art which so disposes and adorns the edifices raised by man, for whatsoever uses, that the sight of them may contribute to his mental health, power and pleasure."[17] We are not far from the Proustian conception of literature, particularly where the spiritual function of the novel as cathedral is concerned (cf. the preface to *Sésame et les lys* and the long meditation on literature, *Le Temps retrouvé*). As a matter of fact, of the five classes of architecture which Ruskin proposes (Devotional, Memorial, Civil, Military, and Domestic), the one which most resembles Proust's novel is the "Devotional" class.

The personal privations and the cossetting of a work of art to which the Narrator looks forward make one think of the first of Ruskin's lamps, that of Sacrifice. Proust had already written in an article in 1900 which he was to incorporate in the preface to *La Bible d'Amiens:* "The words of a genius, just as well as a chisel, can give an immortal form to things. Literature too is a 'lamp of sacrifice' which is consumed to light our descendants" (*La Bible d'Amiens*, 46), and he refers again to this chapter further on (*La Bible d'Amiens*, 52). One could speak of a lamp of Truth and a lamp of Beauty in Proust, but not always in the Ruskinian sense. In fact they are not two but one in Proust, the Beautiful being located not in the Good as with Ruskin, but in the True. This perpetual adoration of beauty, but of an essentially outward beauty, leads according to Proust to idolatry (cf. the preface to *La Bible d'Amiens*, 52–53). For Proust truth and beauty are inward, constituting for the writer as artist the essential light which is shed on his work and on the very subject matter of his book.

In the chapter on the lamp of Power Ruskin says, "I do not believe that ever any building was truly great unless it had mighty masses, vigorous and deep, of shadow mingled with its surface," and he establishes a connection between architecture and literature: "As the great poem and great fiction generally affect us most by the majesty of their masses of shade and cannot take hold upon us if they affect a continuance of lyric sprightliness, but must be often serious, and sometimes melancholy, else they do not express the truth of this wild world of ours, so there must be, in the same way, in this magnificently human art of architecture, some equivalent expression for the trouble and wrath of life, for its sorrow and its mystery" (*Seven Lamps*, 154). These sentences find an echo in Proust, particularly in the sentence in which the Narrator is thinking of creating a novel "like a new world without reflecting those mysteries whose explanation is to be found probably in worlds other than our own and the presentiment of which is the thing that moves us most deeply in life and in art" (*RTP* 3:1032–33; *RTPK* 3:1089).

The chapter on the lamp of Life is very probably the one which most caught Proust's attention. It is from this chapter that there come the quotations in connection with the tympanum of Saint-Maclou at Rouen with its mixture of the spirit "of Orcagna and Hogarth" (cf. the preface to *La Bible d'Amiens* and p. 233), and above all the important text on the little figure over the Booksellers' Porch in Rouen Cathedral).[18] In this chapter, Ruskin looks forward to the Proust of *Contre Sainte-Beuve* in the distinction between the creative personality and the social persona (*Seven Lamps*, 191–92). Ruskin likes the irregularity which turns architecture into a living architecture, and, in this a precursor of Impressionism, he recommends that a sculptor should not cut a *shape* into the stone but should rather cut the *effect* of a shape (*Seven Lamps*, 215).

In the chapter on the lamp of Memory, Proust would certainly have

felt the presence of a kindred spirit. Certainly the evocations of flowers—
"the oxalis troop by troop, like virginal processions of the Mois de Marie"
(*Seven Lamps*, 222) remind us of the flowers of the Month of Mary in Combray. It is in this same chapter that Ruskin proclaims: "There are but two
strong conquerors of the forgetfulness of men—Poetry and Architecture;
and the latter in some sort includes the former and is mightier in its reality:
it is well to have not only what men have thought and felt, but what their
hands have handled and their strength wrought, and their eyes beheld, all
the days of their life" (*Seven Lamps*, 224). In this Proust will not follow his
Master. It would be precious to know *spiritually* what men have thought
and felt, but not to possess the objects themselves. To possess them in the
way a Ruskin, a Montesquiou, or a Swann did would be idolatry. For
Proust objects only relieve memory of its duty. Therefore it is necessary to
contemplate an object profoundly—whether a picture, a church, or a cathedral—and then leave it in order to be able to find it again, finally reduced
to its immaterial essence, in the impalpable structure of memory (*RTP* 1:47;
RTPK 1:51). The great criticism which Proust levels at the position of Ruskin concerning architecture in his translation of *The Bible of Amiens* and
concerning literature in his translation of *Sesame and Lilies* is that
architecture and poetry lead us to the brink of spiritual life but do not replace it.

However, there are many points in common between Ruskin and
Proust in these pages on memory. For example, we know from the interview with Elie-Joseph Bois that Proust tried to isolate "this invisible substance of time" and give it "this beauty of certain Versailles leads covered
with patina and sheathed by time in a scabbard of emerald" (*EA*, 557). For
indeed, this conception of time and memory is quite Ruskinian: "The greatest glory of a building is not in its stones nor in its gold. Its glory is in its
Age. . . . It is in that golden stain of time that we are to look for the real
light and colour and preciousness of architecture; and it is not until a building has assumed this character, till it has been entrusted with the fame,
and hallowed by the deeds of men, till its walls have been witnesses of suffering, and its pillars rise out of the shadows of death, that its existence,
more lasting as it is than that of the natural objects of the world around it,
can be gifted with even so much as these possess, of language and of life"
(*Seven Lamps*, 233–34). And Ruskin pursues his ideas about the ethics of
the artist: "For this period, then, we must build; not, indeed refusing to
ourselves the light of present completion, nor hesitating to follow such por-
tions of character as may depend upon delicacy of execution, to the highest
perfection of which they are capable, even although we may know that in
the course of years such details must perish; but taking care that for work
of this kind we sacrifice no enduring quality, and that the building shall not
depend for its impressiveness upon anything that is perishable" (*Seven
Lamps*, 234).

Certainly Proust's many texts on the work of the artist and particularly the important texts of *Le Temps retrouvé* corroborate the notions expressed here. It would be in this way that we must understand the work of Proust as an architect of Time, whose masterpiece will be the cathedral-novel. Thus Proust resembles his Narrator who says at the end of *Le Temps re-trouvé* that he will give his novel the shape of which he had had "a presentiment in the church of Combray and which ordinarily, thoughout our lives, is invisible to us, the form of Time" (*RTP* 3:1045; *RTPK* 3:1103).

Ruskin brings this septet of lamps to a close with the lamp of Obedience. In this, Ruskin, as an idolator, obeys what is exterior to him, but he concludes by saying that "all men are Builders, whom every hour sees laying the stubble or the stone" (*Seven Lamps*, 265). The Proustian architect obeys his creative personality, his deep personality, the originality of his own vision which Ruskin was on the verge of recommending (253) before falling back into the snares of idolatry. But the idea that we are all architects, whether we are creators or readers, deserves to be retained. It is in this way that Françoise, that Michelangelo of the kitchen, can be placed side by side with the Narrator in the midst of his work in the building yard of his cathedral-novel; whether what is involved is creating a book like a cathedral or like a dress (*RTP* 3:1033; *RTPK* 3:1090), the quality of the work is the same.

It is clear that this book intended to form the ethics of young architects sheds light on many aspects of the conception of the writer as architect in Proust.[19] Before going on to consider the cathedral-novel we should linger over three similes that are fundamental to Proust's aesthetic and also central to the question of the novel as cathedral: the artist as quarry, the artist as prophet, and the artist as Creator.

The artist bears within himself a vast quarry that he is the only one to be able to utilize. In *Le Temps retrouvé* the Narrator says, "I knew very well that my brain was like a mountain landscape rich in minerals, wherein lay vast and varied ores of great price" (*RTP* 3:1037; *RTPK* 3:1094). A work of art, for example the cathedral-novel, would be the assured positioning (i.e. a book) of these elements with the help of the cement of style (i.e. vision) and the light of the spirit.[20] The artist is the only one who can translate this spiritual world so that others may see it: "The essential, the only true book, though in the ordinary sense of the word it does not have to be 'invented' by a great writer, for it exists already in each one of us, has to be translated by him. The function and task of a writer are those of a translator' (*RTP* 3:890; *RTPK* 3:926). This idea crops up again and again in Proust: "I have put an end for ever to the era of translations favored by my mother. And as for translations of myself, I no longer have the courage . . ." (*Lettres à une amie*, 105). The materials of the cathedral-novel emerge from the obscure crannies of one's self; the work progresses in the building-yard of the creative personality under the illumination of the spirit. The person of the artist is nothing more than the place where a work is being accomplished (cf. Gustave Moreau, *EA*, 506–20).

In an important note to *La Bible d'Amiens*, Proust develops Ruskin's idea that prophets and true geniuses can be ignorant of what is in the depths of their souls and their destinies: "but that future which men do not see is already contained in their heart. And it seems to me that Ruskin never expressed it in a more mysterious and beautiful way than in this sentence on the child Giotto when, for the first time, he saw Florence: 'He saw deep beneath, the innumerable towers of the City of the Lily, the depths of his own heart yet hiding the fairest of them all' (that is, the Campanile)."[21]

Like the prophets, then, artists of true genius have a sacred mission that they may misunderstand or fail to recognize at the outset. But when he discovers his mission, when he is in possession of his vision, the artist must reply like the prophet Nehemiah on the ramparts of Jerusalem when he was interrupted in his work: "Non possum descendere magnum opus facio," which should be, according to Proust, the motto of every artist, whom it is as absurd to reproach with shutting himself up in his ivory tower, as people say, as it would be to reproach bees in their hive of wax or caterpillars in their cocoon (cf. Cahier 57, 9v°). In connection with this same quotation, Proust wrote to Gaston Gallimard in September 1921: "If 'magnum' is taken in a complimentary sense, I cannot apply it to *A la recherche du temps perdu*. But if it applies to length, Jacques Rivière has no idea of the amount of work I have put into this book."[22] Certainly, "magnum" applies to Proust's novel and in a complimentary sense. But it is the word "opus" which merits closer scrutiny. What is at issue is not only intense work but also the transformation of the material. The intense work of bees creates at the same time the container (the hive with its honeycombs and cells) and the contents (honey), which is as marvelous a transformation as that of a caterpillar which works on itself, transforming a shapeless, greyish matter into a structure with polychromatic ribbing. It is by this same work that the constructive personality creates itself, manifests itself and stabilizes itself in the structure of a work which is perceptible to others. Nehemiah's ramparts, Giotto's Campanile, or Proust's cathedral-novel are so many fruitions of structures long carried in the heart of a prophet-artist. There where a vacuum had once been they have created a lasting work.

Like bees which transform matter in order to make honey out of it, artists, according to Proust, transform the world to create a new one out of it. In *Jean Santeuil*, the novelist C . . . transforms the reality around him into artistic material as Christ transforms water into wine.[23] In *A la recherche du temps* we read, "if God the Father had created things by naming them, it was by taking away their names or giving them other names that Elstir created them anew" (*RTP* 1:835; *RTPK* 1:893). According to Proust new artists unleash real geological catastrophes (*RTP* 2:327; *RTPK*

2:339). Certainly the transference of attributes from the Divinity to the artist would appear as blasphemy in the context of the Christian religion (the sin of Pride, for instance). This is not the case in the conception of the artist and art according to Proust. Let us quote in support this text from *La Bible d'Amiens:* "The parallelism between different sorts of arts and different countries was not the profoundest one at which he (Ruskin) was to stop. In pagan symbols and Christian symbols the identity of certain religious ideas was to strike him. M. Ary Renan has pointed out, with profundity, how much of Christ there already was in Gustave Moreau's *Prométhée*" (*La Bible d'Amiens*, 63). This kind of parallelism may equally well be applied to Proust's novel. Like God the Father, the Narrator at the end of *Le Temps retrouvé* is going to create his novel "like a world," a phrase that should not be taken lightly, for there is only one step to take to transform the word architect into Architect with a capital A. The artist is comparable to the Divine Architect, to Him who was the Word and created the world. Christ, according to Ruskin, is the supreme and gentle artist who works with his hands to make the dwelling of men more beautiful (Autret, 13). In Mâle's text we read, "The universe is a thought which God bore within himself at the beginning, as the artist bears within his soul the idea of his work. God has created, but he has created by his Word or by his Son. It is the Son who has actualized the thought of the Father, who has made it pass from potential to act. The Son is the true creator" (Mâle, 39).

We have an amusing visual example of this conception in a drawing which Proust traced from a reproduction of a stained glass window in Emile Mâle's *L'Art religieux du XIIIe siècle*, "Jesus Christ and the gifts of the Holy Spirit (Le Mans)" (cf. Hahn, 73 and Mâle, fig. 75, 198). Proust explains his drawing as follows: "Jesus Christ symbolizes poor sickie-wickie Marcel and the gifts of the Holy Spirit the treasures of genius and kindness which Reynaldo never fails to breathe into him. (Under Jesus Christ's arm is some pretty book, always left behind by Reynaldo)." Proust is joking. But under this amusing appearance we find many ideas which are connected with this conception of the artist as creator. In fact, the seven gifts of the Holy Spirit, Wisdom, Understanding, Fortitude, Counsel, Knowledge, Piety, and Fear of the Lord, can complete the seven lamps of the spirit of the novelist as architect. In the chapter "Le Miroir historique" ("The Mirror of History") Mâle gives the explanation of this window. It represents Elisha, a type of Jesus Christ, and in the window the artist shows Christ: "Jesus comes like Elisha to complete the work of salvation. He stretches his body upon the corpse and unites it with his limbs, which means that he unites himself with human nature by taking on a mortal body. He breathes out seven times upon the dead child the spirit of life, which means that he brings the seven gifts of the Holy Spirit to dead humanity, and finally he raises himself up with the living child, as humanity rose from the tomb at the same time as Jesus Christ" (Mâle, 196).

The resurrection of a being and even of a world which was "dead forever" repeats itself every time that an original artist appears: "You triumph, Van Dyck, prince of calm gestures, in all the beautiful beings who will shortly die," wrote Proust in a poem of his youth (*PJ*, 81). Without the Narrator-novelist, the death of Charles Swann would have been final: "and yet, my dear Charles, whom I used to know when I was still so young and you were nearing your grave, it is because he whom you must have regarded as a young idiot has made you the hero of one of his novels that people are beginning to speak of you again and that your name will perhaps live" (*RTP* 3:200. *RTPK* 3:199).

Here we come once more across Proust's ideas on life, on death, on art, and on the spirit—beliefs, dogmas, what word is the right one?—the *truths*, in short, which seem to have always haunted Proust since *Les Plaisirs et les jours* and *Jean Santeuil* and which he sought to integrate into the context of his edifice, which, like the metaphoric edifices of which Mâle speaks, must "edify" others: "the idea of the edifice I had to construct did not leave me for an instant. Whether it would be a church where little by little a group of the faithful would succeed in apprehending verities and discovering harmonies or perhaps even a grand general plan, or whether it would remain, like a druidic monument on a rocky isle, something for ever unfrequented, I could not tell."[24] Proust seems to have conceived his aesthetic, that which certain critics nowadays call his "religion of art," according to the principles of the Judeo-Christian tradition.[25] The essential doctrines of this tradition may be found in the Old and New Testaments, and the cathedral, such as the cathedral of Chartres or the "Bible of Amiens," with its images of the prophets, of Christ's followers and of the Saints, and with its parables, apocryphal stories, and legends, is the illustration of this tradition and this faith. With Proust, the essence of his aesthetic doctrine is found in *A la recherche du temps perdu*, and in this sense one could say that this vast text, like the Bible in the Judeo-Chrisitian tradition, represents the Book. But at the same time Proust gives in his text many illustrations of his doctrines. It is these illustrations which form the whole entity which we identify by the term the cathedral-novel. So, in a metaphorical manner, *A la recherche du temps perdu* is at the same time Bible and Cathedral.

III. THE CONCEPT OF THE CATHEDRAL-NOVEL

It is now time to embark on the third aspect of our subject, the concept of the cathedral-novel. We can eliminate right away the decorative religious elements in the novel (the descriptions of the churches of Combray, Saint-André-des-Champs, and Balbec), the comparative or allusive elements (characters compared to statuary, Legrandin as a St. Sebastian of snobbery), the attributes of different characters (the steering wheel of the chauffeur as a consecration cross), and finally the thematic elements or the motifs (the Codes of Combray, the Credo of the Verdurins or the Last Supper of the Guermantes, "a name as luminous as a stained glass window," "the pictures of memory—so many predellas in altar-pieces consecrated to memory," the Mass, the altar-table of Aunt Léonie, the Madeleine, the epiphanies) which find a place in the context of our inquiry into the cathedral-novel but which have been sufficiently evoked or studied by Proust critics in general for us not to linger over them now.[26] However, all these images form an integral part of the vast repertory of images and metaphors which in its coherence and extent recalls that other system of writing through images, medieval iconography.

Certain texts by Ruskin on architecture have served us as foils to elucidate Proust's thought on the problem of the novelist as architect. Emile Mâle's work, *L'Art religieux du XIIIe siècle en France: étude sur l'iconographie du moyen âge et sur ses sources d'inspiration*, gives an admirable commentary on Gothic cathedrals in France, but at the same time, this book from which Proust quotes approximately twenty times in the notes to his edition of *La Bible d'Amiens* and in which he found the inspiration for two dozen drawings sent to Reynaldo Hahn can provide us with valuable help in our considerations on the concept of the cathedral-novel.

The opening sentences of Mâle's work deserve to be quoted, for they sum up not only the concept of the medieval cathedral but also, in a metaphorical way, Proust's concept of the cathedral novel. "The Middle Ages conceived of art as teaching. Everything that it was useful to man to know, the history of the world since its creation, the dogmas of religion, the examples of the saints, the hierarchy of the virtues, the range of the sciences and of the arts and trades, all these were taught to him by the stained glass windows of the church or by the statues of the porch. The cathedral would have deserved to be called by that touching title which was invented by the printers of the fifteenth century for one of their first books, 'The Bible of the Poor.' The simple, the ignorant, all those who were called 'the holy plebs of God,' learned through their eyes everything they knew of their faith. Its great figures, which are so religious, seemed to bear witness to the truth of the Church's teaching. These innumerable statues, arranged according to a carefully thought out plan, were like an image of the marvelous order that St. Thomas established in the world of ideas; thanks to art, the highest conceptions of theology and science could be grasped, albeit in a confused way, by the most limited intelligence."[27]

Proust conceives of art as a method of teaching; thanks to art we learn, not the elevated concepts of theology and science, but to see a world which is different from our own (*RTP* 3:895–96; *RTPK* 3:931–32). In this sense, Proust is just as dogmatic as the medieval theologians and artists: "At last I have found a reader who has had the *intuition* to understand that my book is a dogmatic work and a construction!" he underlines in a letter to Jacques Rivière (*Choix de Lettres*, 197). In point of fact, we find in *A la recherche du temps perdu* as in its analogue, the cathedral, the history of the world since its creation (how the first pages of *Combray* resemble the book of Genesis!), the dogmas of the religion of art and of truth (the death of Bergotte, the "Intermittences of the heart"), the examples of the "saints" and the hierarchy of the virtues ("the Vices and Virtues of Padua and Combray"), and to conclude, the works of man. If the way the various parts of a Gothic cathedral are arranged can make us think of the absolute order of the world of ideas of a St. Thomas, the way in which the various parts of Proust's cathedral-novel are arranged makes us think of the new order of the ideas of the twentieth century, the relative order of an Einsteinian universe.

Like the cathedral of the thirteenth century, Proust's novel is at one and the same time a vast encyclopedia of Man[28] and a mirror in which every man can see himself, scrutinize himself, and know himself.

Like a cathedral, Proust's novel is not easy to read, all the more so as the reading we must apply to this monument is less that of the plastic or linguistic surfaces than that of the depths hidden in ourselves, for "Reading stands at the threshold of the spiritual life; reading can lead us into it; reading does not constitute it" (Preface to *Sésame et les lys*, 35). The mere fact of entering a cathedral does not necessarily constitute an entry into the spiritual life of the place or, for that matter, of oneself. It is not enough to admire in a detached manner the beautiful external shapes of a cathedral; one has to become oneself the abstraction, the harmonies, the teachings, the truths which it represents, that is to say, the Bible. Proust quotes Ruskin in this connection in his preface to *La Bible d'Amiens:* "Look back now to the central statue of Christ and hear his message with understanding. He holds the Book of the Eternal Law in His left hand; with His right He blesses, but blesses on condition: 'This do and thou shalt live': nay, in a stricter and more piercing sense, 'This be and thou shalt live: to show mercy is nothing—thy soul must be full of mercy; to be pure in act is nothing—thou shalt be pure in heart also.' "[29] We must become the Bible, become its incarnation as does the cathedral. In the same way with Proust, we have to become what we read. From the very first sentences of the novel we learn that the Narrator became the subject of the book he was reading: a church, a quartet, an historical rivalry. According to Proust, one finds oneself in a church, a quartet, an historical rivalry. If we do not attempt to find our own lost selves in these works of art or in these realities, the relationship we have with a church, a quartet, an historic fact, or a book would only be of an aesthetic or scholarly nature, nothing more: "But we play a symphony over and over again, we go back repeatedly to see a church until—in that flight to get away from our own life (which we do not have the courage to look at) which goes by the name of erudition—we know the symphonies and the church as well and in the same fashion as the most knowledgeable connoisseur of music or archaeology. And how many art-lovers stop there, without extracting anything from their impression, so that they grow old, useless and unsatisfied, like life-long bachelors!" (*RTP* 3:891–92; *RTPK* 3:927). In this connection the dialogue between the Narrator and M. de Charlus, a celibate of art, erudite and idolatrous in the style of a Ruskin or a Montesquiou, deserves to be quoted. In this passage, Proust underlines the distinction between the symbolic statues of a cathedral and the fact that it is necessary to embody in ourselves the teachings and the truths which it represents: " 'I do not know whether the raised arm of St. Firmin is still intact today or whether it has been broken. If so the loftiest affirmation of faith and energy ever made has disappeared from this world.' 'You mean its symbol, Monsieur,' I interrupted. 'And I adore certain symbols no less than you do. But it would be absurd to sacrifice to the symbol the reality which it symbolizes. Cathedrals are to be adored until the day when, to preserve them, it would be necessary to deny the truths which they teach. The raised arm of St. Firmin said, with an almost military gesture of command: "Let us be broken if honour requires." Do not sacrifice men to stones whose beauty comes precisely from their having for a moment given a fixed form to human truths' " (*RTP* 3:795; *RTPK* 3:822–23).

Like the medieval sculptors—like those who sculpted the St. Firmin of Amiens and the little fellow in the Booksellers' Portal in Rouen cathedral, Proust too has attempted to give a firm expression to life and certain human truths in his cathedral-novel. As a cathedral is a living thing in whose life believers share (read in this connection the moving text "La Mort des cathédrales"), in the same way a cathedral-novel is a living thing as soon as the reader begins to read and discover the truths, the harmonies, and the great general plan which are to be found in the cathedral-novel and in himself. The miracle of reading occurs if one can say to oneself, "I myself am the subject of this work, a church, a quartet, a rivalry. . . ."

In order to explain this vast encyclopedia of the creation of God, this summa that a cathedral is, Mâle has recourse, for the structure of his own work, to the divisions of the *Speculum majus* of Vincent of Beauvais (mid-thirteenth century), and he studies the iconography of the cathedral in these four mirrors of medieval thought, the Mirror of Nature, the Mirror of Knowledge, the Mirror of Morals, and the Mirror of History. If the Seven Lamps of Ruskin have helped us gain insights into the concept of the writer as architect, these Four Mirrors of Mâle help us gain new insights into the encyclopedic totality of Proust's cathedral-novel.

In a Gothic cathedral, Mâle writes, "the Mirror of Nature is inscribed everywhere—on the pinnacles, on the balustrades, on the recessed arches over the portal and on the least important capital." (Mâle, 39) and further on, "Our great sculptors despised nothing; in the depths of their art, as in the depths of every true art, we find fellow-feeling and love" (Mâle, 71). Is it necessary to remind ourselves of all the fauna and more particularly of all the flora, all this flourishing nature which decorates the novel and attracts the reader, especially at the beginning of the novel?[30] In actual fact, as he says in the letter to Jacques Rivière quoted above, Proust engages in meticulously detailed paintings, just like the whimsical artists of the Middle Ages who have left us hundreds of little people in the Booksellers' Portal of Rouen cathedral. Of these last, Ruskin isolated three on which he commented at length in his chapter on the Lamp of Life, and it is precisely with these same figures that Mâle concludes his study of the Mirror of Nature. Vitality according to Ruskin, Nature according to Mâle, it is basically the eternal, joyous human spirit which emanates from these holy, ancient stones. This flora, this fauna, these grotesques, these caprices, these vagaries of the human mind with which Proust decorates his novel also have their place in a cathedral-novel. I rather like the description by Louise Pillion of the little people on the Booksellers' Portal which, because of its style, could have been inspired by the texts of Ruskin and Proust on the little figure, for she quotes them on the previous page of her study. Proust, if he had read this sentence, would certainly have appreciated if not made a mental note of it; not only does it express that intense life which we see in the bas-reliefs, but it develops the metaphor of the cathedral as a dress which Proust outlines immediately after talking about the cathedral-novel: "Doubtless so many weird, grimacing, half-naked contorted, caricatural and provocative silhouettes seem like a very strange introduction to the majesty of this place, but then after all is it not natural that on this centuries-old breakwater where all the waves of life used to beat, a little of the foam of human fancies should have remained! Everything at that time led up to the cathedral. The fact that it has kept the memory of the frolics of its children, their games and their merry remarks, proves that it was the house of mankind as well as the house of God! Besides, the august physiognomy of the monument has not changed for the worst because of it; this delicate embroidery in stone, which has to be viewed almost with a magnifying glass, only distracts our gaze if we really choose to let it, and the venerable grande dame continues her march across the centuries, quite unperturbed by drawing along after her, cut into the hem of her cloak, the mischievous signature of a few artists who were her enfants terribles."[31]

In Proust the concept of the cathedral-novel is vast enough to include a whole crowd of people, so many scenes and so many merry remarks. They do not detract in any way from the majesty of the whole. On the contrary, they bring to it a remarkably truthful testimony of life.

Let us go on to the "Mirror of Knowledge." The word knowledge, according to Mâle, means work in all its forms, even the most humble, and the cathedral glorifies the work of man—the Works and Days displayed in the calendars and zodiacs of the churches, the manual labor represented by the stained glass windows of Chartres: "From manual labor man rises to knowledge . . . The Seven Arts open seven ways (the Trivium and the Quadrivium) to human activity: in grammar, rhetoric, and dialectic on the one hand, in arithmetic, geometry, astronomy, and music on the other hand, is contained almost all the knowledge that man can acquire outside of revelation" (Mâle, 102). Above the seven arts towers Philosophy. Proust's novel glorifies this labor, from the work of Françoise in the kitchen to the work of Elstir in his studio. In the arches of a portal at Chartres one can see each branch of knowledge accompanied by its inventor or by the man who has acquired most glory by cultivating it: Grammar: Donatus or Priscian; Rhetoric: Cicero; Dialectics: Aristotle; Music: Pythagoras; Astronomy: Ptolemy; Geometry: Euclid; Arithmetic: Pythagoras again or else Boethius (Mâle, 117–121). And on certain cathedrals one can see Medicine, the mechanical arts, the trades and professions, the occult sciences, the architect and the painter (Mâle, 127). In the same way Proust enriches his book, not with young virgins holding the symbols of the sciences and the arts (and he had thought of it for Saint-André-des-Champs in a rough draft of the Cahier 57, 65v°, where he puts in parentheses "look in Mâle for Laon, etc., or somewhere else, or the frescoes of Sienna"), but with real representatives of the contemporary branches of human knowledge: philology: Brichot; criticism: M. Verdurin; the theater: la Berma; and with realistic and productive creators: painting: Elstir; literature: Bergotte; music: Vinteuil. These characters, and particularly the three last, like the representatives of the Old Law in the iconography of a cathedral, are types in the sense that they are at one and the same time real characters and precursors of the Narrator-author who, as custodian of the New Law, will construct his novel like a church and borrow comparisons "from the loftiest and most varied arts" (RTP 3:1032; RTPK 3:1089). Certainly the great quantity of studies on Marcel Proust and the fine arts, music, theater, and particularly literature, has revealed to what extent Proust's work finds a place in the context of the most noble and most different arts. Contrary to what people generally think, Proust's novel is also a real compendium of modern knowledge and particularly of the modern sciences.[32]

Under the heading of knowledge Mâle includes the theme of the ages of life and he elaborates at some length on the image of Fortune's Wheel: "In this way the Wheel of Fortune at Amiens provides the Christian with a new subject of meditation. The royalty bestowed by riches, glory, power, only lasts a moment. The king whom we envy is seated on a wheel: tomorrow another will have replaced him. Our work, our knowledge, all our efforts should not tend towards the possession of such fragile goods. We need a stronger basis from which to act: this world will not give it to us and we will only find it in God" (Mâle, 131–32). This basis "will only be found in us, in the kingdom of the spirit" Proust will say. Proust sets going in his novel a series of wheels analogous to those spoken of by Mâle and seen by us in the plates of his book. We are present at ascents: Odette becomes Mme Swann, then Mme de Forcheville; Mme Verdurin becomes the Duchesse de Duras and then the Princesse de Guermantes, and we are also present at the downfall of Swann and Charlus. Death marks the inevitable end of all. The Narrator participates inevitably in these movements, and he realizes this at the end of *Le Temps retrouvé* where the Reader finds him perched on the dizzy summit of time. Like the Narrator, the reader too becomes dizzy on looking down beneath him and yet within him, as though from a height of "many leagues, at the long series of the years" (*RTP* 3:1047; *RTPK* 3:1106).

In the chapter "Le Miroir de la morale" ("The Mirror of Morals") Mâle analyzes the diverse representations of the Vices and Virtues. Ruskin dwelled on this struggle between the Vices and the Virtues, the Psychomachia, at some length in his interpretation of "The Bible of Amiens," Proust went to Padua to see Giotto's Chapel of the Arena with its celebrated psychomachia and he added considerably to Ruskin's already abundant notes on the psychomachia of the cathedral of Amiens.

As always and almost in order to free himself from his idolatries, Proust was able to derive amusement from the plastic representation of the Vices and the Virtues. In a drawing made up of four plates from Mâle's book and to which Proust gives the title "Synthèse du gothique prétentieux" ("Synthesis of pretentious Gothic") we see "The anger of the young Reynaldo against Bininuls" (Hahn, 75). It is just a game, but a revealing game, for we see Proust in the process of constructing a psychomachia which is far more complex than the medieval psychomachias.

Proust had thought in 1913 of giving part of his book the title "The Vices and Virtues of Padua and Combray."[33] Most certainly it was not for reasons of idolatry in the style of Charles Swann but rather to show among other things the considerable gap which separates the plastic conception of a psychomachia in a world of absolute values such as obtained in the fourteenth century from Proust's own conception, which is that of the twentieth century and where relativity comes into play.

Let us take a close look at the three psychomachia systems; that of Amiens, that of Padua, and that of Proust. At Amiens, the Vices and Virtues frolic, in isolation one from the other, in their little quatrefoils. Above each of these little psychomachias is the saint who embodies the virtue in question.[34] The spectator contemplates these mute scenes, but he does not participate in the psychomachia.

In contrast, Giotto's cycle at Padua involves the spectator; their battleground is the very space we occupy, the nave of the chapel. In order to see a virtue we have to turn our backs on the corresponding vice. As we leave the chapel, the Christ in Judgement who towers over the exit is the symbol of our own judgement—on which side have we lived? On the side of the vices or of the virtues? This vision of things finds its place in the eschatological conception of the Middle Ages: beginning, middle, end.

The psychomachia which is at work in *A la recherche du temps perdu* is more complex because it is constantly active in the heart of every reader in the immaterial dimension of Time: "You know that there is a plane geometry and a three dimensional geometry. Very well, for me the novel is not only plane psychology but psychology in time" (*EA* 557). Thus, in that part of *Combray* where the Vices and Virtues of Giotto are evoked we see Françoise as a Virtue: "the kitchen maid involuntarily made the superior qualities of Françoise shine with added lustre, just as Error by force of contrast, enhances the triumph of Truth" (*RTP* 1:82–83; *RTPK* 1:89). But the conception of the psychomachia in Proust's cathedral-novel is more complex than this "plane psychology," and so we learn with the Narrator that "the virtues of François concealed many of these kitchen tragedies, just as history reveals to us that the reigns of the Kings and Queens who are portrayed with their hands joined in prayer in the windows of churches were stained by oppression and bloodshed" (*RTP* 1:122; *RTPK* 1:132–33). In contrast, the "vicious" girl of Combray will release from papers that are "more illegible than strips of papyrus dotted with a cuneiform script, the formula, eternally true and forever fertile, of this unknown joy, the mystical hope of the crimson Angel of the Dawn," the Septet of Vinteuil (*RTP* 3:262–63; *RTPK* 3:264). Through Proust's letters to Mauriac and Souday, we know to what an extent this person forms an integral part of an "obscene capital" or of a "cornerstone" which further on holds up several vaults, this "vicious girl," in the perspective of time, in the vast and complex psychomachia of the novel, is revealed at the end to be "virtuous" because of this charitable act.

And as for this "veiled composition" of which Proust speaks, does it not stem from the fact that Proust's novel is largely conceived as an allegory? The Vices and Virtues form an integral part of the cathedral of Amiens or of the chapel of Giotto. Proust was perfectly familiar with the different allegorical cycles thanks to his readings in Ruskin and Mâle; he also knew the allegorical texts of Dante, Spenser, Bunyan, and France. By no means do I intend to claim that everything in Proust can lend itself to an exegesis at four levels like the biblical exegesis of the Middle Ages, for we have just ascertained that a certain part of a cathedral (the Mirror of Nature) or of a novel could be composed of purely decorative elements.

But let us observe more closely this problem of the allegory and take by way of example the first distinct episode of the novel, the scene of the magic lantern.[35] It seems that this text contains several levels and that these levels are in perfect accord with the most typical system of allegory.

At the first level, the *sensus litteralis*, or the literal level, the human, natural level which belongs to the domain of the novel, we learn that on certain evenings in Combray his family placed a magic lantern on the Narrator's lamp in order to show him pictures and tell him stories about Golo and Geneviève de Brabant and Bluebeard. These evenings stand out from the others in that they constitute a disturbing intrusion into the customary life of Combray. Now let us go on to a consideration of the "higher" levels of this text which in allegory are called *sensus spiritualis*. In a typical allegory one could distinguish in these higher levels the allegorical meaning, the moral meaning, and the anagogic meaning.

The allegorical meaning of the passage, which is progressively revealed throughout the novel, is vast. Because it represents the introduction of the Narrator to the world of pictures and reading, the episode of the magic lantern is the key which opens the cathedral-novel. This magic lantern "after the fashion of the master-builders and glass-painters of Gothic days . . . substituted for the opaqueness of my walls an impalpable iridescence, supernatural phenomena of many colours, in which legends were depicted as in a shifting and transitory window" (*RTP* 1:9; *RTPK* 1:9). Golo's body is also composed of a "supernatural essence." It was able to accommodate itself to "every material obstacle—everything that seemed to bar his way—by taking it as an ossature and embodying it in himself: even the door-handle, for instance, over which, adapting itself at once, would float irresistibly his red cloak or his pale face, which never lost its nobility nor its melancholy, never betrayed the least concern at this transvertebration" (*RTP* 1:10; *RTPK* 1:10). Thus Golo represents those fictitious characters through which "the novelist's happy discovery was to think of substituting for those opaque sections, impenetrable to the human soul, their equivalent in immaterial sections, things, that is, which one's soul can assimilate" (*RTP* 1:84; *RTPK* 1:91), and these impalpable iridescences, the literary images, so many stained glass windows interiorized by the reader "upon the sort of screen dappled with different states and impressions which [his] consciousness would simultaneously unfold while [he] was reading" (*RTP* 1:84; *RTPK* 1:90). The episode of the projections of the magic lantern is therefore an allegory of reading.

The magic lantern and the projections which emanate from it represent the author and his work. In the gallery belonging to the Guermantes, where the Narrator plunges into contemplation of the Elstirs, we read this: "I had before me fragments of that world of new and strange colours which was no more than the projection of that great painter's peculiar vision, which his speech in no way expressed. The parts of the walls that were covered with paintings of his all homogenous with one another, were like the luminous images of a magic lantern which in this instance was the brain of the artist, and the strangeness of which could never have been suspected so long as one had only known the man, in other words, so long as one had only seen the lantern boxing its lamp before any coloured slide had been slid into its groove." (*RTP* 2:419; *RTPK* 2:435) The canvases of the artist-priest Gustave Moreau which cover the walls of his church-house (*EA* 671) and the innumerable frescoes of Giotto which cover the walls and the vaulting of the chapel of the Arena would therefore also be the projections of the unique "magic lantern" of the painter.

Finally this scene is a type of the novel which we are in the process of reading. Proust, who is the architect and master glass-painter of the novel as cathedral, substitutes for the opacity of "real" life as Françoise would say, that is to say of our habitual life and our habitual vision, this new, wholly spiritual structure composed of an "impalpable iridescence, supernatural phenomena of many colours, in which legends were depicted as in a shifting and transitory window." These characters, Golo or Swann, immaterial, impalpable, exist nowhere but in our minds, in the kind of screen dappled with different states of our consciousness. This cathedral-novel is created by each reader as he reads the book, that is to say as he becomes the book.

Now let us go on to the moral level of the episode. In the context of the story, once the projections are over the Narrator flings himself into the arms of his mother, for Golo's crimes made him examine his own conscience more scrupulously. What is at issue here is obviously some juvenile peccadillo. But things get worse and later the Narrator will forget the truths learned at Combray. On the road to idolatry he will see the name of Guermantes like a stained glass window, the Duchesse de Guermantes through Geneviève de Brabant, etc. If the child examines his boyish crimes, the Narrator-to-come, before the revelation of his vocation, seems unaware of the intellectual sins that he is in the act of committing.

With the revelations of *Le Temps retrouvé,* the Narrator realizes that he must capture the precious immaterial instants which he has rediscovered in himself in a work of art, and so we come back to the idea of constructing the novel like a church. While the focus of the spirit still shines in him, the Narrator must make the most of his inner quarry where he will find blocks of stone for his labors as architect and minerals for his labors as master glass-worker. At the anagogical level we do not find God in Proust's work, as in the Middle Ages, but the Spirit. If a cathedral stands entirely under the aegis of God, the cathedral-novel stands under the aegis of the Spirit. Its most insignificant parts invite us to enter into this world where we cease to feel mediocre, contingent, and mortal.

As in a medieval cathedral, the psychomachias and the allegories of *A la recherche du temps perdu* require the active participation of the reader. Like the Narrator who, thanks to reading, became the rivalry of François I and Charles V, that is to say the psychic tension between the two historical characters, so each reader of Proust's novel becomes at one and the same time the battleground and the combattants of this vast psychomachia which makes up *A la recherche du temps perdu.* Thus it is inaccurate to speak of this novel as the "novel of a vocation," particularly if one gives the name of Marcel to the individual who is seeking the truth and a vocation, for that would mean failing to understand the aim of the work. One should use the moral mirror of a cathedral or of a cathedral-novel, not to scrutinize the acts of other people, but to scrutinize oneself: "For it seemed to me that they would not be 'my' readers but the readers of their own selves, my book being merely a sort of magnifying glass like those which the optician of Combray used to offer his customers—it would be my book, but with its help I would furnish them with the means of reading what lay inside themselves" (*RTP* 3:1032–33. *RTPK* 3:1089).

Let us return to Emile Mâle and the fourth mirror, the historical one, which takes up nearly two thirds of his work. In "Le Miroir historique" ("The Mirror of History"), Mâle studies the Old Testament, the Gospels, the legendary traditions added to the Old and New Testaments, the Saints and the Golden Legend, antiquity and secular history, and the end of the story: the Apocalypse and the Last Judgment. Proust's novel, it is hardly necessary to state, involves all these elements, whether at the historical level of the novel, the *sensus litteralis*, or at the allegorical level, the *sensus spiritualis*. At first sight, secular literature, that is to say the pleasures and days of Combray and its inhabitants or of Paris and the Guermantes, seems to predominate. But, as we have just seen with the scene of the magic lantern, we are often brought face to face with something else—a parable, an exemplum in which the objects are symbols and in which the characters are typological.

The Church has been able to assimilate the beliefs of the religions which preceded it. St. Michael replaced the Roman god Mercury and the Egyptian tetramorph may be supposed to represent the Gospels in the form of an ox for Luke, a lion for Mark, an eagle for John, a man for Matthew. In the same way in Proust's cathedral-novel we are in the presence of multiple metempsychoses. The Narrator who was at different moments whatever the work he was reading was talking about identifies with the stories of the past—Adam in the Bible, Dante in the *Divine Comedy*, Parsifal in the opera by Wagner. A cathedral is not only the Bible in stone, it is encyclopedic, it is the book of all the books, where the legends of Aristotle and Campaspe or of Vergil rub shoulders with the sacred story.[36] In the same way, in Proust's cathedral-novel, the most diverse stories, the *Arabian Nights*, the fairy-plays of Shakespeare, Geneviève de Brabant, and Golo have all left their mark on his work. Like all the different stories which are sculptured into the stones of a cathedral or painted on its stained glass windows, all these stories which Proust incorporates into his text bring with them a slanting light which throws into relief the central truths of the cathedral-novel. Thus the Mirror of History is the most important part of Proust's novel as it is in the vast and erudite programs of Chartres or of the Sainte-Chapelle.

It has been impossible in the restricted limits of this article to do more than take a rapid survey of this conception of a cathedral-novel. Nevertheless it is clear that this encyclopedic novel, *A la recherche du temps perdu*, can be read with great profit in the four mirrors Mâle uses to explain the encyclopedic works which the Gothic cathedrals are. Bending over these four mirrors, these four outer aspects of a cathedral, medieval man found God and the eternal. In Proust these four mirrors reveal to the reader the recesses of an inner space in which, while discovering the kingdom of the spirit, he ceases, like the believer in a cathedral, to feel mediocre, contingent, and mortal. Thus the function of a cathedral and the function of a cathedral-novel would be to a considerable extent analogous.

CONCLUSION

In his 1920 article "Pour un ami (remarques sur le style)" which was reprinted as the preface to *Tendres stocks* by Paul Morand (1921), Proust wrote that "all merely approximate metaphors do not count" (*EA* 616). The handful of aspects of the image of the cathedral-novel which we have evoked demonstrate that it could serve to describe *A la recherche du temps perdu*.[37] Proust was very familiar with the treatment of history, the technique and the iconography of Gothic architecture, but he was particularly interested in what one can find in this architecture, that is the presence of the creative human spirit: "In the Middle Ages every form clothes a thought. One might say that this thought is at work within the building materials and shapes them. The form cannot be separated from the idea which creates and animates it. A work of the thirteenth century interests us, even when the workmanship is inadequate, for we feel there is something in it which resembles a soul" (Mâle, iii). This thought, this form, this soul had already been discovered by Proust in the texts of Ruskin and in the Booksellers' Portal of Rouen Cathedral in the form of the figure which only measures ten centimeters but to which Ruskin devoted some moving pages in "The Lamp of Life." Like the architects, the master glassworkers, and the sculptors of the Middle Ages who worked arduously in the building yards of the cathedrals, Proust, instinctively following his inner voice and finding in his inner depths, as he continued to make progress, "the universal spirit," labored to give to his thought a form, a "material representation," as Germaine Brée puts it, "an imperfect and fragmentary representation of this vision of the spirit which had become incarnate for a moment, a 'cathedral' or a 'Bible,' in any case a manifestation of the spirit albeit incomplete."[38]

Like the French cathedrals of the thirteenth century, Proust's work is encyclopedic. As a work of synthesis it includes everything. Before the unity of a cathedral Mâle felt ill at ease: "We separate what has been joined together: from the sacred text we can detach neither the symbol nor the legend" (Mâle, 266). We find this unity again in Proust. His book is "a block of stone, a totality from which nothing can be removed" (Brée, 209).

If Proust's work can be read according to the four great "mirrors" of medieval thought, it is not medieval for all that. Proust does not reconstruct a medieval cathedral in the manner of a Viollet-le-Duc: "You can make a new version of what you love only by first renouncing it" (*RTP* 3:1043; *RTPK* 3:1102). Ruskin was not able to renounce what he loved. It is true that any page by Ruskin is "mysterious, full of images belonging both to beauty and religion like this same church of St. Mark where all the types of the Old and New Testament appear against a background of a kind of splendid shadowiness and changing luster" (*La Bible d'Amiens*, 83). But this beauty in Ruskin's writing rests on something false: idolatry. Proust attempts to found his work on something true and therefore secure: the impression—insubstantial, elusive—but the only criterion of truth (*RTP* 3:880; *RTPK* 3:914). So that one would be wrong to conceive of Proust's novel as a "fabled St. Mark's."

The parallels we have established throughout this article between the architecture of the thirteenth century and Proust's novel have all been at bottom metaphorical. Most frequently the word "church" evokes in Proust's readers an image of the medieval church, such as the church of Combray or the cathedral of Chartres. And to make our analysis easier we have pursued our study with this image before us. It served us as a temporary basis on which to establish certain analogies. And perhaps, at certain moments, Proust may well have thought of these edifices as he constructed his work. It is time to abandon this image, for everything in the work suggests a different structure, a structure so new that even nowadays we have not yet been able to discern it in its totality. In 1921 Proust wrote "The imitators of the classics, in their most inspired moments, do nothing but provide us with a pleasure of erudition and taste which does not have much value. One cannot doubt that those innovators who are worthy of one day becoming classics obey a severe inner discipline and are constructors before all else. But precisely because their architecture is new, it happens that one can wait a long time before being able to discern it" (*EA* 617). The architecture of *A la recherche du temps perdu* is new. Viollet-le-Duc, the imitator of the classics of the thirteenth century, has given us constructions which may provide us with a pleasure of erudition and taste. But his monuments are only pastiches. The architecture of Proust's novel is not derived from pastiche. It is much more like the space-time of the cubists and the luninous projections of kinetic art than it is like the pastiche of a cathedral in the Ile-de-France. "And so it is essential that the artist (and this was what Vinteuil had done), if he wishes his work to be free to allow its own course, should launch it, there where there is sufficient depth, boldly into the distant future." (*RTP* 1:532; *RTPK* 1:572) Thus it is clear that those who accuse Proust of living in the past are mistaken. Chartres Cathedral illustrates the conception of the universe according to Ptolemy; Proust's novel as cathedral confirms Einstein's conception of the universe. The passage on the steeples of Martinville where what is involved, according to Cattaui, is this "esthetic enjoyment partly occasioned by the displacement of the architectonic shapes and volumes in space and time"[39] is one of the numerous key passages in *Combray*. As the reader progresses through the novel, he becomes more and more aware of this phenomenon of the parallax—occurring in time as well as in space. It is from this parallax—what Proust calls "the psychology of space or psychology in time"—that a large part of his aesthetic enjoyment is derived. It is true that one can find stable "stained glass windows" such as the scene of the magic lantern at the beginning of the novel. But most of the "stained glass windows" have been reduced to fragments and scattered throughout the narrative, and one finds oneself moving in a vast kaleidoscope: "like a kaleidoscope which is every now and then given a turn, society [but let us read Proust for a moment] arranges successfully in different orders elements which one would have supposed immutable and composes a new pattern" (*RTP* 1:517; *RTPK* 1:556). So it is the reader who must retain all the fragments that he discovers while reading the book, and it is he who will construct the cathedral-novel, immaterial and intangible but existing within himself and in Time. The vocation at issue in the novel is less that of a Narrator than it is ours. It is we who must decipher the text, as one deciphers a piece of music. "What we have not had to decipher, to elucidate by our own efforts, what was clear before we looked at it, is not ours" (*RTP* 3:880; *RTPK* 3:914). And once the text has been understood and the piece of music deciphered, we begin to cross the threshold which leads to the kingdom of the spirit and penetrate more deeply at the same time into the work and ourselves. In a passage intended for *Sodome et Gomorrhe* Proust speaks of the mirage of an artificial existence which is no more "the depths of things" than the depths of the narthex which in certain romanesque monuments gives so much by its extent the illusion of being the real church that we are completely dazzled when the sacristan opens up the far end, which is only the second portal, the real one, of the nave, and the nave opens up to us in its immensity (cf. *Sodome et Gomorrhe*, Ms, 4, 86V⁰). With Proust it is this second portal that we have to seek. Perhaps it is not in the work but in ourselves. We will have found it if we can utter, like the Narrator, this sentence which is now ours: "I was myself what the work was talking about: a church, a quartet, the rivalry of. . . ."

Notes

1. Georges Cattaui, "L'Œuvre de Proust: son architecture, son orchestration, sa symbolique", *Critique* (March 1958), pp. 197–213, seems to have had the best grasp of the different aspects of the question. Proust never gave the title of "the Porch" to the first chapter of his novel as Magda Lempart claims in *La Transposition esthétique des valeurs chrétiennes dans l'œuvre de Marcel Proust* (s.l.: Desclée de Brouwer, 1968), pp. 55 and 70. The connection which R. M. Albérès establishes in *Métamorphoses du roman* (Paris: A. Michel, 1966), between *Le Temps retrouvé* and a porch is quite as little based on fact. M. Robert Vigneron says that the novel is an immense cathedral consecrated to love and suffering, but it is difficult to suppose like him that it is a monument which Proust, in secret, wished to raise to Agostinelli. See on this subject his article "Genèse de Swann", *Revue d'histoire de la philosophie et histoire générale de la civilisation*, n.s., fasc. 7 (15 January 1937), p. 115. Antoine Adam took this formula of Vigneron's up again in his article "Une Vie laboratoire d'une œuvre", in *Proust* (Paris: Hachette [Collection Génies et Réalités] 1965). Among those who have written about this problem, the solution of Elisabeth de Gramont, in her article "La Jeunesse de Marcel Proust," *La Revue des deux mondes* (February 1948), p. 486 and reprinted in her *Marcel Proust* (Paris: Flammarion, 1948), pp. 54–55, is typical of a certain way of conceiving the novel as cathedral which is very personal but bears little relationship to the texts: "The choir is reserved for his mother, in perpetual adoration. The great east window is Combray and its landscapes. The great west window is Balbec and its seascapes. The pillars are Swann, Odette de Crécy, Gilberte, Albertine, Robert de Saint-Loup, Françoise, the Duchesse de

Guermantes, the Duc de Guermantes, the Baron de Charlus, the Verdurins. In the porch of his cathedral he has carved girls in bloom. Some of them have angels' wings and cloven hooves. All around grimace singular spirits of the night. In the nave the crowd of supernumaries is about to move around in perpetual motion while the great organ will rhythmically accompany the march of Time" (p. 486). In *Les Œuvres d'art imaginaires chez Proust* (Univ. of London: Athlone Press, 1964), Michel Butor sees in this image of the cathedral "a fabulous St. Mark's . . . a work in 'n' parts which death, which the narrator feels drawing near, will prevent him from continuing, hyperprism and variation," (p. 43). The solutions of Georges Poulet and Joseph Frank appear to be more theoretical, more abstract, and also more distant from the work. Bruce Lowery provides us with an important chapter, "La Notion architecturale," in his book *Marcel Proust et Henry James* (Paris: Plon, 1964), pp. 237–46. An early version of the present article was presented to the accompaniment of numerous slides on the occasion of the literary Colloquium at Illiers, September 9, 1973. It brings together several elements of a work which I am presently preparing on the question of Marcel Proust and the visual arts.

2. Sybil de Souza, *L'Influence de Ruskin sur Proust* (Montpellier: Université de Montpellier, Faculté des Lettres, 1932), p. 44.

3. *Lettres à une amie. Recueil de quarante-et-une lettres inédites adressées à Marie Nordlinger*, 1899–1908 (Manchester: Editions du Calame, 1942), pp. 5–6 and 14. From now on all the references to the works of Proust and to the volumes of the correspondence will be given in the text with the usual abbreviations. On the question of Proust and Ruskin, see also Jean Autret, *L'Influence de Ruskin sur la vie, les idées et l'œuvre de Marcel Proust* (Genève: Droz et Lille: Giard, 1955) and Philip Kolb, "Proust et Ruskin: nouvelles perspectives", *CAIEF*, no. 12 (1960), pp. 259–73.

4. For a complete list see the biography by George B. Painter. For the question of Proust and architecture see Jacques Levron, "Marcel Proust et l'archéologie," *BSAMP*, no. 4 (1954), pp. 45–56; P-L Larcher, "Chartres à travers l'œuvre de Marcel Proust", *BSAMP*, no. 4 (1954), pp. 61–67; Yves E. Glogenson, "Le Thème de la cathédrale dans Proust", *BSAMP*, no. 14 (1964), pp. 152–59, and Jean Autret, "La Dette de Marcel Proust envers Emile Mâle," *Gazette des Beaux-Arts*, VIᵉ période, II (janvier 1958), pp. 49–59. See also Gabrielle Friedman, "Le Symbole de la sculpture mortuaire chez Proust," *The French Review*, XXX, no. 1 (October 1956) 5–12. The question of Proust and the Middle Ages has been treated by William Enloe Cunningham in his thesis "The Role of the Middle Ages in Proust," Diss. University of North Carolina, 1971, and by Richard Martin Bales in his important thesis, "Proust's Interest in the Middle Ages and its Impact on his Works, with Especial Reference to Architecture," Diss. University of London, 1973. I am glad to have the opportunity to thank Mr. Bales for having sent me a copy of his thesis while I was working on this paper.

5. Emile Mâle, *L'Art religieux du XIIIe siècle en France: Etude sur l'iconographie du Moyen âge et sur ses sources d'inspiration*. Paris: Ernest Leroux, 1898, p. 17. All the references are to this first edition, the one Proust quotes in his edition of *The Bible of Amiens*. A study of the first editions of Mâle's work (1898, 1902, and 1910) and of the drawings Proust traced on the plates reveals that Proust also had in his own collection the second edition, that of 1902.

6. See Samuel Borton, "A Tentative Essay on Dante and Proust," *Delaware Notes*, XXXI (1958), 33–42 and Bales, *op. cit.*, pp. 278–317.

7. *La Cathédrale* in XIV of the *Œuvres complètes* (Paris: Crès et Cie, 1931), vol. 1, p. 315.

8. François René de Chateaubriand, *Les Mémoires d'Outre-Tombe*, éd. Maurice Levaillant et Georges Moulinier (Paris: Gallimard, Pléiade, 1958), I, 7.

9. Victor Hugo, *Notre-Dame de Paris*, éd. Marius-François Guyard (Paris: Garnier, 1959), p. 222. Mâle includes several quotations from this novel by Hugo in his *Art religieux de XIIIe siècle*. We have only quoted a few examples out of several of the tradition of ek-

phrasis—the imitation or the transposition in literature of a plastic work of art—the importance in France of which we know, from Gautier and Baudelaire down to Montesquiou. The young Proust's *Portraits de peintres* belong to this tradition. Proust comments at length on Victor Hugo's "A l'Arc de Triomphe" in a note to his translation of *Sesame and Lilies*, p. 95. At the beginning of the century Péguy and Rilke transposed the porches of Chartres into poems. In the domain of the novel Proust alludes to Hardy: "Another example of Vinteuil's key phrases is that stonemason's geometry in the novels of Thomas Hardy" (*RTP* 3:376; *RTPK* 3:382). Here I should like to thank Professor Peter Casagrande who obligingly sent me a copy of his unpublished essay "The Architectural Matrix of Thomas Hardy's *Mayor of Casterbridge*" while I was preparing this article.

10. Marcel Proust, *Lettres à André Gide* (Neuchâtel et Paris: Ides et Calendes, 1949), p. 25.

11. Letter to Paul Souday, November 10, 1919, *Choix de lettres*, éd. Philip Kolb (Paris: Plon, 1965), p. 250; letter to Jacques Boulenger, December 21, 1919, *CG* 3:200; and "A propos du style de Flaubert," *Essais et Articles* (Paris: Gallimard [Pléiade], 1971), p. 598.

12. Quoted by François Mauriac, *Du côté de chez Proust* (Paris: La Table ronde, 1947), pp. 21–22.

13. *Choix de lettres*, p. 250. Obviously Proust is using the term "cornerstone" in a metaphorical way; see his text on the statue of Christ as a "cornerstone" of the edifice, not in figurative sense but in the proper sense, *La Bible d'Amiens*, p. 35.

14. *Correspondance de Marcel Proust avec Jacques Rivière*, annotée par Philip Kolb (Paris: Plon, 1956), p. 114.

15. The drawing of the facade of Amiens Cathedral is reproduced in *Lettres à Reynaldo Hahn*, éd. Philip Kolb (Paris: Gallimard, 1956), p. 117. Proust traced from Mâle's book the prophets of Chartres and of Rheims, the Virgin of Amiens and of Paris, the Paris choir screen, a capital representing the psychomachia of Notre-Dame-du-Port at Clermont, a bas-relief from Le Bourget, the gargoyles of the Sainte-Chapelle (after Viollet-le-Duc), two birds (after Villard de Honnecourt) and the stained glass windows of Paris, Le Mans, Lyons, Chartres, Laon, and Bourges. Proust "drew" Notre-Dame de Paris, the Mont Saint-Michel, and the church of Dordrecht. He invented a series "Notre-Dame-des-Flots." Finally, several of the little indications Proust uses to facilitate references from one text to another in the labyrinth of his notebooks are inspired by ecclesiastical architecture. There are only two real drawings of churches in the Cahiers: Cahier 46 (93v⁰) and Cahier 55 (42v⁰).

16. Unpublished letter from Marcel Proust to Jacques Hébertot, *BSAMP* no. 23 (1973), p. 1571.

17. John Ruskin, *La Couronne d'Olivier sauvage. Les Sept Lampes de l'architecture*, trans. George Elwall (Paris: Société d'Edition artistique, s.d. 1900), p. 85. [Editor's note: This is the reference given in the original French version of this article, but for the benefit of English-speaking readers all quotations from Ruskin in this English version will be given in Ruskin's own words. Consequently the reference for this quotation as given is as follows: John Ruskin, *The Seven Lamps of Architecture*, vol. 8 of *The Works of John Ruskin*, ed. E.T. Cook and Alexander Wedderburn (London: George Allen, 1903), p. 27.]

18. See on this subject my article, "Proust, Ruskin et la petite figure au portail des Libraires à la Cathédrale de Rouen," *BSAMP*, no. 23 (1973), pp. 1721–1736.

19. And in Ruskin who has characterized his work as a "many towered city." Hélène Lamaître concludes her study *Les Pierres dans l'œuvre de Ruskin* (Caen: Association des Publications de la Faculté des Lettres et Sciences Humaines de l'Université de Caen, 1965) by comparing the works of Ruskin to a cathedral (pp. 218–19).

20. For Proust, the entire work has to come from within the artist, and in this way he differs from Ruskin who tried to find Truth and Beauty outside himself, which explains the fact that Ruskin made "some memory of the Bible enter into the construction of his sen-

tences, as the Venetians interpolated in their monuments the sacred sculptures and precious stones that they brought back from the East" (*La Bible d'Amiens*, p. 12). In this Ruskin is close to Montesquiou; see "Un Professeur de Beauté," *EA*, pp, 506–20.

21. John Ruskin, *Giotto and His Works in Padua*. [Vol. XXIV of *The Works of John Ruskin*, p. 18], quoted by Proust in *La Bible d'Amiens*, p. 227, fn. 1. [Editor's note: The phrase "that is, the Campanile," was added by Proust.] In *The Seven Lamps of Architecture* under the heading "The Lamp of Beauty," Ruskin analyzes his admiration for Giotto's campanile.

22. *Lettres à la NRF*, (*Les Cahiers Marcel Proust*, VI), p. 174. This quotation is also found in the pastiche of Faguet. In his critical edition of the pastiche, Jean Milly gives the exact quotation: "Opus grande ego facio, et non possum descendere."

23. *Jean Santeuil* (Paris: Gallimard [Pléiade], 1971), p. 194. See also Larkin B. Price, "Marcel Proust's 'dieu déguise': The Artist Myth in *Jean Santeuil*," *L'Esprit Créateur*, XI, no. 1 (1971), pp. 61–73.

24. *RTP* 3:1040; *RTPK* 3:1098. Victor Hugo expresses a similar idea in *Notre-Dame de Paris*: "The Celtic dolmen and cromlech, the Etruscan tumulus, the Hebrew galgal, are words. Some of them, particularly the tumulus, are proper names. Sometimes even, when people had a great deal of stone and a vast beach, they would write a sentence. The huge pile of stones at Karnac is already an entire phrase" (p. 211).

25. Barbara J. Bucknall, in *The Religion of Art in Proust* (Urbana: University of Illinois Press, 1969) also indicates analogies between Proust's aesthetic and several Eastern mystical sects.

26. The allusions to the Bible have been dealt with by Marcel Gutwirth, "La Bible de Combray," *La Revue des sciences humaines*, n.s. fasc. 143 (July-September 1971), 417–27. The different images have been pointed out by Victor Graham in *The Imagery of Proust* (Oxford: Basil Blackwell, 1966), while the philosophical extensions have been suggested by Pauline Newman-Gordon in her *Dictionnaire des idées dans l'oeuvre de Marcel Proust* (La Haye: Mouton, 1968), or they have been examined in studies concentrating on one aspect of the work of Proust, such as the studies of Chernowitz and Monnin-Hornung on painting, Mendelsohn on glass, Autret, Richard, Quémar and most of all Bales for the medieval side, etc.

27. Mâle, p. 10. Almost the same words are used in the text on the nature of the faith of the Baron de Charlus (*RTP* 2:1040; *RTPK* 2:1073–74).

28. Northrop Frye classifies Proust in the encyclopedic mode in his *Anatomy of Criticism* (New York: Atheneum, 1969), pp. 55–61.

29. *La Bible d'Amiens*, p. 43. [John Ruskin, *The Bible of Amiens*, vol. XXXIII of *The Works of John Ruskin*, p. 170. Editor's note: It has been necessary to add this footnote, which does not appear in the original article as printed. Consequently the footnotes numbered 29 to 38 in the original article have been renumbered 30 to 39.]

30. Many critics have already dealt with this aspect, which one could call the Mirror of Nature, in Proust. A considerable number of books, theses, chapters, and articles have been devoted solely to the study of flora in Proust. The Colloquium held September 2, 1962 had as its theme "Marcel Proust as a lover of flowers and gardens." See the articles of MM. Costil, Larcher, and Kopman in the *Bulletins* nos. 13 and 19.

31. Louise Pillion, *Les Portails latéraux de la Cathédrale de Rouen: Etude historique et iconographique sur un ensemble de bas-reliefs de la fin du XIIIe siècle* (Paris: Picard, 1907), p. 164. Let us mention as a reminder that Proust read the very long article, "Cathédrale" in Viollet-le-Duc's *Dictionnaire de l'architecture*, and that in this article we learn that "the cathedrals in the thirteenth century were not reserved exclusively for worship; assemblies were held there, also debates, mysteries were performed, courts of Justice were held, things were for sale there, and purely secular entertainments were not refused a right of entry" (2:298). Proust's cathedral-novel includes things just as diverse. Finally in this same article Viollet-le-

Duc develops at some length a comparison between medieval architecture and music, particularly harmony (pp. 384–87). Mâle makes the same comparison several times (e.g. "Dante's Paradiso and the porches of Chartres are symphonies," p. 29). Like the thirteenth-century cathedral, Proust's work combines the sacred and the profane, architecture and music.

32. See in particular Reino Virtanen, "Proust's Metaphors from the Natural and Exact Sciences," *PMLA*, LXIX, no. 5 (December 1954), 1038–59; Roger Shattuck, *Proust's Binoculars* (New York: Random House, 1963); William C. Carter, "The Role of the Machine in *A la recherche du temps perdu*," Diss. University of Ohio, 1971; Georges Cattaui, "Proust et les sciences: les métaphores scientifiques de Proust", in *Proust et ses métamorphoses* (Paris: Nizet, 1972), pp. 243–61; John D. Erickson, "The Proust-Einstein Relation: A Study in Relative Point of View," in *Marcel Proust: A Critical Panorama*, ed. Larkin B. Price (Urbana: University of Illinois Press, 1973), pp. 247–76; Sandra S. Beyer, "The Sciences in the Works of Marcel Proust," Diss. University of Kansas 1973; and James A. Boon, *From Symbolism to Structuralism: Lévi-Strauss in a Literary Tradition* (Oxford: Blackwell, 1972). In his brilliant study Boon situates Proust's work not only in the contexts of symbolism and structuralism but also in the context of anthropology, thereby opening up rich new perspectives for the understanding of the work.

33. Albert Feuillerat, *Comment Marcel Proust a composé son roman* (New Haven: Yale University Press, 1934), pp. 218–21 and p. 273 (reproduction of the half title). I have studied this problem in "Proust and Giotto: Foundations for an Allegorical Interpretation of *A la Recherche du Temps perdu*," in *Marcel Proust: A Critical Panorama*, ed. Larkin B. Price (Urbana: University of Illinois Press, 1973), pp. 168–205.

34. *La Bible d'Amiens*, pp. 290–92; 295–306 and the diagram of the west porch, p. 341.

35. I have studied the allegorical levels of this text in my article *"La Lanterne Magique: Proust's Metaphorical Toy,"* *L'Esprit Créateur*, XI (Spring 1971), 17–31. Several episodes in the novel, particularly at the beginning, are allegorical, and I am in agreement with Caludine Quémar when she says that the church of Combray has a "metaphorical bearing—that of an archetypal Church, an image of Time and an allegory of the work—which defines its principal function in the novel." See her article, *"L'Eglise de Combray, son curé et le Narrateur* (trois rédactions d'un fragment de la version primitive de *Combray*)," *Etudes Proustiennes*, I, Cahiers Marcel Proust VI (Paris: Gallimard, 1973), 287.

36. Cf. *RTP* 1:151 [*RTPK* 1:164—reference added by editor], and Mâle, pp. 428–30.

37. It is true that there is still much to be said about this image. For example, those who have worked on Proust's manuscripts know how greatly extensions of the image are appropriate to describe their work. The manuscripts and the documents deposited in the Bibliothèque Nationale are like a vast building yard, an immense lapidary museum beside the cathedral. The first digs revealed to us *Jean Santeuil*, some pastiches, fragments of *Contre Sainte-Beuve*. The first scientific labors were made thanks to the meticulous care of Mme Callu and the center for restoration. Like archeologists facing unearthed ruins and numbered objects, we are now at the stage of hypotheses and reconstructions, and we are studying *Jean Santeuil*, that first "romanesque basilica," the "scholastic" theories and arguments of *Contre Sainte-Beuve*, the "stained glass windows," the "capitals," "the meticulous paintings" that are to be found in this building yard and which were intended to take their place in the "cathedral-novel." A study of the different documents with their physical characteristics—watermarks, paper of such and such quality, margins—tell us much about the construction of the work. All these widely differing texts interest us because of the quality of the spirit to be found in them, the very one which illuminates the texts of *A la recherche du temps perdu*.

38. Germaine Brée, "La Conception proustienne de l'espirit," *CAIEF*, no. 12 (June 1960), p. 209.

39. George Cattaui, "L'Œuvre de Proust: son architecture, son orchestration, sa symbolique," *Critique* (March 1958), p. 200.

Proust and Painting

J. Theodore Johnson, Jr.*

By the time young Proust decided to become a writer during the final decades of the 19th century, the tradition of the interrelations of literature and painting was well established in France. That tradition had produced the *salons* by Diderot and Baudelaire, poems on painters by Gautier and Baudelaire, novels, plays, and short stories that dealt with the painter and his artistic milieu such as *Le Chef-d'œuvre inconnu* of Balzac, Zola's *L'Œuvre*, or *Manette Salomon* by the Goncourts. Proust continues that tradition through his essays on painters, his poems *Portraits de peintres*, and the fictive painter Elstir in *A la recherche du temps perdu*, as well as his contributions to Ruskin studies. Proust moved in the fashionable circles of the Belle Epoque where he frequented the established art critic and novelist Edmond de Goncourt, the novelist Alphonse Daudet whose son and Proust's intimate friend Lucien was an art student, and the painter Madeleine Lemaire who was, as Dumas *fils* put it, the one who had created more roses than anyone else after God, and it was she who provided the numerous illustrations for Proust's extravagantly elegant first volume, *Les Plaisirs et les jours*. In the descriptions of certain society salons published in *Le Figaro* in 1903 and 1904 which he signed "Dominique" or "Horatio," Proust mentions the artists of this particular milieu: the Comtesse Aimery de La Rochefoucauld, the Princesse Mathilde, Mme Herbelin, and Mme Nélie Jacquemart-André, as well as the established painters Madeleine Lemaire, Hébert, Bonnat, Forain, Frédéric de Madrazo, and the distinguished painter of the Belle Epoque who was one of Proust's seconds at his duel with Jean Lorrain in 1897, Jean Béraud.[1] Proust's hosts often had rich collections of paintings, allowing him therefore, like the narrator in *Le Temps retrouvé*, to compare Chaplin's portrait of the Comtesse de la Rochefoucauld with Renoir's portrait of Mme Charpentier and her children, to study at first hand the Monets in the collections of Charles Ephrussi, Emile Straus, or the Prince de Polignac, or even, during one evening in 1916, to help unpack crates of freshly painted Picassos.

As befitting any professional upper-middle class Parisian family, a number of paintings hung on the walls of Professor and Mme Adrien Proust's apartment: copies of paintings by Frans Snyders, a Roman History, a Gabriel Metsu, *Tobias and the Angel* by Govaert Flinck, and a painting of *Esther and Haman* identified by Professor Kolb as being perhaps by Frantz Franken or Franken the Younger and against which, according to Mme Mante-Proust in whose collection the painting is today, young Marcel apparently threw an eraser *(une gomme)* that, much to the consternation of Robert and Marcel, stuck to the painting and left a mark when removed.

*This essay was written specifically for this volume and is published here for the first time by permission of the author. Quotations from *A la recherche du temps perdu* are from the Kilmartin translation. All other translations are by the editor.

There was a pseudo-Velasquez portrait of a shepherdess, visible in the often reproduced photograph of Proust's drawing room in the apartment on the rue Hamelin, and which Proust described as a little old woman with an air at once monstrous and true to stock of some Spanish Infanta. There was the rather somber portrait of Jeanne Proust done in 1880 by Mme Beauvais, although the Pléiade *Album Proust* identifies the artist as Landelle. The portrait of Adrien Proust by Lecomte du Nouÿ shows Proust's father dressed in the academic regalia of a professor of medicine who has taken a moment from his work as hygienist, professor, and writer of treatises (the sandclock to the viewer's right is an important element in the picture) to confront the viewer. In 1891 Laure Brouardel did a portrait of Adrien Proust, and Paul Nadar photographed the family members. The very fashionable Edwardian painter Jacques-Emile Blanche drew a portrait of Proust in October, 1891 and painted his full length portrait in 1892. According to Professor Kolb the picture was exhibited in the Salon du Champ-de-Mars in May, 1893.[2] Later the portrait was cut down to a bust.

The dozen years (1874–1886) during which the Impressionists waged and won their battle for recognition coincided with Proust's childhood and early adolescence. During these years Proust made many trips to the Louvre, but not to these exhibitions. According to several questionnaires he filled out at the time, his tastes ran from Leonardo da Vinci and Rembrandt to Meissonnier. André de Billy recalls that Marcel would often wax lyrical and even philosophic before certain paintings, in particular those by Van Dyck, and later Lucien Daudet remembers Proust's perceptive comments on the pictures in the Louvre. In a letter to his grandmother written at age 14 or 15 Proust attempts a verbal portrait of young Mme Catusse, and the way he makes reference to a "painter in love with perfect beauty" suggests neoclassicism or the manner of Ingres. We gather from certain references to Ingres and to Gleyre in later texts that this corresponds to a youthful need for forms admirable in themselves, and that eventually gives way to the acceptance of beauty in banality, in the lessons of Chardin.[3] In a letter to his mother written at sixteen, Proust mentions a trip to the Louvre and recounts discussions between his uncle Louis Weil and "Nuna" about Ingres. Proust refers to a discussion of the previous week when his uncle confused Raphael with Dürer.

A few years later Proust's visits to the Louvre produced four poems on northern painters of the 17th and early 18th centuries brought together as *Portraits de peintres*. The poems continue the tradition of *ekphrasis* promoted by Charles Baudelaire in his famous statement in the *Salon de 1846* to the effect that if a painting be "nature reflected by an artist," then criticism should be "that picture reflected by an intelligent and sensitive mind," so the best account of a picture might well be a sonnet or an elegy. Proust's poems, indeed reflections by an intelligent and sensitive mind, and at times elegiac in tone, and enhanced by Reynaldo Hahn's intelligent and sensitive musical settings, are moving accounts of works by great masters. These pieces were often performed in the spring of 1895; the poems were published in *Le Gaulois* on June 21; the poems on Cuyp, Potter, and Watteau were published in *L'Année des poètes* for 1895, and an elegant folio edition with the dedication of the poems to the distinguished Parnassian poet José-Maria de Heredia and the music to the painter and society hostess Madeleine Lemaire was published in 1896.

Already at work in the four poems which constitute *Portraits de peintres,* "Albert Cuyp," "Paulus Potter," "Antoine Watteau," and "Antoine Van Dyck," are the aesthetic principles of Proust's mature work. "Cuyp," a poem inspired by *Promenade* and *Departure for the Promenade* in the Louvre, but applicable to a number of paintings by Cuyp, such as the *Horsemen and Herdsmen with Cattle* in the National Gallery of Art in Washington, turns around the theme of profound moments: elegant cavaliers contemplate a radiant landscape bathed with light. Hahn's music captures the final line of the poem, "They ride off to breathe in these profound minutes," in shimmering chords played *pp* that open and close the piece which otherwise rigorously follows the "program" of Proust's poem.[4] In "Potter" Proust admires the melancholy poetry of the simple country scene in the tiny *Horses at the Door of a Cottage*. The theme of poetry and beauty in simple subjects will dominate the essay on Chardin and underlies all of Proust's fiction from *Les Plaisirs et les jours* through *A la recherche du temps perdu*. If in "Van Dyck" Proust evokes the tragic fate of the aristocratic models (*Charles I* and the *Royal Children*) who, as Proust apparently supposed, would all soon be killed by Cromwell, and the enigmatic, epicene beauty of the young aristocrat holding a fruit, the so-called *Duke of Richmond,* on the other hand he celebrates the triumph of the artist: "You triumph, Van Dyck, in the gestures . . . in all these beautiful beings who are soon to die." *Ars longa, vita brevis* is central to Proust's aesthetics: like Van Dyck, the narrator will rescue out of oblivion the aristocratic Guermantes, but also the bourgeois Swanns, the worker Françoises, and all of Combray laid waste by the ravages of World War I, from the inexorable, destructive sweep of men and time. The wistful melancholy of Watteau with his almost neurotic compulsion for disguises in love finds resonances in the vignettes of *Les Plaisirs et les jours*, particularly in "Fragments de comédie italienne," the recently recovered novella *L'Indifférent* whose title according to Philip Kolb may have come from the Watteau painting, and in the mascarades and gestures of Swann and Odette (Watteau peignoirs and "do a catleya") or the perverse scenarios set up for the pleasures and pains of the Baron de Charlus.

Proust's concerted effort to get these poems performed widely during the spring and summer of 1895 and then to bring them out in three different publications underscores the importance he attached to these poems despite a certain detached air. For example, Colette found his glosses on painters lovely, but deplored Proust's ruining them by reciting them poorly (*Cor.* 1:383), and that August Proust's mother goes to see Watteau and Van

Dyck paintings in the Louvre on behalf of her son and Reynaldo (*Cor.* 1:422). This flurry of activity in the area of painting may well have been part of a plan to launch a career in the arts and criticism rather than as a librarian at the Mazarine to which he was named on June 24 and in which he was to assume his functions as of August 1st. Probably at the time Proust was having his portrait done by Blanche as a young socialite, his parents must have begun to put pressure on him to choose a proper career. In response to that pressure Proust drafted a vignette destined for *Les Plaisirs et les jours* and understandably unpublished wherein a painter and writer B. defends Honoré's choice of a career as a man of letters (*Textes retrouvés* [Cahiers Marcel Proust, Nouvelle série, no. 3] pp. 104–06). Seven letters to Charles Grandjean dated by Philip Kolb as being written during November 1893 show that Proust seems to have considered fairly seriously doing something in museum work (*Cor.* 1:244, 250–51, 253–54, 254–55, 256–57, 258–59, and into December, 260–61).

Proust never assumed his position as librarian at the Mazarine, nor did he pursue the possibility of being attached to a museum. The sojourn with Reynaldo in Brittany (he signs into the hotel designating himself as "Marcel Proust, man of letters") inspired a number of texts which were to be part of a novel, and Proust seems to have taken a new interest in essay writing. Upon his return to Paris, his social connections brought him into contact with Edmond de Goncourt, whose writings and conversations were undoubtedly important for his understanding of 18th century art, although he severely criticizes a number of Goncourt's attitudes in a letter to Reynaldo Hahn written just after a dinner party in mid November (*Cor.* 1:441–43). The important essay on Chardin, written that same month and proposed to Mainguet as an article to appear in the *Revue hebdomadaire,* may well have been written in partial response to Goncourt and that particular dinner. The other article mentioned in the letter, "Contre l'Obscurité," did get published in *La Revue Blanche* on July 15, 1896 and separated Proust from the Symbolists of the day. In both the article against obscurity and in the article on Chardin, Proust firmly commits himself to an aesthetic much like that of the Realists or the Impressionists who find beauty in everyday life as opposed to the erudite and arcane obscurations of the Symbolists. Chardin's *Ray-Fish, Cat and Kitchen Utensils* which might be considered repulsive to 18th century rococo or Belle Epoque neo-rococo sensibilities becomes for Proust "a delicate and vast architecture, tinted with red blood, blue nerves and white muscles, like the nave of a polychrome cathedral" (*CSB* 376).

The general thrust of the article on Chardin is that thanks to the painter's lessons we can fully appreciate the beauties of a banal, bourgeois apartment or something as seemingly repulsive as a ray or as dull as a kitchen; later Proust will explore the beauties of Combray as well as Sodom and Gomorrah. Proust sees Chardin in terms of a light that floods into the world and quickens objects that had faded into eternal night. Thus a "still

life" (the French is even more somber, *nature morte* or "dead life") becomes living, like itself *(la nature vivante)*. Proust concludes his article by
evoking the transcendent world of Rembrandt, like Chardin, always
grounded in realism, but tending to move to a higher plane. Proust discusses the artists' peculiar gift of transforming the humble into the sublime,
bringing back to life people and things absorbed by nothingness. That the
1895 essay on Chardin should end with such thoughts, and that at the same
time Proust should compare the artist's transformation of reality to Christ's
transformation of water into wine as in Rembrandt's *Pilgrims at Emmaus*
(Proust has confused the events at Emmaus with those at Cana, but no matter, it is the idea and the Rembrandt allusion that are important; see *JS*
194), underscores Proust's description of this essay in the letter to Pierre
Mainguet as a "philosophy of art."[5]

Proust comes back to Rembrandt in an essay (*CSB* 659–64) written
probably just after his trip to Amsterdam in October, 1898. Artistic pilgrimages are important elements in Proust's religion of art, and thus to his own
real pilgrimage to see one of the grandest exhibitions of Rembrandts ever
assembled, he adds the fictitious pilgrimage of the aged John Ruskin, who,
much as Bergotte will make a supreme effort to go to see a Vermeer exhibition in *La Prisonnière*, goes to the exhibition to bathe one last time in the
warm glow that emanates from Rembrandt's work. Proust often refers to
the "light" that emanates from certain works of art, and thus in *Le Temps
retrouvé* Vermeer and Rembrandt are compared to dead stars who continue to send us their light, "leur rayon spécial" ("their special radiance,"
RTP 3:896; *RTPK* 3:932), through their paintings.[6]

Proust develops the idea that the unique vision of an artist survives in
his art in his essay on Gustave Moreau (*CSB* 667–74). The painter died on
April 18, 1898, and Proust seems to have visited the house in November
of that year, writing the essay immediately after that visit. The almost mystical language of the Rembrandt essay returns as Proust develops the idea
that the painter explores the innermost vision of a mysterious inner landscape he bears within himself, illuminates it, extracts it to bring it up to
the surface, and then spreads it across the canvas. In this essay, and in the
fragment on Elstir's work which derives from it, Proust develops the idea
that the painter sets forth a mythological instant and recounts the fable in
the *preterite* (*RTP* 2:422; *RTPK* 2:438). In the works of Moreau, as later in
the mythological pictures of Elstir, androgynous beings move in a world
illuminated by the setting sun, the whole in accord with mysterious laws of
the inner world of the painter's mind. Proust's pantheon of great artists includes both the frank, open poetic realism of Chardin and the mystic, hermetic, and private symbolism of Gustave Moreau, and this despite the objections raised in the essay against obscurity.[7]

In the brief biographical sketch about Antoine Watteau (*CSB* 665–67),
Proust defends the view that we should be indulgent towards the private
life of the painter, a position central to Proustian aesthetics and which he

first expressed at age thirteen or fourteen when, to the question: "For what fault have you most toleration," he answered: "For the private life of the genius" ("Pour la vie privée des génies," see *Album Proust*, 91). Still, however adamantly Proust refuted Sainte-Beuve's position about the intimate relationship of "the man and the work," Proust seems always keenly interested in the private life of an artist, such as in this essay, or in his review of Gabriel Mourey's book on Gainsborough in 1907, or his private inquiries as to sexual orientations of artists.[8]

The most significant texts Proust left on a contemporary artist are the three drafts he wrote in 1899 on Claude Monet.[9] Upon returning to Paris from Beg-Meil in 1895, Proust, Reynaldo Hahn, and Maria Nordlinger, a young artist who was the cousin of Reynaldo, went to see the painter Harrison in his Paris studio, and they often went to the Louvre and to art galleries, where they discovered Claude Monet. Proust's good friends Emile and Geneviève Straus acquired *Branch of the Seine, near Giverny, at Dawn*, one of the *Mornings on the Seine* series Claude Monet painted in 1897 and exhibited in 1898. Proust refers to this painting in several of his letters and in one of the three drafts about Monet written most likely after seeing an exhibition of paintings by Monet, Pissarro, Renoir, and Sisley at the Galaries Durand-Ruel in April, 1899. In these drafts Proust hesitates between the essay form and fiction, a hesitation which runs through his work down to *A la recherche du temps perdu*, whose primitive form may well have been an aesthetic treatise, in dialogue form, against Sainte-Beuve. The resounding theme in those fragments on Monet, and here Proust reiterates what he had written in his essay on Chardin, is that the painter initiates us into the awareness of our world, making us see beauty where we heretofore did not. Proust urges the reader to make artistic pilgrimages to view certain effects in nature such as a field of poppies, cliffs by the sea, ice floes on a thawing river, and the like.[10]

Although Proust publishes neither *Jean Santeuil* nor these fragments on Monet and Sisley, he will come back to these fragments, both for the general ideas and for the specific examples, when he constructs his painter Elstir in the mature novel. These three manuscript fragments, now separated into two volumes of manuscripts at the Bibliothèque Nationale as well as into two separate volumes of the Pléiade editions of Proust's works, were once to be found gathered together within a folded sheet of paper with the title: "Le Peintre.—Ombres [i.e. *A l'ombre des jeunes filles en fleurs*]— Monet." Thus, while none of the essays on the painters Chardin, Rembrandt, Moreau, Watteau, and Monet were published during his lifetime, they nonetheless constitute important first drafts for a number of the major aesthetic concerns that underlie *A la recherche du temps perdu*.

Proust puts into practice the program of the artistic pilgrimage, about which he wrote in his essays on Rembrandt and Monet, in 1898 when he discovers Ruskin and French medieval architecture. In the days just after Ruskin's death on January 21, 1900, Proust travels with the young sculptress Madeleine Yeatman and her husband Léon to Rouen to view the little figure carved on the portal of the booksellers, and during May of the same year he sojourns in Italy in order to see Venice and the Giotto frescoes at Padua. In the Arena chapel at Padua, Giotto designed a veritable viewing box upon which he projected images of the life of Christ, the life of the Virgin, and the Last Judgment, with the figures of the Virtues and Vices below. Of the fourteen virtues and vices, Proust retains Charity, Envy, Injustice, and Idolatry in the mature novel where it is Swann who introduces the young narrator to these works. The concept of the Psychomachia or the "Battle within the soul" is such an important one that Proust had thought about calling a subsection of *Le Temps retrouvé* "Les Vices et les Vertus de Padoue et de Combray." As in the article "Contre l'Obscurité," Proust rejects the hierarchical medieval symbolic system in favor of a more humanistic and relative view of man in his world. Still, this close work with allegory as he dealt with Ruskin, Emile Mâle, and medieval iconography and architectural systems in preparation for his translation of *The Bible of Amiens*, as well as his own curious and playful interpretations (e.g. "Synthèse du gothique prétentieux" in *Lettres à Reynaldo Hahn*, p. 75) prepared him for writing a much richer and deeper work.[11]

Towards the end of Proust's Ruskin activity, the large Whistler retrospective exhibition opened in Paris (July 1905). Thanks to Marie Nordlinger, Proust seems to have read or at least been aware of the general lines of Whistler's *The Gentle Art of Making Enemies and the Ten O'Clock Lecture* (*Cor*. 4:53–54 and *Cor*. 5, 41–42). His impassioned remarks about Whistler in a letter to Marie Nordlinger (*Cor*. 5:260) and his enthusiastic letter to his mother about which Whistlers to see in the exhibition show Proust favorably disposed to this great American impressionist whom he had met at a soirée. It has often been pointed out that "Elstir" is an anagram of Whistler, or as Proust spells it, "Wisthler," without the ungallic W and *h*. Just as Gustave Moreau's mythologies eventually provide the mythological background for Elstir, so does the Japanese phase of Elstir derive in great part from the Japonism of Whistler as the rough drafts demonstrate. As Proust sought to reconcile Ruskin and Whistler at a certain level, so does he in his "representative" painter Elstir bring together several artistic trends of the second half of the 19th century.

In many respects the marvelously humorous Ruskin pastiche "La Bénédiction du Sanglier. Etude des freques de Giotto représentant l'Affaire Lemoine à l'usage des jeunes étudiants et étudiantes du Corpus Christi qui se soucient encore d'*elle* par John Ruskin" closes the Ruskin period.[12] Rather than deal with Giotto as painter of the events, Proust has his Ruskin typically bury the matter under a welter of extraneous detail. The pastiche stands as a critique of Ruskinian aestheticism but at the same time builds in those spectacular errors Proust found so delightful. Proust's Ruskin finds the basilica of Sacré-Coeur, because of its romano-byzantine forms, to be earlier than the gothic Notre-Dame, and the Eiffel Tower, because it is really Wotan's spear stuck in the ground, is the earliest monument of the three. There is also a good deal of playful modernism in the pastiche. If Ruskin counseled his cockneys on how to travel by train to Amiens, in the pastiche Proust's Ruskin brings his cockney tourists to Paris in an airplane, a really nice bit of futurist thought on Proust's part, given that Blériot's darling solo crossing of the English Channel in a monoplane takes place in the summer of that year, 1909. Proust seems also to be responding to the Futurist manifesto which had been published in *Le Figaro* of February, 1909. In any case, there is something remarkably modernist, perhaps Fauve, perhaps even Cubist in the Orphic manner not yet painted by Robert Delaunay nor yet named by Apollinaire, in the spectacularly drawn view of flying over Paris by plane and observing the color streaked townscape, and again, this before Gertrude Stein's texts about Picasso, Cubism, and flying. Proust will revive this concatenation of Giotto and airplanes when the narrator will see Giotto's angels in flight at the Arena chapel in Padua and compare them to pupils of Roland Garros doing loop the loops (*RTP* 3:648; *RTPK* 3:663).

Picasso's *Demoiselles d'Avignon* dates from 1907, and in the six years running from that historical work to 1913 with the full flowering of Cubism, painting turned definitively away from the nineteenth century. Whether in painting (Futurism, Cubism, Orphic Cubism), film (camera displacement and montage), or science (Einstein and the theory of relativity), artists of the new century were developing with tremendous vigor a new vocabulary, grammar, and syntax for dealing with time and space.[13] In "Impressions de route en automobile" of 1907, Proust describes the steeples of Caen not *fixed* in their usual medieval cartographic space, but, thanks to the displacement of the car over a circuitous route, and the effects of parallax, shifting perspectives, relative time and space, in *motion*. Their metamorphoses from one image to another resemble Emile Cohl's pioneering work with the animated cartoons (this development of one image out of another is brought to full flower in Disney's *Fantasia* of the late 1930s), while the displacement of point of view might be compared to the camera displacement coupled with montage techniques in cinema. This article in *Le Figaro* was written and published just months after Proust had published in the same paper his review of *Les Eblouissements*, a volume of poetry by Anna de Noailles, a work which Proust called "le chef-d'oeuvre peut-être, de l'*impressionnisme* littéraire" ("the masterpiece perhaps, of literary *impressionism*." Proust's emphasis on *impressionism;* I personally find the "perhaps" quite significant). Proust's conception of the primacy of the literary image and of the impression as the sole criterium of truth coupled with his gifts of genius, intellectual vigor, and expansive vision would allow him in the years ahead to surpass the graceful but fairly limited vision of Anna de Noailles who ultimately is concerned with her own *éblouissements* (or bedazzlements) and not with the reader's. As Valéry so aptly put it, a painter paints not what he sees but what will be seen. The same goes for writers / writing.

The tiresome, sterile erudition of Ruskin and Montesquiou or the highly personal, restrictive view of Anna de Noailles gave little room for the impressions of the reader and the viewer, and it was towards the enhancement of his reader's view of the world, much in the same way as Monet in painting, that Proust most deliberately strove. Style, Proust was soon to write, like color for a painter, is a question not of technique, but of vision, and if the year of the pastiches gave him the chance to develop the vision of other writers, 1909 was devoted to a meticulous examination of the style of Sainte-Beuve, of Balzac, of literature in general, and intensive work on drafts of A la recherche du temps perdu whose style, that is, vision, turns out to be compatible with both the Cubists at their most analytical and with the Impressionists at their most sensual.

There seems always to have been a place for "the painter" in Proust's conception of a work, often in order to corroborate views on literature and the arts. In Les Plaisirs et les jours there was to have been the dialogue in which the painter and writer B. argue with the parents of Honoré (read Proust) about the possibility of an artistic career.[14] While the events at Beg-Meil that lead Proust and Hahn to meet Harrison become, in Jean Santeuil, Jean's meeting with the novelist C. (eventually the material reverts back to Elstir), the major painter in Jean Santeuil is Bergotte, a painter whose work resembles much of what we call the "academic" school of the 19th century or the kind of art generally exhibited in the official salons of the 1880s and the 1890s in France. Bergotte does portraits, a marine, two still lifes (a vase of flowers and a pheasant on a table), a landscape (a road at Fontainebleau), and Electra, Eurydice, Salome with a Black Slave, and statues of Venus. Considerable attention is given to his social life as well.

By 1909 Proust seems definitely to have thought about including a painter in his novel. In one of the small note-books Mme Straus gave to Proust in 1908, and which Philip Kolb has published as Le Carnet de 1908, Proust refers several times to Harrison as well as to Carpaccio, Giotto, and other painters who will eventually contribute much to the allegorical or structural underpinnings of the novel. Claudine Quémar dates certain texts called "Le Peintre" in Cahier 28 between 1909 and 1910, and the texts she reproduces (folios 1 to 13) derive from certain Impressionist works, paintings by Moreau, and Whistler and Turner, and include a rough draft of what will become the Port of Carquethuit.[15] Jo Yoshida, in his article "La Genèse de l'Atelier d'Elstir à la lumière de plusieurs versions inédites," in Bulletin d'Informations Proustiennes (no. 8, Autumn 1978, pp. 15–28) examines closely notebooks 7 and 6 (1909) and 25, 12, 29, 32, 28 and 7 (ca. 1909–1910). Douglas W. Alden in Marcel Proust's Grasset Proofs: Commentary and Variants (1978) and Alison Winton in Proust's Additions: The Making of "A la recherche du temps perdu" (2 volumes, 1977) have studied the evolution of Proust's text beyond the publication of Du côté de chez Swann in 1913.

When the adolescent narrator meets Elstir in his studio, that studio is described as if we were somehow inside a veritable *camera obscura* or a block of rock crystal with here and there a mirror-like surface (read a painting), and when he views Elstir's paintings in the Guermantes picture gallery, he realizes that the pictures are projections of the "magic lantern" or the brain of their creator (*RTP* 2:419; *RTPK* 2:435), ideas with sources as diverse as the essay on Gustave Moreau, the essay on Monet where the pictures in a private collection are compared to magic mirrors like an astrologer's *lunette* or speculum, the visit to the Réveillons' gallery of Monets, and undoubtedly Proust's readings of Ruskin on Giotto. The Arena chapel in many ways is the prototype of Elstir's studio (as is also Moreau's studio), or the Guermantes picture gallery, or the narrator's bedroom transformed under the influence of the magic lantern: the frescoes are literally "projections" of Giotto's original way of viewing his material.[16] His iconographic interpretation of the traditions of the Psychomachia is original, and he makes the viewer deal with it in a fresh way. If Proust thought about calling a section of *Le Temps retrouvé* "Les Vices et les Vertus de Padoue et de Combray", it was to show us the considerable distance that separated his from the fixed, medieval view of the world.

Swann gives the narrator reproductions of the Giotto paintings of the Virtues and the Vices, but tied to idolatrous textuality, Swann seems incapable of descending to a deeper understanding either of the images or of himself and limits himself at the level of "naming" the kitchen maid "Giotto's Charity," a point the narrator makes patently clear in the statement that Swann always stops just this side of art (*RTP* 1:852. *RTPK* 1:911), becoming one of those "celibates of art" Proust refers to in *Le Temps retrouvé* (*RTP* 3:811–92. *RTPK* 3:927–28). While idolatry can be delightful at a certain level, such as lucid awareness of enjoying being in the presence of a descendant from some distant grand name, as Proust points out in his notes on idolatry in the "P.S." of the preface to his translation of *The Bible of Amiens* or his article on Robert de Montesquiou as a "Professor of Beauty," ("Un Professeur de Beauté," *CSB* 506–20), idolatry can lead to a perversion of intellectual sincerity, idolatry being "the art of serving with the best of our hearts and minds some dear and sad image we have created for ourselves" (*CSB* 129). Swann falls in love, not with the woman Odette, but with his images of her as a Botticelli (after his death, Odette will assume Botticellian poses), Elstir marries his "belle Gabrielle" (in the same way that the painter Bergotte in *Jean Santeuil* falls in love with Mme Delven) because she corresponds to his aesthetic idea of beauty, and if Swann's idolatry keeps him "this side of art," in the same sentence the narrator foresees the day when Elstir will succumb to idolatry of certain forms (*RTP* 1:852. *RTPK* 1:911).

If Swann's idolatry is typical of much of the "bad" aesthetics of the characters in the novel, in that he compares "reality" and paintings, as when he finds the nose of M. de Palancy in a Ghirlandajo[17] or soldiers from Mantegna in the footmen at the Saint-Euverte soirée, then the reader must

constantly ask him or herself who is doing the comparing, what the character derives from such a comparison, does this comparison deepen or not
our own understanding of the characters, the text, art, reality, or ourselves,
and if so, how.

The narrator (or is this really Proust—author and idolator?) makes frequent references to paintings in the text, and it is one of the disconcerting,
duplicitous elements of the Proustian view of fiction and life that the reader
must deal with. For example, at the end of the text dealing with the marriage in the church of Combray during which the narrator perceives the
Duchesse de Guermantes, the text resolves with a highly imagistic, poetic
text of reds on reds and synaesthesia: "that sort of tenderness, of solemn
sweetness [douceur in French also means gentleness, softness, smoothness,
pleasantness, slowness, or tenderness] in the pomp of a joyful celebration
which characterizes certain pages of Lohengrin, certain paintings by Carpaccio, and make us understand how Baudelaire was able to apply to the
sound of the trumpet the epithet 'delicious' " (RTP 1:178. RTPK 1:194).
From the perspective of the "ideal" reader who makes all the associations
Proust intends in such a text, who knows Wagner's opera, who remembers
the Carpaccio paintings Proust is thinking about in this text (the manuscript
is more specific about which ones), and who has read Baudelaire's "L'Im-
prévu" in Les Epaves, the text is beautiful and makes sense, but isn't it
beautiful and coherent precisely because we bring to it our "dear and sad
images" of erudite idolatry? For certain undergraduates and graduates,
these references to Wagner, Carpaccio, and Baudelaire couldn't be more
sterile and opaque, in the same manner that the text would be opaque for
a western reader of non-western artists were substituted for Wagner, Carpaccio, and Baudelaire. In other words, for certain readers the cultural re-
ferentiality lessens their own feeling of joy while reading the text.

In "Contre l'obscurité" Proust urges the writer to use words in such a
way that they quicken our memories, and elsewhere Proust refers to the
need of building a "caisse de résonance" (sound-box) within the memory of
the reader. What Proust is really talking about is a method of "imprinting,"
or getting the reader to make certain associations or synapses. This, of
course, resembles any kind of training ranging from simple memory building to connoisseurship. Proust develops at considerable length the aesthetic
qualities attached to the "recognition" of a picture as being a Gustave Moreau in his essay on the painter. In a later text in which he deals with several pictures by Vermeer, Proust explores this zone between two paintings
in which the viewer experiences an ideal picture (CSB, ed. de Fallois, 302–
03; cf. RTP 3:377–78. RTPK 3:384–85). All art, Proust maintains, urges us
to enter this zone where we abandon our personal moi or ego to float in a
general zone of consciousness. Unlike the celibates of art who are compared to vehicles unable to fly, Swann begins to "take off" since he realizes
that Diana and Her Companions is not by Nicolas Maes but by Vermeer

(connoisseurship), but he does not let his *moi* or inner self float in this enriching metaphysical state.

Proust clearly establishes the primacy of memory in dealing with paintings and texts, but he is vague, ambiguous, even contradictory as to where we draw the line between connoisseurship, erudition, taste, impressions, sentimentality, idolatry, nostalgia, "artistic celibacy", and the like. It is only the mature narrator, remembering the marriage scene in Combray, who has heard Wagner, who has viewed Carpaccio paintings, and who has read Baudelaire (none of the three artists figure in the young narrator's experiences, and as far as Carpaccio goes, the episode involving the Fortuny dress inspired by Carpaccio was not even written until 1916, and it was only then that Carpaccio was decided upon), and who colors his past impressions of joy with these erudite references to works of art.

If Carpaccio is associated with great joy at the end of the marriage scene in Combray, a work of his unleashes great pangs of pain and loss later in the novel when the narrator, disconcertedly viewing Carpaccio paintings in Venice, is about to move away from the painting of the *Patriarch of Grado Exorcizing a Possessed Man* when he recognizes on a Cavalier of the Calza a cloak resembling the very one Albertine wore during their last evening together. Here Proust effectively uses a painting to trigger the mechanism of involuntary memory.[18] To sum up, then, there is no "one way" to deal with the references to a painting in the Proustian novel. An exhaustingly close analysis allows the reader to explore the associative patterns in Proust's psyche; in a more relaxed reading the reader draws connections sentimental, idolatrous, or irrelevant between his or her own psyche and the connections the narrator makes; for the general reader they might be construed as so many opacities no different from the "beryls" of the symbolism Proust cited in "Contre l'obscurité" or as dreary as the brittle and idolatrous comparisons Montesquiou draws between art and reality, and which are criticized by Proust in "Un Professeur de Beauté."

In Belle Epoque society, painters and paintings were above all commodities, and Proust incorporates this in *A la recherche du temps perdu*. That the painter in the Verdurin circle, from their perspective a commodity and whom they have labeled Biche, turns out to be the genius Elstir is yet another illustration of Proust's distinction between the superficial social self and the profound creative self. (*Biche* means hind or doe; in familiar language, *ma biche* means my darling or dear, generally used for a young girl, and perhaps, in this sense, he is one of the "darlings" of the Verdurin clan; the term may also come from the slang verb *bicher*, meaning to be happy, satisfied, or in the impersonal, as in *ça biche*, to have things go smoothly or well). Elstir's little "speech" about a painting he admires is full of slang, much like the speech of Vuillard whom Proust knew and whose speech mannerisms he had recorded in a letter to Reynaldo Hahn (*Lettres à Reynaldo Hahn*, pp. 145–46; cf. *RTP* 1:212–13, *RTPK* 1:232, *RTP* 254–55,

RTPK 1:277–78), but Elstir's enthusiasm for the work of the master is sincere. When Elstir abandons the Verdurin circle, ostensibly to devote himself to more high-minded pursuits and to his wife Gabrielle, the Verdurins quickly replace him with the practical joker "Ski." But nothing is ever exactly as it seems in Proust, and we learn through the pseudo-Goncourt journal that M. Verdurin was a highly respected and perceptive art critic who wrote a book on Whistler, and later we learn that his death sorely grieved Elstir.

To participate in Belle Epoque society, whose rituals Proust reviews in the opening pages of *Un Amour de Swann* or shares with us in the long dinner scene in *Le Côté de Guermantes,* aesthetic counterfeiting in the salons was *de rigueur.* There were accepted lists of what was to be seen, and thus when paintings are mentioned the Duc de Guermantes exclaims "If it is to be seen, I've seen it" (*RTP* 2:524. *RTPK* 2:544). When Mme Cottard meets Swann in the omnibus, she makes conversation about the Machard portrait on exhibition (*RTP* 1:374–75. *RTPK* 1:407–08). While she allows that Leloir might be superior to Machard, she still prefers Machard, and the Machard to the portrait Elstir did of her husband with a blue mustache. Mme. Cottard's position is that if one pays 10,000 francs for a portrait, as is the case with Machard, then the portrait must resemble the sitter. Socialites prefer to have their portraits done by fashionable artists like the Bouguereaus or the Chaplins rather than the more original Whistlers, Renoirs, or Elstirs (cf. *PJ* 52 and *RTP* 3:722, *RTPK* 3:742). Other texts in Proust deal with the acquisition of paintings, and thus the Duc de Guermantes acquires a pseudo-Velasquez or Philippe de Champaigne (it turns out to be a fake), and St. Loup sells part of his family estate to buy art nouveau furniture, polychrome objects by Gérome, and paintings by Lebourg and Guillaumin (Cahier 30, 30r^0 and *RTP* 1:757, *RTPK* 1:813).

Unlike Zola who gives us a very clear picture of the financial situation of the painter Claude Lantier, Proust is not concerned with the question of how an artist survives, only that his vision might survive through his art. Since all of Proust's unpublished texts on painters turned around the question of the artist's unique *vision* and the *lessons* the viewer learns, understandably he sought to incorporate as much as he could in Elstir. An original vision, Proust implies, comes with time, with experience, and considerable effort, before one arrives at the stage of a master (*RTP* 1:863–64; *RTPK* 1:922–24). Elstir's first manner is mythological. Complex manuscript versions and certain variants and texts published in the Pléiade versions of the novel deal with this phase of Elstir's art and demonstrate to what extent Proust was thinking of Turner and Gustave Moreau when he conceived of this aspect of Elstir's art. This world of epicene poets, muses, or a centaur carrying an exhausted poet on his back, where Hercules kills the hydra from Lerna, where Bacchantes tear apart Orpheus, or where heroes occupy a small place in an immense landscape, are all directly inspired by specific works by Gustave Moreau and Turner (*RTP* 2:421–22. *RTPK* 2:437–38 and *RTP*, 2:1162).

In his second manner alluded to ever so briefly in the published text, Elstir is influenced, as were so many artists during the second half of the 19th century, by Japanese art. Although at the house of Gustave Moreau Proust may have seen several interpretations Moreau did of works seen in an exhibition of Japanese art, and although Proust undoubtedly read the article / interview of Roger Marx about Claude Monet in the *Gazette des Beaux-Arts* of June 1909 where Monet refers to his admiration for 18th century Japanese masters, Proust seems particularly to have had in mind the works of Whistler he had seen in the 1905 exhibition, as is amply evident in the texts contained at the outset of Cahier 28, sections of which have been published by Claudine Quémar (see footnote 15).

Elstir's mature style is Impressionist, and here Proust concerns himself not with the historical developments of Impressionism but rather with a loose and fairly poetic interpretation of illusionism in the visual arts. Taken at face value, Proust's text on the "metaphors" of Elstir read more like descriptions of a Mannerist such as Tintoretto or Arcimboldo, or a Neomannerist and Surrealist like Dali.[19] Whether it is the illusionistic qualities of the *Port of Carquethuit* and its "metaphors" (Proust's use of rhetorical terms is fairly loose) of land terms for the sea and sea terms for the land, or the transvestism of Odette as *Miss Sacripant* in male dress, Elstir's art is one that at times relates more to the complex seascapes of Turner at the outset of the 19th century or the photograph of Réjane as the Prince de Sagan in the Marquis de Massa's review at the Epatant than it does to works by traditional Impressionist painters. And yet many of the subjects of Elstir's oeuvre derive from those of the Impressionists: *Cliffs of Creuniers* (Monet); *Cathedral* (Monet, Sisley); *Fête at the Water's Edge* (Monet, Renoir); *Ice Floes on a River* (Monet); *Sunrise* (Harrison, Monet); *A Wave* (Harrison, Whistler, Renoir); *Horse Races* and *Jockeys* (Manet, Degas), *Regattas* (Monet, Helleu); *Nudes in a Southern Landscape* (Renoir), *A Bunch of Asparagus* (Manet), *Variations in Opal* (Whistler), and so forth. But there are also connections to be made between numerous other painters ranging from Chardin to Monticelli.

In his essays on painters in the 1890s Proust insisted on the lessons painters teach us about reality (Chardin, Monet, and Rembrandt) and an abstract, inner world of thought (Rembrandt and Moreau). Like the various figures in the sculptural program of a gothic cathedral, Elstir's function as the painter in Proust's cathedral novel is didactic and assumes an integral role in the structure of the entire system of Proust's religion of art.[20] Elstir is one in the series of the "Professors of Beauty" who initiate the narrator into the world of art, beginning with the grandmother and Swann to go on to Bergotte and eventually to Vinteuil. Elstir teaches the narrator about the beauty of the modern world of fashions and is an authority in such diverse areas as medieval iconography or the proper furnishing of a yacht (*RTP* 1:898–99; *RTPK* 1:959–60). He fulfills Baudelaire's insistence that the artist deal with the heroism of modern life, and it is in this respect that, if Guys was "le peintre de la vie moderne" (the painter of modern life) for Baudelaire, Elstir for the narrator reveals the beauty in contemporary regattas in the same way that Carpaccio celebrated the splendors of early 16th century Venice, or else in a modern hospital or a modern school building.

Original artists, like Renoir, writes Proust in his preface to Paul Morand's *Tendres Stocks*, proceed in the same way as the oculist: their works are like new glasses, sometimes painful, but they allow us to see the world anew (*CSB* 615). Elstir is such an artist / oculist, and although socialites such as Mme. Cottard or the Guermantes find his works painful, the narrator learns from the paintings how to discover in life and in his environment beauties he had missed, overlooked, or ignored. It is in this sense that Elstir functions as a foil for the narrator, and at a different level as a foil for Proust, who, through his own unique style is able to rival in his literary "impressionism" the greatest of the Impressionist masters in a way far more subtle, far more intense, far more vigorous than the somewhat insipid surface intensities of the Comtesse de Noailles. In his preface to *Calligrammes*, Guillaume Apollinaire had boasted "et moi aussi je suis peintre" ("and I'm a painter, too"). Proust very subtly says the same thing in his work. Through his descriptions, his vignettes, his consummate use of the subtleties of the French language whether in its syntactic intricacies or in exquisite tonalities, he emulates the subtle harmonies of Whistler and Monet, brings to life the commonplaces of experience like Chardin, threads through the complex elegancies and amorous masquerades of Watteau, sets down broad luminous strokes like Rembrandt, or patiently layers mythic, symbolic, and allegorical meanings over great washes of color like Gustave Moreau. Painters contributed much to the aesthetic formation of Marcel Proust; if they showed him beauties in the world, Proust would soon occupy a place alongside as one who also proceeds as an oculist and who transforms the world for the readers through the imaginative beauty and painful perceptions he offers us in *A la recherche du temps perdu*.

Notes

1. Herbert de Ley has examined closely the place of these and other painters in his article " 'L'Hôpital sans style vaut le glorieux portail': Salon Painters in *A la recherche du temps perdu*," *L'Esprit Créateur* 11, no. 1 (Spring 1971): 32–41. An excellent selective survey of the general question of Proust and painting down to the early 1970s is to be found in the subsection on "The Arts" in the entry "Marcel Proust," in *A Critical Bibliography of French Literature*, 20th Century (Syracuse, N.Y.: Syracuse Univ. Press, 1980), vol. 1, nos. 2238–2305, and related rubrics as well. See also the essay and bibliography with 43 items in Elizabeth Russell Taylor, *Marcel Proust and His Contexts: A Critical Bibliography of English-Language Scholarship* (New York & London: Garland Publishing Inc., 1981), pp. 181–97. Philip Kolb has developed the notion of the artist as Baudelairian "phare" (lighthouse) in Proust in several articles, notably "Les 'Phares' de Proust," in *Entretiens sur Marcel Proust*, led by

Georges Cattaui et Philip Kolb, International Cultural Center of Cérisy-la-Salle (Paris, La Haye: Mouton & Co., 1966), pp. 105–14, followed by discussions, pp. 114–28, and "Proust's Protagonist as a 'Beacon,' *L'Esprit Créateur* 5, no. 1 (Spring 1965): 38–47. See also Juliette Hassine, *Essai sur Proust et Baudelaire* (Paris: Nizet, 1979) and Simone Kadi, *La Peinture chez Proust et Baudelaire* (Bruges: La Pensée universelle, 1973). Jeffrey Meyers deals with Proust and painting in two chapters of his *Painting and the Novel* (Manchester: Manchester University Press / Barnes & Noble, 1975): "Bellini, Giotto, Mantegna, Botticelli and *Swann's Way* (pp. 96–111) and "Vermeer and *The Captive*" (pp. 112–23). Christian Robin draws connections with Van Eyck's *Ghent Altarpiece* in "Le Retable de la cathédrale," in *Etudes Proustiennes*, vol. 3, Cahiers Marcel Proust, Nouvelle Série, 9 (Paris: Gallimard, 1979), pp. 67–93. See the chapter "Comparing Styles: Proust and Fénéon, Fénéon and Huysmans," in Joan Ungersma Halperin, *Félix Fénéon and the Language of Art Criticism*, Studies in the Fine Arts: Criticism, no. 6 (Ann Arbor: UMI Research Press, 1980), pp. 149–84, and "Proust and the Metaphor of Painting" in Lee McKay Johnson, *The Metaphor of Painting: Essays on Baudelaire, Ruskin, Proust, and Pater*, Studies in the Fine Arts: Criticism, no. 7 (Ann Arbor: UMI Research Press, 1980), pp. 147–91. The most important recent publications are the two articles by Helen O. Borowitz listed below (notes 5 and 6) and J. M. Cocking's important essay "Proust and Painting" in his *Proust: Collected Essays on the Writer and His Art*, Cambridge Studies in French (Cambridge: Cambridge Univ. Press, 1982), p. 130–63. This essay is twice as long as the one originally published in *French 19th Century Painting and Literature*, ed. Ulrich Finke (Manchester: Manchester Univ. Press, 1972), pp. 305–24.

2. See *Correspondance de Marcel Proust*, ed. Philip Kolb (Paris: Plon, 1970), 1:173–74. Subsequently references to the correspondence will be to the volumes in this edition and will be included in the text. Proust and Blanche kept somewhat in touch over the years, but they disagreed profoundly over the beuvian "man and the work" question and allowed that disagreement to show in their publications about each other's work. Although Proust did eventually keep some of the family paintings (see his letters to Mme. Catusse in this regard in 1906), in general he did not seek to collect paintings, and only kept a picture of Versailles when Helleu dedicated the picture to him. See Paulette Howard-Johnston, "Bonjour M. Elstir," *Gazette des Beaux-Arts* 69 (1967): 247–50 for Proust and Helleu, written by the painter's daughter.

3. See *Contre Sainte-Beuve*, preceded by *Pastiches et mélanges* and followed by *Essais et articles*, ed. Pierre Clarac with Yves Sandré (Paris: Gallimard [Pléiade], 1971), p. 677. Unless indicated otherwise, all references to Proust's texts are to the five volume Pléiade edition and will be included with appropriate abbreviations in the text.

4. Proust's verses in French with an English prose translation accompany a colored reproduction of this work in *Masterpieces of Painting from the National Gallery of Art*, ed. Huntington Cairns and John Walker (New York: Random House, 1944), pp. 108–09. These poems with substantial variants are to be found in *Poèmes*, ed. Claude Francis et Fernande Gontier, Cahiers Marcel Proust, Nouvelle Série, 10 (Paris: Gallimard, 1982), pp. 29–33 and 161–64. See also the humorous variation on "Potter" for Céleste Albaret on p. 152. For a detailed analysis of these poems and the music of Hahn see J. Theodore Johnson, Jr., "Proust's Early *Portraits de peintres*," *Comparative Literature Studies* 4, no. 4 (1967): 397–408.

5. *Cor.* 1:444. Proust's essay on Chardin has been dealt with by Gita May, "Chardin vu par Diderot et par Proust," *PMLA* 72 (1957): 403–18; Kyuichiro Inoue in "Proust et Chardin," *Etudes de Langue et de Littérature Françaises* (Tokyo) 1 (1962): 1–15; Jean Roudaut, " 'Par qui nos yeux sont déclos'ou la vie profonde des 'natures mortes' ", *L'Arc*, no. 47 (1971): 27–31; David Backus, "La Leçon d'Elstir et la leçon de Chardin," in *BSAMP*, no. 32 (1982): 535–39, and the excellent study by Helen O. Borowitz, "The Watteau and Chardin of Marcel Proust," *Bulletin of the Cleveland Museum of Art* 69, no. 1 (January 1982): 18–35.

6. The Rembrandt material in Proust has been discussed by Helen O. Borowitz in "The Rembrandt and Monet of Marcel Proust," *Bulletin of The Cleveland Museum of Art* 70,

no. 2 (February 1983): 73–95. See also Henri Bonnet, "Maria ou l'épisode hollandais," *BSAMP,* no. 28 (1978): 602–14. For Proust and Vermeer see the chapter "Vermeer and *The Captive*" in Jeffrey Meyers' book mentioned above. Hélène Adhémar's "La Vision de Vermeer par Proust, à travers Vaudoyer," *Gazette des Beaux-Arts* 68 (November 1966): 291–94 is followed by "Vermeer de Delft" by Jean-Louis Vaudoyer, pp. 295–302. See also Germaine Brée, "Proust's Combray Church: Illiers or Vermeer?" *Proceedings of the American Philosophical Society* 112, no. 1 (January 1968): 5–7, and "L'Eglise de Combray: Présence de Vermeer," in *RHL* 71 (September-December 1971): 965–71; and Diana Culbertson, "A la recherche de Vermeer: Proust and the 'Sphinx of Delft'," *Southern Humanities Review* 9, no. 1 (Winter 1975): 77–87.

7. For a discussion of Proust and Gustave Moreau see the following: Mizuho Hokari, "Proust et Gustave Moreau, à propos de l'échec de *Jean Santeuil*," *Etudes de Langue et de Littérature Françaises* 14 (1969): 34–48; Patrick Gauthier, "Proust et Gustave Moreau," *Europe,* nos. 496–97 (August–September 1970): 237–41; Richard Bales, "Proust et Gustave Moreau: la 'Descente de Croix' de Decazeville," *RHLF* 74, no. 6 (December 1974): 1032–37; and J. Theodore Johnson, Jr., "Marcel Proust et Gustave Moreau," *BSAMP,* no. 28 (1978): 614–39.

8. For the Watteau essay see the article by Helen O. Borowitz "The Watteau and Chardin of Marcel Proust" cited in note 5. Regarding Proust's curiosity about the private life of an artist, see for example his letter to Robert de Billy written in 1910, just a year after the "Contre Sainte-Beuve" venture, in which he inquires about Thomas Hardy and James Matthew Barrie: "quels hommes ce sont, mondains, amateurs de femmes etc." [what sort of men they are, men about town, fond of women, etc.] (*Cor.* 10:55).

9. For Monet and Proust see particularly J. Theodore Johnson, Jr., "*Débâcle sur la Seine* de Claude Monet: source du *Dégel à Briseville* d'Elstir," *Etudes Proustiennes,* Cahiers Marcel Proust, Nouvelle Série, 6, (Paris: Gallimard, 1973), 1:163–76 and the article by Helen O. Borowitz cited above, "The Rembrandt and Monet of Marcel Proust," note 6.

10. These ideas become such a commonplace for Proust that they seem to churn out spontaneously, such as in a letter to the artist Maxime Dethomas of April 1903 when, having seen the exhibition of his works, Proust writes that from them he received a "profound initiation to the understanding of nature and love of life." He continues "it seems that one has gotten from you new eyes to look at life and men and even down to those little windows on the Grand Canal that I would like to juxtapose with yours." He concludes this section by saying that artists innoculate us with a "great desire of realities . . . by covering reality with a particular beauty (that they simply have extracted from it, forcing it, so to speak, to remove its mask and fly its flag)." See *BSAMP,* no. 26 (1976): 201–02, and reprinted in *Cor.* 3:306–07. These are almost the exact terms Proust will use for Elstir's influence on the narrator in *A la recherche du temps perdu.* In *La Fugitive* just a few lines after mentioning the *lessons* of Chardin and Veronese, and in a context of a discussion of bad painters who do not properly capture Venice, Proust makes an exception for Maxime Dethomas, as well he had to since Dethomas had illustrated Proust's article "Les Mille et un Matins: Mme de Villeparis à Venise," and subsequently titled "A Venise" with the Dethomas illustrations in *Feuillets d'art* (15 December 1919), pp. 1–12.

11. For the question of Giotto, allegory, and Proust's drawings see particularly J. Theodore Johnson, Jr., "Proust and Giotto: Foundations for an Allegorical Interpretation of *A la recherche du temps perdu*," in *Marcel Proust: A Critical Panorama,* ed. Larkin B. Price (Urbana: Univ. of Illinois Press, 1973), pp. 168–205. Chapter Three "Reading (Proust)" of Paul de Man's *Allegories of Reading: Figural Language in Rousseau, Nietzsche, Rilke, and Proust* (New Haven and London: Yale Univ. Press, 1979), pp. 57–78 deals particularly with Giotto and the question of allegory. For Proust drawings see also Claude Gandelman, "The Drawings of Marcel Proust," *Adam, International Review,* nos. 394–96, 40th year (1976): 21–57.

12. See the excellent critical edition of this pastiche by Jean Milly in his *Les Pastiches de Proust: édition critique et commentée* (Paris: Armand Colin, 1970), pp. 321–34.

13. Proust was aware of cubism (cf. *RTP* 1:532, *RTPK* 1:573 and *RTP* 3:307, 946, *RTPK* 3:311, 983), and in "M. Jacques-E. Blanche critique littéraire" of 1914 Proust quotes Blanche's reaction to *Du côté de chez Swann* when Blanche writes of Proust: "Je dirais presque qu'il suggère la quatrième dimension des cubistes" ("I would almost say that he suggests the fourth dimension of the cubists") (*Textes retrouvés*, p. 371). He was aware of comparisons made between his work and Einstein's, and in a letter to Benjamin Crémieux of August 6, 1922, he refers to an interval of time and writes, humorously, "Einsteinisons-le si vous voulez pour plus de commodité." ("How about Einsteining it, if you like, if that is easier.") See John D. Erickson, "The Proust-Einstein Relation: A Study in Relative Point of View," in *Marcel Proust: A Critical Panorama*, ed. Larkin B. Price (Urbana: Univ. of Illinois Press, 1973), pp. 247–76. According to Louis Gautier-Vignal in *Proust connu et inconnu* (Paris: Robert Laffont, 1976), Proust got to see a number of Picasso paintings come out of their crates in the apartment of Eugenia Errazuriz in 1916, but he found them "insignificant" (pp. 102–04), although publicly in his preface to Blanche's *Propos de peintre* Proust finds Picasso's portrait of Cocteau "admirable" and of such a "noble rigidity" that it makes the most charming Carpaccios seen in Venice fade in his memory (*CSB* 580). For Proust and modern art, see J. Theodore Johnson, Jr., "Proust's 'Impressionism' Reconsidered in the Light of the Visual Arts of the Twentieth Century," in *Twentieth Century French Fiction: Essays for Germaine Brée*, ed. George Stambolian (New Brunswick, N.J.: Rutgers Univ. Press, 1975), pp. 27–56; Reinhold Hohl, "Marcel Proust in neuer Sicht," *Die Neue Rundschau* (Berlin), no. 1 (1977): 54–72; Claude Gandelman, "Proust as a Cubist," *Art History*, no. 3 (September 1979): 355–63; Diane R. Leonard, "Proust and Virginia Wolf, Ruskin and Roger Fry: Modernist Visual Dynamics," in *Comparative Literature Studies* 18, no. 3 (September 1981): 333–43; and Paola Placella Sommella, *Marcel Proust e i Movimenti pittorici d'Avanguardia*, in Biblioteca dei Quaderni del Novecento Francese I (Roma: Bulzoni Editore, 1982).

14. See Larkin B. Price's presentation of the text "Conversation" in *BSAMP*, no. 17 (1967): 523–30. The text has been republished in *Textes retrouvés*, ed. Philip Kolb, Cahiers Marcel Proust, no. 3 (Paris: Gallimard, 1971), pp. 104–06, as dating from 1893–1895.

15. Nos. 3 / 4 of *Cahiers critiques de la littérature* (Summer 1977) is largely devoted to Proust and painting. Manuscript pages of Cahier 28 are reproduced on pp. 7 and 20. The text itself, edited by Jacques Bersani and Claudine Quémar, is called "Marcel Proust, Le Peintre," and is published on pp. 8–19. See also Jean-François Chevrier and Brigitte Legars, "Pour un ensemble pratiques artistiques dans la *Recherche*," pp. 21–69.

16. The episode of the magic lantern has been dealt with in the following articles: J. Theodore Johnson, Jr., "*La Lanterne magique:* Proust's Metaphorical Toy," *L'Esprit Créateur* 11, no. 1 (Spring 1971): 17–31; Emily Zants, "Proust's Magic Lantern," *Modern Fiction Studies* 19, no. 2 (Summer 1973): 211–16; and Marcel Muller in *Préfiguration et structure romanesque dans "A la recherche du temps perdu"* (Lexington, Kentucky: French Forum Publishers [French Forum Monographs, 14], 1979) who discusses the magic lantern, reproduces several slides, and in general deals with a number of ideas relevant to the question of Proust, the visual arts, Swann, medieval architecture, and iconography.

17. *RTP* 1:223. Here Proust ascribes to Swann, as he frequently does, his own "idolatrous" way of seeing pictures. Lucien Daudet recounts how Proust would stop in front of the Ghirlandajo portrait and exclaim: "But it's the living portrait of M. du Lau. It really is an unbelievable resemblance! How nice it would be if it were he! Ah! *mon petit . . .* it really is fun looking at paintings." See Lucien Daudet, *Autour de Soixante lettres de Marcel Proust*, Les Cahiers Marcel Proust, (Paris: Gallimard, 1929), pp. 18–19.

18. See J. Theodore Johnson, Jr., "La Place de Vittore Carpaccio dans l'œuvre de Marcel Proust" to appear in volume 3 of *France et Italie dans la Culture Européenne, Continuité et Renaissances, Mélanges à la Mémoire de Franco Simone* (Torino, Italy). Jean Milly has reproduced the letters to Maria de Madrazo in his edition of *La Prisonnière* (Paris: Flammarion, 1984), pp. 47–50, and he has discussed this material relevant to Carpaccio in a section of his preface, "Albertine et le motif Fortuny," pp. 28–36. See also Kazuyoshi Yoshikawa, "Genèse

du leitmotif 'Fortuny' dans *A la recherche du temps perdu*," *Etudes de Langue et de Littéra-ture Françaises* (Tokyo), no. 32 (1978): 99–119.

19. For the "baroque" elements in Elstir see P. W. M. Cogman, "Reading a Painting by Elstir: Fanciful Descriptions in Proust and some Baroque Poets," *French Studies* 30, no. 4 (October 1976): 419–32 and Giorgetto Giorgi, "Barocco e impressionismo in Proust," in *Stendhal, Flaubert, Proust: (proposte e orientamenti)*, (Milano: Istituto Editoriale Cisalpino, 1968), pp. 107–29. Arnold Hauser discusses the Mannerist aspect of Proust in the final pages of his *Mannerism: The Crisis of the Renaissance and the Origins of Modern Art*, translated in collaboration with the author by Eric Mosbacher (New York: Knopf, 1965), "Proust and Kafka." For a general survey of critical assessments as to what constitutes literary Impression-ism, see J. Theodore Johnson, Jr., "Literary Impressionism in France: A Survey of Criticism," *L'Esprit Créateur* 13, no. 4 (Winter 1973): 271–97. For additional materials on Elstir: Charles Newell Clark, "Elstir: The Role of the Painter in Proust's *A la recherche du temps perdu*," Diss. Yale University (1952); Raymond Riva, "A Probable Model for Proust's Elstir," in *Modern Language Notes* 78, no. 3 (May 1965): 307–13; Philip Kolb, "The Birth of Elstir and Vin-teuil," in *Marcel Proust: A Critical Panorama*, ed. Larkin B. Price (Urbana: Univ. of Illinois Press, 1973), pp. 147–67; and Diana Festa-McCormick, "Proustian Aesthetics of Ambiguity: Elstir's 'Miss Sacripant'," *International Fiction* 3, no. 2 (July 1976): 92–99.

20. On Proust's religion of art, see Barbara J. Bucknall, *The Religion of Art in Proust*, Illinois Studies in Language and Literature, 60 (Urbana, Chicago and London: Univ. of Illi-nois Press, 1969), and J. Theodore Johnson, Jr., "Against 'Saint' Proust," in *The Art of the Proustian Novel Reconsidered*, ed. Lawrence D. Joiner Winthrop, Studies on Major Modern Writers, no. 1 (Winthrop, South Carolina: Winthrop College, 1979), pp. 105–43.

Proust and Theater   Louise M. Jefferson*

Among the arts celebrated in *A la recherche due temps perdu*—litera-ture, music, and painting—theater has been integrated into the novel with perhaps the most variety and complexity in its structural aspects, both for-mal and metaphorical, as a body of literature, and as a performing art.

The prestige and the importance of the theater during Proust's lifetime have been well documented.[1] In his formative years it was only natural that Proust would be attracted by the theater and want to associate himself with it in some fashion. His experiments with theatrical form began fairly early, according to the introduction of his first published work, *Les Plaisirs et les jours* (1896), in which he states, "if some of these pages were written when I was twenty-three, many others ('Violante,' almost all the 'Fragments de comédie italienne,' etc.) date from my twentieth year."[2] The metaphor of the theatrical "type" in the manner of the *commedia dell'arte*, is basic to all of the "Fragments. . . ," but in "Personnages de la comédie mondaine" (which is in the literary tradition of the Caractères of La Bruyère) it most forcefully binds theater to society. The "Fragments" also boast an actual attempt at theatrical writing, a "Scénario." It is a self-conscious, affected

*This essay was written specifically for this volume and is published here for the first time by permission of the author. Quotations from *A la recherche du temps perdu* are from the Kilmartin translation. All other translations are by the editor.

piece, studiedly simple, borrowing a bit from fairy tale and symbolist drama. Whatever the literary influences, the basic Proustian pattern of a love affair is already established: coquetry and flight of the Beloved, jealousy and suffering of the naïve, and too eager, lover Honoré.

Among the "pages written at the age of twenty-three," there is a selection entitled "Un dîner en ville" that has special interest in the light of similar dinner scenes in the *Recherche*. The dinner at the home of M. et Mme Fremer has Verdurin touches, but has not yet been endowed with the animation, lively dialogue, and graphic descriptions of gesture or mannerism common to the mature work. It is nonetheless in the spirit of the *comédie mondaine* that Proust will develop so admirably.

From time to time Proust made a tentative step in a strictly theatrical direction. Such a step is the seven-page dialogue "Vacances," published in 1949 by Harry Levin, who estimates that it was written between 1896 and 1904.[3] The dialogue, in two scenes, occurs between Henri and Françoise, who meet, have a love-affair, quarrel, but seem ultimately on the verge of reaching an understanding. The jealous, spoiled Henri is told at one point, "I am sure that you could write a play if you weren't so spineless, my dear."[4]

To the extent that Proust shared with his characters, or rather distributed among his characters, his own faults and virtues, the criticism voiced by Françoise concerning Henri's lack of will and drive to write a play is significant. Proust never had, to use his own word, the "courage" to write a play.[5] He may have realized as early as 1896 or as late as 1906, when the last nostalgic references to play-writing are found in his correspondence, that a play in the contemporary mold was not the original work he was to create.

Subsequently in his abandoned novel *Jean Santeuil* (1896–1900), in his pastiches of the Lemoine Affair (1908–1909), and even in his unfinished critical study *Contre Sainte-Beuve* (1905–1912), theatrical form—melodramatic plots, dialogues, or conversation—will be present in one guise or another. When Proust found the unifying narrative principle that would allow him finally to encompass his diverse literary interests, his sense of theatre was transformed, but not lost.

Proust's view of role-playing as endemic to society and to all human relationships made of him a keen, at times pitiless, observer with an eye for significant decor and gesture and an ear for the most subtle intonation and colorful expression, who presents the characters of his major novel at different moments in time in typical "scenes," ranging from massive society receptions, to aristocratic and bourgeois salons, to jealousy-ridden boudoirs. That the nature of these scenes is purely dramatic, that is presented for the intrinsic comic, tragic, and psychological value *per se,* is a factor which contributes to the originality of the novel. For the *Recherche* is essentially a descriptive novel, and the best means found by Proust to illustrate his narrator's progressive and ultimately complete disenchantment with all social relationships was to let society speak for itself at length, in detail, and repeatedly.

Lester Mansfield points out in his study *Le Comique de Marcel Proust* (1953) that the author sees society as basically comic, in the Bergsonian sense, and often as hypocritical and fatuous.[6] He contrasts the shifts in literary emphasis that take place in a serious work, where the intrigue is the all-important factor, and in a comic one, where details of gesture and language are the elements needed to produce a humorous effect. Proust's art is in the latter category.

Later studies have revealed further, and equally persuasive, aspects of the multiple meanings of the French term *comédie* as it applies to Proust's novel.[7] And in so doing have shown that the concept of *comédie* and ritual—all subsumed under the rubric of theatre—is fundamental to the *Recherche*.

The significance of the Proustian social scenes *(les scènes mondaines)*, in particular, has been emphasized by Michel Raimond, who called for a systematic study of this unique scenic pattern. He defines the *scène mondaine* as "the detailed account, interspersed with *numerous dialogues*, of the limited number of hours which, at some particular time of the day, the Narrator spends 'in society,' on the occasion of an afternoon reception, of a dinner or of an evening reception to which he has been invited and where it has been given to him to meet, in a brief span of time, a great number of characters who belong either to the Guermantes circle or the Verdurin circle" (my emphasis).[8] He examined only the six major social events from *Lé Côté de Guermantes* through *Le Temps retrouvé* and, earlier omissions notwithstanding, the first and most striking fact is that they occupy one-third of these two volumes to which Proust gave his full attention from 1914 to 1922. Undoubtedly, then, they are of great import in the design and aesthetic effect of the work. While Raimond's analysis was only preliminary, he remains convinced that "one could find some fine effects of composition in the totality of this *Corpus*."[9]

Another of the impressive compositional effects in the *Recherche* that has been constant, whatever the narrative transformations, is the patently theatrical dialogue, either on a large scale or in a *tête-à-tête*. In the total Proustian *corpus*, in addition to the more complex social scenes, the lovers' quarrel, already seen in *Les Plaisirs et les jours* and in the dialogue "Vacances," is a telling example. Within the framework of the novel it is illuminating to trace the evolution of this standard Proustian landmark.

It is in the abandoned novel *Jean Santeuil* that the character of "L'Aveu," as the chapter is entitled, becomes set. In a vain attempt to secure his hold on happiness, and to reassure himself of the fidelity and constancy of his mistress, the anxious lover will question her minutely and insistently about her past. Here Proust makes one of his best uses of the short, dramatic dialogue. Its pace is rapid; the underlying emotions and reactions of the speakers are conveyed as much by their words as by the few explanatory remarks that serve to give additional weight and bite to their exchanges. Here, too, the theme of homosexuality is joined, as it will be in the *Recherche*, to that of the querulous jealousy of the lover. In *Jean Santeuil*, the scene is more markedly theatrical because even the unspoken commentary reads more like stage directions than do the psychologically astute reflections of Charles Swann or Marcel:[10]

> They waited, they were quite alone and close together. He took her head in his hands and looked at her for the third time as he had done on the day of the sonata and the day of the theatre. Then he stepped back a few paces like someone who has been pushed, and then, standing still, he said to her: "Françoise, have you never loved anyone but me?" "You know that quite well, darling." "Don't tell me, you know, tell me, I have never loved anyone but you." She said, as if she were repeating a lesson: "I have never loved anyone but you, is that good enough for you?" "Do you swear to it?" (*JSF* 3:213)

And with this touch, reminiscent of Molière's Agnès, the scene continues, and the lovers play out what will become a classic moment in every Proustian love affair. The scene has its own dramatic unity, from the onset of the questioning to the climactic moment of avowal of homosexual relations in the past, with Françoise's outraged indignation, when her difficult confession is badly received, as the dénouement.

In *the Recherche*, Proust will rework and amplify *l'aveu* between Jean Santeuil and Françoise, assigning their roles first to Swann and Odette, then to the Narrator and Albertine. The fully developed background of the characters in *the Recherche* immediately gives the dialogue greater interest and permits the use of more specific detail. It becomes increasingly evident that the fatal drama is the result of the lover's slowness to recognize, in the case of Swann, or to admit, in the case of the very cognizant Narrator, that the fallible, socially determined object of his desire is not the ideal, unattainable object of his imagination. In dramatic terms, inspired by Eros (or, in the Narrator's case, conceivably by Narcissus as a literary or homosexual equivalent), the subject Swann or the Narrator pursues Odette or Albertine, who embody sexual gratification, when the object desired is actually Zipporah or the Goddess of the beach at Balbec. This in no way lessens the suffering jealousy; it simply makes the situation more discordant as they play their roles and struggle with the rules of the game. This awareness on the part of the reader gives added insight into the workings of the Proustian "law of love."

The form of the dialogue undergoes inevitable narrative modifications from *Jean Santeuil* to *the Recherche*. Swann is certainly a much more mature man-of-the-world than was Jean when he confronted Françoise. Still, the difference in age and experience, both in the character and the author, is shown more in Swann's reflections and in Proust's analyses than in the dialogue itself, which is quite similar to that of the original scene:

"Odette, my darling," he began, "I know I'm being simply odious, but I must ask you a few questions. You remember the idea I once had about you and Mme Verdurin. Tell me, was it true? Have you, with her or any-one else, ever?"

She shook her head, pursing her lips, a sign which people commonly employ to signify that they are not going, that it would bore them to go. . . . But this shake of the head thus normally applied to an event that is yet to come, imparts for that reason an element of uncertainty to the denial of an event that is past. . . . When he saw Odette thus signal to him that the insinuation was false, Swann realised that it was quite possi-bly true.

"I've told you, no. You know quite well," she added, seeming angry and uncomfortable.

"Yes, I know, but are you quite sure? Don't say to me, 'You know quite well'; say, 'I have never done anything of that sort with any woman'."

She repeated his words like a lesson learned by rote, in a sarcastic tone, and as though she hoped thereby to be rid of him: "I have never done anything of that sort with any woman."

"Can you swear to me on the medal of Our Lady of Laghet?" (*RTP* 1:362; *RTPK* 1:393–394)[11]

And Swann, like every Proustian lover, continues to question his mis-tress until she makes an avowal that will only cause him further suspicion and pain.

Comparing the Swann-Odette confrontation with a jealous quarrel of a somewhat similar nature between Marcel and Albertine, the most striking difference is the volume of unspoken, analytical commentary from one to the other. The differences are dictated by the nature of the quarrels and the traits of the characters. Swann visits his mistress and questions her about possible amorous relations with women in the past. His suspicions are confirmed. It is his reaction and some of its ramifications that accom-pany their reflections. In the case of Marcel and his mistress, they are liv-ing together in an uneasy atmosphere of alternating affection and distrust. He has just returned from a musical evening at the Verdurins', and Alber-tine's anger over not having been informed of his plans touches off the ar-gument. Marcel's immediate defense is the countercharge that Albertine hides many of her activities from him. This accusation and her replies lead to the same area and manner of questioning seen in the Swann-Odette quarrel. Only here, the Narrator's sensitivity and subsequent shock cause him to react in a more extreme fashion than did the urbane Charles Swann. Albertine's guarded comments reduce Marcel to tears; and, to hide the real cause of his weeping, he attributes his emotion to a sudden decision to end their relationship. He skillfully manages, therefore, to bring her around to his real desire, a continuation of their current arrangement. But this *com-édie de rupture* (sham drama of separation), which they have played, con-tains no theatrical surprises for the reader. A full psychological explanation accompanies it, revealing an even more intense drama going on behind the one enacted. This unplayed, veridical version occupies, within the text of the scene, twice the place of the actual dialogue. The explanation of Marcel's motives, then, is a necessary accompaniment to retain the sympathy (and comprehension) of the reader.

Dialogue, nonetheless, continues to fulfill a distinct and consistent function. It presents, in this case, a very fascinating dramatic study in character analysis. Taken alone, and because of the very *revirements* (reversals) of which the Narrator speaks, it emphasizes the lack of understanding, the conflict of the participants, and, in short, the *comédie* (play-acting) on which this relationship is based. In a sense, the Narrator has outdistanced Swann in his involvement with a woman who is not his *genre* (type); and his sufferings and machinations exceed Swann's as well. Thus, it is that the *comédie de rupture* is definitely reminiscent of the Swann-Odette episode, but is much more laden with possibilities to hurt the players. Moreover, it was from Swann himself that, years earlier, the adolescent Marcel heard the warning: ". . . the danger of that kind of love, however, is that the woman's subjection calms the man's jealousy for a time but also makes it more exacting. After a while he will force his mistress to live like one of those prisoners whose cells are kept lighted day and night to prevent their escaping. And that generally ends in trouble." (*RTP* 1:563; *RTPK* 1:606–07). In effect, the final irrevocable drama is precipitated by the *comédie de rupture*. And how familiar it sounds. There is the standard request for reassurance by the lover: "Albertine, can you swear that you have never lied to me?"

But the answer affords the Narrator more than the expected shock.

> Yes . . . that is to say no. I was wrong to tell you that Andrée was greatly taken with Bloch. We never met him."
> "Then why did you say so?"
> "Because I was afraid that you believed other stories about her, that's all."
> She stared once again into space and then said: "I ought not to have kept you from a three weeks' trip I went on with Léa. But I knew you so slightly on those days!"
> "It was before Balbec?"
> "Before the second time, yes."
> (*RTP*3:349–50; *RTPK* 3:357)

The recognizable form and content of the Proustian lover's knot is there. The petulant give-and-take comes through in passages such as the foregoing. Still, although it remains the core of the entire episode, proportionately, the dramatic scenario as such has a lesser place in the scene, as narrative and analytic passages increasingly dominate.

As indicated earlier, Proust is most theatrically impressive in scenes of society (or *scènes mondaines*), where he mingles spectacle, dialogue, monologue—Brichot, Norpois and Charlus are the great protagonists here—and even pantomime (*RTP* 3:317–18; *RTPK* 3:322).[12] Though the dramatic quality may be obscured in many instances by an abundance of critical analysis or poetic digression, the fact remains that an actual scene, be it with family, friend, or social group, is the focal point of the major part of the novel.[13] Time, his major character and the novel's catalyst, is an elusive, subtle figure whose messages are best understood not by action and intrigue, which the novel lacks, but by periodic examinations of time's effect on the Narrator and the world about him. The varied scenes are of social and vocational significance in fixing the Narrator's values. By intrinsic and stylistic design, they are meant to stand out as textual events: musical evenings, where guests came to be seen as much as to listen; dinners characterized by elegant service and banal conversation; lovers' quarrels full of deceit and pain; and all too distant times of warmth and affection within the family circle. To recapture the full flavor of these memories, they are consciously dramatized with a theatrical awareness stemming from Proust's wide knowledge of theatrical literature and his interest in the theater of his day.

In addition to this major structural integration of theater into the *Recherche,* Proust's novel is rich in theatrical quotation, analogy, and metaphor.[14] The density and extent of this phenomenon have yielded many extremely perceptive stylistic, semiotic, and thematic studies, some specifically dealing with theater, others of a more general nature.[15]

On a completely referential level, along with an abundance of references to the theater of the Golden Age, a review of the metaphors and allusions of the *Recherche* is also a review of the theatrical history of the late 19th and early 20th centuries: the roster of players of the Comédie Française, the stars of the Théâtre du Boulevard, opera singers, the traditional and a few foreign, avant-garde playwrights and producers, the Ballets Russes, the song stylists of the day are all given a place in the *Recherche*. The result is a chronologically identifiable art, whose fictitious elements are rendered more believable due to their factual surroundings.

A reading in depth, involving a full appreciation of the semiotic and semantic elements of the text, will reveal an equally extensive use of theatrical material. John Gaywood Linn's essay on "Proust's Theater Metaphors" (1958) was one of the earliest to focus on the pervasiveness of theater imagery. Linn found that Proust uses "upwards of 270 theatrical metaphors" and 500 direct allusions to theater. The metaphoric function, he determined, is three-fold: to connect and refer to greatly separated events in the novel; to establish the rapport between art and life; and to lower subtly the reader's opinion of the characters.[16]

Subsequent analyses by exponents of *la nouvelle critique* have given even further insight into the aforementioned process of connection and referral. Gérard Genette has demonstrated that metonymy is the prevailing trope that precedes and / or follows any metaphoric postulation, creating the narrative substance of which metaphor is but a privileged moment:

". . . it is metaphor which recovers lost Time, but it is metonymy which reanimates it and sets it in motion once more: which restores it to itself and to its true 'essence,' which is its own flight and its own Search. Here then, here alone—by metaphor but *in* metonymy—here begins the Account."[17]

Pursuing further the analysis of Genette's diagetic metaphor . . . that is, a metaphor metonymically founded . . . Jean Ricardou analyzed the role of what he terms the "structural metaphor," which posits resemblances between separated fictional "cells" of a similar nature, and that of the "generative metaphor," which posits similarities between contiguous elements of a seemingly different nature. This latter metaphoric function is, in effect, a reflection of the functioning principle of the *Recherche* itself, the outstanding example being the discovered contiguity of the two seemingly separate ways—le côté de chez Swann and le côté de Guermantes.[18] The theatrical metaphors show these processes at work as admirably as do the choices made by Genette and Ricardou. Without specifically evoking these theorists, in an article on "The Hôtel de Balbec as a Church and Theater," Peter V. Conroy has illustrated the multiple possibilities Proust drew from this generative theatrical metaphor.[19] Indeed from the beginning of the *Recherche*, after the formal opening or prologue, to its closure or, differently put, from the unsuccessful bed-time distraction furnished by the *surnaturelles apparitions* (supernatural apparitions) of Marcel's magic lantern at Combray to the *coup de théâtre* which presented him with the initially unrecognizable guests at the *matinée* (afternoon reception) of the Princesse de Guermantes in Paris. Proust has superimposed contiguous and disparate elements via generative metaphors from the realm of theater to convey the force and quality of many revelations in the novel.

Proust's notebooks reveal that he even considered having "une pièce de théâtre, une comédie" (a play, a comedy) presented as the attraction at the final matinée instead of a recitation of poetry by Rachel and a musical interlude.[20] One can only speculate on what the content of the *comédie* might have been—possibly a sub-text (or *mise-en-abyme*), a device often used in the novel, portraying the social comedy of which Marcel had so often been a part. Whatever Proust's reason for abandoning this idea, he highlighted in this final, metaphorically developed scene both the structural and thematic resources of the theatrical art and also the ironic fate of its major fictional exponents, La Berma and Rachel.

Again, in connection with the thematic role of theater, it is not only through metaphor that thematic links are established. The impressive sampling of dramatic works of the 17th, 19th, and early 20th centuries provides an opportunity for criticism of both Proust's characters, who are consistently associated with certain authors and opinions, and the plays evoked. In fact, drama criticism in and of itself arises quite naturally and spontaneously in social scenes, where, at the Verdurins', Brichot holds forth in the manner of drama critic Emile Faguet (*RTP* 2:935. *RTPK* 2:966) or, in the face of the duchesse de Guermantes's capricious preferences, the Narrator reflects on the menace of irresponsible critics (*RTP* 2:470–71. *RTPK* 2:488–89), or again, Mme de Villeparisis indulges in Sainte-Beuve-like comments on Hugo's *Hernani* (*RTP* 1:710, 722–23; *RTPK* 1:763, 775–77).[21]

Certain dramatists furnish a consistent thematic code of reference of greater or lesser complexity depending upon the frequency of allusion or quotation. Racine and Maeterlinck play privileged roles in the novel, which will be discussed presently, but, viewed chronologically, among the dramatists who receive more than passing mention are Shakespeare, Corneille, Molière, Hugo, Labiche, Dumas fils, Meilhac, and Halévy.[22] Shakespeare's *Hamlet* is given on four occasions as an ideal of artistic achievement, while four other allusions relate either to the theme of homosexuality or to one of its proponents (the Charlus-Jupien encounter is a case in point (*RTP* 2:627; *RTPK* 2:651). Corneille, even when referred to humorously, is the playwright of forbearance and duty and the poet of the grandiose declamation, associated in the latter connection with the salon of Mme de Villeparisis (*RTP* 2:195; *RTPK* 2:199). On the other hand, Proust manifests great literary kinship with the 17th century's foremost writer of comedy, Molière. Proust is not merely tacitly allied to Molière by his scenically comic technique and his choice of similar social targets, he openly invites the reader to witness the unchanging character of human nature from Molière's day to his own. By paraphrasing and quoting Molière's lines, referring to his characters, or the traditional portrayal of certain stock roles, Proust associates Molière with the human comedy of all time.

In the 19th century, Hugo, the poet and dramatist, is evoked, as indicated earlier, as a victim of criticism *à la Sainte-Beuve*, while the theater of Eugène Labiche offers the stereotype of the lower middle class, to which Swann at one point allied the Verdurins, when they excluded him from their salon and separated him from Odette. Alexandre Dumas fils represents the contemporary playwright who is highly esteemed by the bourgeoisie and the aristocracy, but found mediocre and over-rated by the artistic spokesmen of the novel, Swann and Marcel. Even so, his theater has an important thematic association with the *Recherche* due to the central role played in both by the courtesan. The play *Francillon*, discussed at length in the Verdurins' salon, concerns just such a woman; and Odette, Rachel, and, to a certain degree, Albertine mirror the importance of Dumas' typical protagonist. Michael Finn has convincingly drawn parallels between *La Dame aux camélias* and the Swann-Odette love affair, demonstrating that Dumas fils' work is used as a *mise-en-abyme*, and contested in the process by Proust, whose courtesan Odette lacks the redeeming qualities of the self-sacrificing Marguerite Gauthier.[23] Finally, Meilhac and Halévy, the collaborators on witty, spirited, society theatre, are the models for the conversation and wit of the Duchesse de Guermantes.

It falls to Racine and Maeterlinck to illustrate time's effect on dramatic works of art. Racine is Marcel Proust's literary beacon of all time, both stylistically and thematically.[24] This has been amply commented upon by me and others;[25] but it bears repeating that, at the outset, Racine is associated with two of the youthful Narrator's artistic idols, La Berma in theatre and Bergotte in literature, and, throughout the novel, Racine's theater remains the pinnacle of dramatic art. Racinian tragedy emerges as well as the exemplary sub-text in which Marcel finally recognizes and is able to evaluate his romantic desires and experiences. And it is Phèdre, the symbol of guilty love, who is the incarnation of those experiences (*RTP* 3:458; *RTPK* 3:467). The generative metaphor that establishes Marcel's identification with this *princesse de tragédie* (tragic princess) (*RTP* 1:145; *RTPK* 1:158) is found in *Du côté de chez Swann* and reaches its culmination in *La Fugitive* (*RTP* 3:458; *RTPK* 3:467). Even Racine's *Esther*, though not exclusively linked to the love-jealousy theme, reflects certain aspects of the unusual relationship between the Narrator and his sequestered mistress Albertine. What is more, *Esther* and Racine's other biblical drama *Athalie* serve Proust in comic as well as tragic episodes, where he finds irresistible parallels between the corps of decorative, superfluous young men at the Hôtel de Balbec (*RTP* 1:706, 2:773–74; *RTPK* 1:759, 2:801–02) or at certain foreign embassies (*RTP* 2:665–66; *RTPK* 2:689–90) and the impressive but unessential choruses of Racine's two tragedies. In this comic vein, the thematic association with homosexual activities among these male choruses is again present, as it is to a lesser or greater degree in Marcel's tragic love affairs, allowing the Narrator to view life through art, which is, for him, the privileged medium.

As a dramatist, Maeterlinck is not proposed as a modern peer of Racine's. His is rather a specific role for the chronological time in which the Narrator lived and sought artistic fulfillment. Maeterlinck is the much-discussed, greatly misunderstood, avant-garde dramatist of Marcel's youth; and his reputation through the years provides insight into the time-lag between the appearance of an original work and popular acceptance of the truly original writer. From the time of Rachel's disastrous recitation of excerpts from *Les Sept Princesses*, in the salon of Oriane de Guermantes (*RTP* 1:784, 2:229–30, 249; *RTPK* 1:841–42, 2:235–36, 257), to the final matinée of the Princesse de Guermantes, when Oriane insists that she alone at the time found the text admirable (*RTP* 3:1013; *RTPK* 3:1065), Maeterlinck the creator of "that poetry of the incomprehensible" (*RTP* 3:1009; *RTPK* 3:1062), is the dramatist whose acceptance is an important demonstration of the effect of time on a work of art, an idea which is at the heart of the Narrator's preoccupations and discoveries.[26]

The theatrical art itself is particularly vulnerable to the effects of time. Still its artistic value is not, as some Proustian scholars believe, negated by the metaphorical use of theater imagery to expose the social comedy in the *Recherche*.[27] The presence of two fictional actresses, the great La Berma and the competent Rachel, balances that of two actual playwrights with whom they are aligned, Racine and Maeterlinck. La Berma's genius in her art is quite a match for the genius of a Racine: "I realised then that the work of the playwright was for the actress no more than the raw material, more or less irrelevant in itself, for the creation of her masterpiece of interpretation . . ." (*RTP* 2:51; *RTPK* 2:47). As for Rachel, an early interpreter of the theater of Maeterlinck, she is seen in a performance of the poetry of La Fontaine in her old age but at the height of her career. And she is judged ultimately to be quite mediocre. Her role in the novel is, however, more complex, showing the attraction exercised by the actress and her art, and repeating with St. Loup a variation on the love / jealousy theme.[28] Proust's repeatedly enunciated theory that a real innovator must create a receptive public and will be appreciated in time is proven in her case, but she is in no way on an artistic par with Bergotte, Elstir, or Vinteuil, all artistic geniuses belatedly esteemed. It is La Berma, forced into the background by age and Rachel's popularity, who is their peer. She has been, as have they, capital in Marcel's artistic apprenticeship, a *porteuse de signes* (bearer of signs), as Deleuze so appropriately indicates, at an early point in his development, enabling him to learn that it is the "essences"—those differences in each entity that constitute being—which her art reveals.[29] The eclipse suffered by La Berma is not the result, then, of lack of genius. Rather, it is the result of lack of permanence. This gifted actress is the one artist whose shrine is in the audience's memory, for her creation is an ephemeral, mobile masterpiece. The Narrator understands this fully during the revelation of the *matinée*, when he pays final tribute to the literary and performing geniuses of theater, Racine (among others) and La Berma:

> In spite of Rachel's words I was thinking myself that time, as it passes, does not necessarily bring progress in the arts. And just as some author of the seventeenth century, who knew nothing of the French Revolution, or the discoveries of science, or the War, may be superior to some writer of today. . . , so Berma was, as the phrase goes, head and shoulders above Rachel, and Time, when simultaneously it had turned Rachel into a star and Elstir into a famous painter, had inflated the reputation of a mediocrity as well as consecrated a genius. (*RTP* 3:1003; *RTPK* 3:1054–55)

Notes

1. Léon-Pierre Quint, *Marcel Proust, sa vie, son œuvre* (1938; rpt. Paris: Editions du Sagittaire, 1946); George D. Painter, *Marcel Proust, A biography*. 2 vols. (London: Chatto & Windus, 1959–1965); John Gaywood Linn, *The Theatre in the Fiction of Marcel Proust* (Columbus: Ohio State Univ. Press, 1966).

2. (rpt. Paris: Gallimard, 1924), p. 5.

3. "An Unpublished Dialogue by Proust," *Harvard Library Bulletin* 2, no. 2 (Spring 1949).

4. Ibid., p. 266.

5. In December 1906, Proust wrote to Mme Caillavet, "Dites à Gaston et à Robert que j'ai en vue une assez belle(!) idée de pièce et que je n'ai pas le courage de la faire." Marcel Proust, *Correspondance générale* (Paris: Plon, 1930), 4:114. The idea in question was described to Reynaldo Hahn in a letter of September 1906 and concerned sadism. The plot,

transformed and attenuated, was used in the *Recherche* in connection with Mlle. Vinteuil and her *amie*.

6. (Paris: Nizet, 1953)

7. Roland André Donzé, *Le Comique dans l'œuvre de Marcel Proust* (Neuchâtel, Paris: Editions Victor Attinger, 1955); Jack Murray, *The Proustian Comedy* (York, South Carolina: French Literature Publications Co., 1980); Rosette C. Lamont, "Le rituel dramatique dans *A la recherche du temps perdu*" in *Marcel Proust: A Critical Panorama*, ed. Larkin B. Price (Urbana, Chicago, London: Univ. of Illinois Press, 1973), pp. 226–46.

8. "Les scènes mondaines dans *A la recherche du temps perdu*" in *Proust et le texte producteur*, ed. John D. Erikson and Irène Pagès (Guelph, Ontario: Univ. of Guelph, 1980), pp. 71–77.

9. Ibid., p. 71.

10. All references to *Jean Santeuil* will be to the edition of three volumes published by Gallimard in 1952 and will be followed by page references in the text.

11. All references to *A la recherche du temps perdu* are to the Paris: Bibliothèque de la Pléiade, Gallimard, 1954 edition, 3 vols., and will be followed by page references in the text.

Concerning the Narrator, his complexity has been convincingly demonstrated by, among others, Marcel Muller, *Les Voix narratives dans la Recherche du temps perdu* (Genève: Droz, 1965). These facts notwithstanding, the convention of referring to him as "Marcel" will be followed here.

12. This particular pantomime, executed by Charlus in a state of panic, following Morel's repudiation of the baron, occurs in what could conceivably be a self-contained drama, namely the musical soirée at the Verdurins. See Louise M. Jefferson, "Proust and Theatre," Diss. Univ. of Illinois 1963, pp. 80–83.

13. The most obvious and vital exceptions are the experiences of involuntary memory, the theories and analyses of the cycle of love, the lack of synchronization between events and emotions, and the appraisal and value of works of art.

14. Jacques Nathan, *Citations, références et allusions de Proust dans A la recherche du temps perdu* (Paris: Nizet, 1953); Linn, op. cit., pp. 23–29; Jefferson, op. cit., pp. 103–97.

15. Ernest Robert Curtius, *Marcel Proust*, trans. Armand Pierhal (Paris: Les Editions de la Revue Nouvelle, 1928); Emeric Fiser, *L'Esthétique de Marcel Proust* (Paris: Librairie de la Revue Française, 1933); Jean Mouton, *Le Style de Proust* (Paris: Editions Correa, 1948); Stephan Ullmann, *Style in the French Novel* (Cambridge, Mass.: University Press, 1957) and *The Image in the French novel* (Cambridge, Mass.: University Press, 1960).

16. *The Romanic Review* 49 (October 1958): 179–90. These early conclusions were developed and refined in his book-length study (note 1), which includes an examination of the entire Proustian *corpus*.

17. "La métonymie chez Proust," *Figures III* (Paris, Seuil, 1972), p. 63. Genette recognizes in a note that Jean Pommier had called attention to the role of contiguity in the Proustian metaphor in 1939 in *La Mystique de Marcel Proust* (rpt. Genève: Droz, 1968), p. 54.

18. " 'Miracles' de l'analogie (aspects proustiens de la métaphore productrice)," *Cahiers Marcel Proust*, p. 7, Etudes proustiennes 2 (Paris: Gallimard, 1976), pp. 15–17.

19. In *Marcel Proust: A Critical Panorama*, pp. 206–25. This particular metaphor is also inscribed, by virtue of its designation as the "Temple-Palace de Balbec," in the metaphoric network of churches via the pun on Méséglise / mes églises, which incorporates all the churches in the novel. Although this Balbec metaphor is not mentioned, Ricardou points to the importance of the church in Proust's text as a "véhicule à voyager dans le temps" (vehicle for time travel) (Ricardou, op. cit., p. 23), and Conroy establishes in his introduction that ". . . this provincial hotel is a half-way house, a neutral zone where two worlds, ordinarily separate, can meet and sometimes intermingle" (op. cit., p. 206).

20. *Matinée de la Princesse de Guermantes: Cahiers du Temps retrouvé*, ed. Henri Bonnet and Bernard Brun (Paris: Gallimard, 1982), p. 29.

21. It was Jean Mouton who initially commented on Brichot's speech as a pastiche of the style of dramatic critic Emile Faguet, op. cit., pp. 60–61.

22. Proust also refers, in a minor vein, to Greek and Roman dramatists—Aristophanes, Plautus—and to figures of Greek mythology—Agamemnon, Oedipus, Theseus (in connection with *Phèdre*)—to aid character study.

23. "Proust and Dumas fils: Odette and La Dame aux Camélias," *French Review* 47 (February 1974): 528–42.

24. There are over fifty references to his theater, nineteen of which contain quotations.

25. Louise M. Jefferson, "Proust and Racine," *Yale French Studies*, no. 34 (June 1965): 99–105; Jack Murray, op. cit.; Carlo Persiani, *Proust e il teatro, con una nota su Proust e il cinematografo* (Caltanissetta-Roma: Edizioni Salvatore Sciascia, 1971); François Kessedjian, "Proust et Racine," in Marcel Proust 2, *Europe*, no. 502–03 (February–March 1971):28–44.

26. In choosing *Les Sept Princesses* (1891) of Maeterlinck as a vehicle for Rachel, Proust's memory undoubtedly failed him. The seven princesses are under a spell and are asleep throughout the play. With the return of the hero at the denouement, all awaken except his love Ursule; but not one speaks a line!

27. Linn, op. cit.; Persiani, op. cit.; Maurice Descotes, "Les Comédiens dans *A la recherche du temps perdu*," *Revue d'Histoire du Théâtre*, no. 2 (1978):168–91.

28. Dennis G. Sullivan has shown very convincingly that, in the *Recherche*, the actress "will be employed to figure every character who is desired by another," p. 534 in "On Theatricality in Proust: Desire and the Actress," *Modern Language Notes* 86, no. 4 (May 1971): 532–554.

29. *Proust et les signes* (Paris: Presses Universitaires de France, 1970), p. 47.

Death of My Grandmother / Birth of a Text

Elyane Dezon-Jones*

It seems that up till now Proust critics have rather neglected studying the genesis and the function of the figure of the grandmother in *A la recherche du temps perdu*, when in fact she takes her place at the point of departure and of arrival of the narrator's literary vocation. She initiates him to aestheticism in *Du côté de chez Swann* ("instead of photographs of Chartres Cathedral, of the Fountains of Saint-Cloud, or of Vesuvius, she would inquire of Swann whether some great painter had not depicted them, and preferred to give me photographs of "Chartres Cathedral" after Corot, of the "Fountains of Saint-Cloud" after Hubert Robert, and of "Vesuvius" after Turner, which were a stage higher in the scale of art") (*RTP* 1:40; *RTPK* 1:43); in *A l'ombre des jeunes filles en fleurs*, she lets him benefit by her connections when she gives him an entrée into "society" by introducing the narrator to Mme. de Villeparisis; she dies in *Le Côté de Guermantes* the

*This essay was written specifically for this volume and is published here for the first time by permission of the author. Translated by the editor, with the exception of the quotations from *A la recherche du temps perdu*, which have been taken from the Kilmartin translation.

better to reappear in *Sodome et Gomorrhe* under the form of an intermittency of the heart, becoming the epicentre of the Proustian approach to seeking a praxis of the "combined forces of memory and imagination."

The grandmother is a character very different from the others from many points of view but chiefly because her function consists of dying that the text may live. It was therefore necessary for Proust to make her stand out in a radical way. He did so by setting her aside from the original group (the family cell), which explains the numerous references to the grandmother's "eccentricities" in *Du côté de chez Swann,* and beyond the reference group (the Guermantes) by presenting her as the constant modifying factor in the narrator's point of view. She had to die—stop incarnating a world where appearances are not misleading—so that the narrator could name the false appearances by their true names.

When he goes to the theater to see la Berma for the first time, the narrator appeals to his grandmother to straighten out the confusion which is inherent to his vision of the world: "I told my grandmother that I could not see very well and she handed me her glasses" (*RTP* 1:449; *RTPK* 1:484). This act will be repeated by the narrator become novelist at the end of *Le Temps retrouvé* when he offers his reader his book as an optical instrument enabling him to see reality more exactly. So the grandmother is the indispensable intermediary who potentializes the focus of the whole work and the clarification of the role of the creative artist. She appears and disappears at strategic moments of the fictional life of the narrator to organize the stages which will lead to the recognition of "the invisible vocation of which this book is the history" (*RTP* 2:397; *RTPK* 2:412).

If she sometimes gives the impression of being a minor character, a convenient marionette, a slightly ridiculous old woman, a mere accompanist, a duplicate of the mother, a fanatical reader of Mme. de Sévigné, an "imbecile," it is because she will be embodied in the narrative only after her death. Before that there will only be brief snatches of a partly glimpsed individual. It is in order to reconstitute this character that the work will be composed. All we see of the grandmother, up till the day of her death, is a cheek that the child kisses and a pair of arms which she protectively folds around him. Her face is never described in its totality but only in terms of the emotions that modify her gaze, the expression of her mouth, and the wrinkles on her forehead. As for her voice, we only hear "fragments" of it.

The grandmother is in a perpetual process of modification even when she is supposed to represent that stabilizing influence in the narrator's life. She is reduced to a simple "face" when Proust depicts the physical sufferings to which her illness subjects her: "her face, worn, diminished, terrifyingly expressive, seemed like the rude, flushed, purplish, desperate face of some wild guardian of a tomb in a primitive, almost prehistoric sculpture" (*RTP* 2:324; *RTPK* 2:335). The grandmother is truly the "guardian of the tomb" constituted by the book which is still to be written. In fact, when Professor E . . . announces to the narrator "Your grandmother is doomed"

("Votre grandmère est perdue"), he states a condition without which the thematics of *A la recherche du temps perdu* could not function. In order to recover his grandmother, which is as much as to say recompose her eternal body, it only remains to the narrator to undo the work of time, by substituting life for death: "Life in withdrawing from her had taken with it the disillusionments of life. A smile seemed to be hovering on my grandmother's lips. On that funeral couch, death, like a sculptor of the Middle Ages, had laid her down in the form of a young girl" (*RTP* 2:345; *RTPK* 2:357).

It really is a question, for the narrator, of *setting down on paper* the body of the grandmother "in the form of a young girl" so satisfying his ambition to isolate "a fragment of time in the pure state" (*RTP* 3:872; *RTPK* 3:905). She goes from being a guardian of the tomb to becoming the goal of the quest. From being a face, she becomes the body of the narrative. She is an avatar of the "mighty goddess of Time" (*RTP* 3:387; *RTPK* 3:393) which the narrator will believe he sees in the sleeping Albertine *laid (or set down)* on her bed.

In a dream, the narrator repeats the voyage of Orpheus, the oneiric journey which is to snatch the grandmother back from oblivion.

> . . . as soon as, to traverse the arteries of the subterranean city, we have embarked upon the dark current of our own blood as upon an inward Lethe meandering sixfold, tall solemn forms appear to us, approach and glide away, leaving us in tears. I sought in vain for my grandmother's form when I had entered beneath the somber portals; yet I knew that she did exist still, if with a diminished vitality, as pale as that of memory; the darkness was increasing, and the wind; my father who was to take me to her, had not yet arrived. Suddenly my breath failed me, I felt my heart turn to stone; I had just remembered that for weeks on end I had forgotten to write to my grandmother (*RTP* 2:760; *RTPK* 2:787–88)

This passage makes it clear that the narrator is in search of the divine afflatus. The grandmother's disappearance is bound up with failure to write. She will only be brought back to the land of the living by the achievement of the literary work whose inspiration she is in every sense of the word:

> "Where is grandmother? Tell me her address. Is she all right? Are you quite sure she has everything she needs?" "Yes, yes," says my father, "you needn't worry. Her nurse is well trained. We send her a little money from time to time, so that she can get your grandmother anything she may need. She sometimes asks what's become of you. She was told you were going to write a book. She seemed pleased. She wiped away a tear" (*RTP* 2:761; *RTPK* 2:788)

In search of the lost grandmother, the narrator will once more attempt "the desperate stratagem of a condemned prisoner" (*RTP* 1:28; *RTPK* 1:30), the same stratagem he had used to get his mother to come to him in the initial scene of Combray, to cancel her absence, to erase the time spent without her: that is by writing, no longer a brief and clumsy note, but three thousand pages organized to form a work of art. Thus he will guarantee eternity to the character of the grandmother, who becomes a determining creation, leading to the fundamental difference between the disorganization of *Jean Santeuil*, from which she is absent and from which a real standard of objective validity is absent in consequence, and the coherence of *A la recherche du temps perdu* for which she provides a structure. It is in fact the grandmother who becomes the focal point for the existential anguish of separation which the narrator will soothe *by recounting it*. This is what puts the scene of the mother's goodnight kiss in its proper perspective: the temporary absence of the mother is only the "rehearsal" of the permanent absence of the grandmother. The "drame du coucher" (bedtime drama) is nothing more than the pale prefiguration of the tragedy which the death of his grandmother—any death— will constitute for the narrator. "There is no reply" to the note sent by Marcel to his mother, for their separation is not permanent. In contrast, the only possible reply to the death of the grandmother is the act of writing which will bring her back to life, showing how true it is that "real life, life at last laid bare and illuminated—the only life in consequence which can be said to be really lived—is literature" (*RTP* 3:895; *RTPK* 3:931).

From the very beginning of *Du côté de chez Swann*, the reader is led to suspect that in order to enter into real life, the grandmother is first of all condemned to die surrounded by misunderstanding.

> But when my father had almost called her an imbecile on learning the names of the books she proposed to give me, she had journeyed back by herself to Jouy-le-Vicomte to the bookseller's so that there should be no danger of my not having my present in time (it was a boiling hot day, and she had come home so unwell that the doctor had warned my mother not to allow her to tire herself so), and had fallen back on the four pastoral novels of George Sand (*RTP* 1:39; *RTPK* 1:42)

The genesis of the episodes concerning the illness and death of the grandmother confirms that as early as 1908 Proust had planned the "loss" of the grandmother in order to justify his search.

It is in a marginal addition to galley number 25 in the 1920 Gallimard proof sheets of *Le Côté de Guermantes* II (N.A. fr. 16763) that Proust introduces the sentence, "Your grandmother is doomed" (in French, "perdue," which means both "doomed" and "lost"). The visit to Professor E. . . constitutes the final addition to the episode of the illness and death of the grandmother which Proust had intended to add to his novel as early as 1908. The text evolves between these two dates, from the rough draft Cahiers numbered 29 and 14 to the manuscript formed by the Cahiers 47 and 48 which will serve as the basis for the three typescripts corrected by Proust in many different ways and of which the last will be used to make up the galleys numbered 24 and 25 in the Gallimard proofs of *Le Côté de Guermantes* I and II. These galleys themselves are covered with additions leading up to the text of the original 1920 edition. Initially, the illness and death of the grandmother form a complete unit which only the hazards of a publication delayed by the declaration of the First World War and a change of publisher will split into two parts, constituting the end of *Guermantes* I and the beginning of *Guermantes* II. As a matter of fact, *Le Côté de Guermantes*, which was to be published by Grasset in 1914 consecutively to *Du côté de chez Swann*, would become the third volume of *A la recherche du temps perdu* since *A l'ombre des jeunes filles en fleurs* would be inserted between them.

It seems that Gallimard had at one time intended to publish *Le Côté de Guermantes* in a single volume, for on the other side of the half title of *A l'ombre des jeunes filles en fleurs* one could read in 1918:

> Publications of the *N.R.F.* Works of Marcel Proust.
> *A la recherche du temps perdu*, 5 volumes
> *Du côté de chez Swann* I
> *A l'ombre des jeunes filles en fleurs* II
> to appear:
> *Le Côté de Guermantes* III
> People's names: the Duchesse de Guermantes.—Saint-
> Loup at Doncières.—The salon of Mme de Villeparisis.
> —Death of my grandmother.—Albertine reappears.—
> Dinner with the Duchesse de Guermantes.—The Guermantes
> wit.—M. de Charlus continues to disconcert me.—
> The Duchesse's red shoes.
> *Sodome et Gomorrhe* IV
> *Sodome et Gomorrhe* V

In the end this volume III of *A la recherche du temps perdu* was subdivided into two volumes for practical reasons. This arbitrary division, due to the fact that the printed book would have been too long, repeats a situation which had already occurred at the time of the publication of extracts from *Le Côté de Guermantes* by the *N.R.F.* In the July 1914 number, these extracts end with the evolution of the grandmother's illness up to the moment where the narrator perceives that "she did not recognize [him]." The readers of this journal had to wait for the number of January 1, 1921 to read the rest of the episode, that is to say the description of the aggravation of her symptoms and, not to mince words, her death, the original outline of which, going back to 1908, is embellished on a large scale by scenes tending to underline the uselessness of medicine and powerlessness before death.

For example, in a letter dated December 10, 1920, Jacques Rivière specifies to Proust: "Immediately upon receiving your letter, I asked Paulhan to recopy the scenes with Professor E. . . They will be added."[1] In exchange, Jacques Rivière asks Proust to remove from this passage Bergotte's visits to the grandmother in her illness. This everlasting haggling about the length of the writings to be published is completely typical of the difficulties Proust was to run into every time he tried to get his publishers to accept the scope and size he wanted. Because of this, it is necessary to understand that the passage which appeared in the 1921 *N.R.F.* under the provisional title *Une Agonie* and which constitutes with a few minor variants the beginning of *Guermantes* II should have been, if Proust had had his way, the conclusion of the Grasset *Le Côté de Guermantes* in 1914 and the conclusion of *Le Côté de Guermantes* I in 1920. Proust indicated this quite unambiguously to Jacques Rivière when he wrote to him in May 1914:

> I was counting on letting you have some marine passages (in contrast to the landlocked landscapes of the first volume) on Balbec and on my disappointment when Balbec turned out so different from what I had expected (plus the night of my arrival with its distress and the consolations of my grandmother). It is a part of the chapter which in the volume will be called Names of Regions: the Region, and which corresponds to the chapter of the first volume: Names of Regions: the Name. Anyway, if you want a little more, I could add to this the pages on the death of my grandmother which will conclude the volume and which could quite easily be connected with these pages on Balbec.[2]

While it is possible to consult the rough drafts, the manuscript, the typescripts, the 1920 Gallimard galleys and the extracts published in the *N.R.F.*, there does not seem to be any trace of Grasset proofs concerning the illness and death of the grandmother. In May 1914 there is another death which directly affects the work in progress: the demise of Alfred Agostinelli has as its immediate consequence Proust's inability to work on correcting the proofs of *Guermantes*, as a letter Proust wrote to Gide on June 20 of the same year bears witness:

> Since the death of my poor friend, I have not had the willpower to open a single one of the packets of proofs which Grasset sends me every day. They are piled up, still in their wrappings, one on top of the other, and I do not know when, if ever, I shall have the strength to get back down to the job. I have arranged the extracts for the next number of the N.R.F. because I was afraid that such a long passage would create too much of a gap by its absence. But that is all I have been able to do.[3]

The passages concerning the stroke in the Champs Elysées, the return to the apartment, and the various stages of the illness had, however, already been set up in type in 1914 since, when he winds up his account with Grasset, Proust reminds him, on August 14, 1916:

> Unless I am much mistaken, I do not owe you anything for the proofs of the second volume, for the following reason: we had agreed to put together a book of around 700 pages or a bit more. In the course of working on it, we stopped it at page 525. The first proofs of 150 pages (represent-

ing the part of the first volume which we were deciding to use as the beginning of the second volume instead of the end of the first) had already been pulled. That is almost everything that has been pulled of the second volume. Now that was in fact paid for in advance, as I had paid for the first volume. It is true that when I wanted to publish extracts in the N.R.F. I asked you to pull a few more proofs a little further on. I cannot swear to it without being able to have the proofs in front of me but I believe they go up to page 18. As for the changes you discuss, I cannot, without being authorized to repeat a secret, tell you what caused them (I am speaking of the most recent ones). In any case, it is impossible that 18 pages of new proofs should make up the entire conclusion of the first volume which I paid for as if it had been done and which has never even been set up in page form (the only proofs I have received of the end of this first volume are big proof sheets called (I believe) galleys. In any case I am only talking to you about our accounts to give you a rough idea. Your books will allow you to see if I am mistaken.

The secret to which Proust is here alluding is of course the transformation of Alfred Agostinelli, the fugitive who had disappeared from Proust's life and from his own, into a character of A la recherche du temps perdu: Albertine, who will play an essential role in the Côté de Guermantes II and in the parts of A l'ombre des jeunes filles en fleurs composed after June 1914, but who is totally absent from the Côté de Guermantes I which was originally supposed to end with the death of the grandmother. The death of the grandmother was "displaced" to the beginning of the second volume of the Côté de Guermantes but already existed in the form of proofs because Proust adds by way of a rider in a letter to Gaston Gallimard written January 11, 1921: "Point out to Bellenand that Guermantes II must be paginated by numbering the first page number 1 and so on. (At the moment the pagination begins on page 25, I believe, but I don't remember it very clearly)."5

One may conclude that the 18 pages Proust is talking about to Grasset more or less correspond to the stroke suffered by the grandmother in the Champs-Elysées and to the first phases of the illness which is to carry her off, while the twenty-five pages discussed in the letter to Gallimard cover in a general kind of way the doctors' treatments, the aggravation of the patient's condition, and her death.

In contrast to Albertine as a character inserted relatively late in the narrative structure of A la recherche du temps perdu, the grandmother as a character goes back to the 1908 project, even though Proust notes down in 1914, in the Cahier number 13, his hesitations about the definitive place to put her death, at a time when he is trying to restructure the whole plan of his work, shattered by the appearance of the new character, Albertine. On leaf 55 of Cahier 13, dated autumn 1914 by Maurice Bardèche, Proust considers the following sequences: "2nd year at Balbec—girls. I meet them through the painter, I am infatuated with ~~Maria~~ Albertine. Will I be seeing you in Paris? Difficult. Sweetness of Andrée. Hunt-the-slipper. ~~See~~ Disappointment. Bed scene. Definite disappointment. Desires looking for an object turn back towards Andrée. Take advantage of her sweetness (perhaps) to have prestige in eyes of Albertine. Give up Andrée. Paris: Mme de Guermantes. ~~Death of my grandmother~~. Visit Mme de Villeparisis. Doesn't the master know who's come? Mlle Albertine. Death of my grandmother. Mlle de Silaria—Visit from Albertine etc . . ."

Maurice Bardèche writes in connection with *Le Côté de Guermantes* that "one has the impression that Proust is engaged in a kind of aimless roaming, one should almost say in a kind of incoherence: not one of the capricious incidents of the novel appears to be justified."[6] In fact it is quite normal that Proust, after having inserted the Albertine cycle in the body of the *Recherche* and thus having broken up what was originally intended to be the second volume, should ask himself how he is going to reorganize his text and which is the most favourable place to introduce the theme of death. This theme will finally conclude *Guermantes* I with the study of the grandmother's heart failure and *Guermantes* II with the announcement of the impending demise of Swann.

It is true that the way Proust shifted the grandmother's death around in the course of the narrative can give the superficial impression that it didn't matter much where it went. It was at the heart of *Le Temps retrouvé* "to appear in 1914" if one refers to the list of contents printed on the other side of the half title of *Du Côté de chez Swann:* "A l'ombre des jeunes filles en fleurs.—The Princesse de Guermantes.—M. de Charlus and the Verdurins.—Death of my grandmother.—The intermittencies of the heart.—The "vices and Virtues of Padua and Combray.—Mme de Cambremer.—Robert de Saint-Loup's marriage.—Perpetual Adoration."

The death of the narrator's grandmother, followed by the description of a relevant phenomenon of intermittency of the heart is roughed out by Proust as early as 1908 in his Carnet published by Philip Kolb. On the left hand side of leaf number 44, Proust jots down "3° After my grandmother's death, apparitions, etc."—and on the right-hand side of leaf number 51:

51   —*And after her death* "all at once the memory of one of her smiles at the dinner table, reminded me of the way she had smiled when sitting opposite me at lunch at Querqueville, to apologize for the request she had addressed to me and which I had just refused to recommend Brichot to Montargis. At that moment the small disappointment I had caused her made such a painful impression on my heart that I could not bear it, and like a foot warmer that needed plugging in I was jolted to one side of the bed on which I was sitting. Of course I knew that she wouldn't have been unhappy, that I put up very readily with being refused things, but from the moment that I could no longer grant her request or take her in my arms, saying but how could you suppose that I was seriously refusing you, ~~a life~~ world where this atonement was no longer possible, was no longer bearable to me, all the pleasures and all the pains of the world

no longer counted compared to the pain of not being able to erase the disappointment, the sad and mocking smile from her face, and from the moment when I could no longer do this I wanted to die.

51v° Without doubt later on this idea was often borne in on me and left me indifferent but that was because it was deprived of this upper part, of this crest that ideas only have for me on certain days, the only ones that count in life, the only ones in which ideas are complete and not insipid truncated fragments.[7]

Of course, the names of places and people will be transformed in the final version into Balbec, Jupien, and Saint-Loup. But in the passage drafted in 1908 Proust is reworking the end of the article that had appeared in the *Figaro* of July 23, 1907 under the title "Une grand'mère." It was written as the funeral eulogy of Robert de Flers's grandmother, Mme de Rozière, and concludes as follows:

"No one will have understood me better than Robert. . . . He would have acted like me. He knows that in the case of the beings one has most loved, one never thinks of them, at the moments when one sheds the most tears for them, without passionately directing towards them the most tender smile of which one is capable. Is it in order to try to deceive them, to reassure them, to tell them that they need not worry, that we will be brave, to make them believe that we are not unhappy? Or is it rather that that smile is only the very shape of the unending kiss which we bestow upon them in the realm of the Invisible?"

At the outset of this article, Proust makes Robert de Flers responsible for the death of his grandmother like a number of his characters who literally bring their parents to the grave and like the narrator of *la Recherche* who will reproach himself with having contributed to the death of his grandmother—"Consumed by the constant anxiety which constitutes a great life-long love (her love for her grandson) how could she have enjoyed good health?"

There is no equivalent for the character of the grandmother in *Jean Santeuil* but she appears, in the *Contre Sainte-Beuve* published by Bernard de Fallois, in the course of a trip to Venice with the narrator. She is present at the very beginning of the 1908 Carnet under the heading "Pages written" on the left hand side of leaf number 7:

Robert and the kid, mama leaves on a trip.
The Villebon Way and the Méséglise Way.
Vice ~~interpr~~ seal and opening of the face. Possession as disappointment, kissing the face.
    My grandmother in the garden, M. de Bretteville's dinner, I go upstairs, the face of mama then and since in my dreams, I cannot go to sleep, concessions, etc.[8]

And Proust foresees that he will dream of her after her death:

My grandmother

Every time I dreamed of her I believed that she had gone to bed without telling me, I was most distressed I saw Françoise go furtively by. She was in bed but not yet asleep, but she quickly sent me away, as if it were too late to want to see her, because during the day I had preferred everyone else to her and now she didn't want to see me, and putting out her light she pretended to go to sleep.[9]

In a similar vein, in the first typescript of the grandmother's illness and death there is a passage which was reduced to a single sentence in the final version[10] concerning the fact that children are far too ready to neglect their duty, which is to spend time with their parents instead of pursuing worldly distractions:

Since we prefer our parents to everything else, how does it happen that this happiness in their company which is so delightful that the deprivation of it forever, at their death, will cause us the deepest suffering we are capable of experiencing, how then does it happen that during all the years that it is miraculously preserved for us we do so little to enjoy it. We are always ready to leave them for the most insignificant friend. Every day we go out, we take trouble to see everybody except them. We do know however that one day we will no longer be able to see them and yet we carried (sic) on tomorrow as we did yesterday. What are we waiting for to act as if they were alive, and not as if they were dead, in order not to anticipate in advance and while they are alive the distress of never seeing them again?[11]

The confusion of values which leads to a bad choice of priorities is a dominant theme in *Le Côté de Guermantes*, which is a kind of chronicle of the death of illusions at the same time as an enumeration of the obstacles to literary creation, "society" in all of its forms being the main one. Because the narrator is unable to go all the way through an experience of involuntary memory, which is as much as to say his writing, because of the arrival of Saint-Loup, he goes off to waste his time along the Guermantes way, being prevented from making full use of "an enthusiasm which might have borne fruit had I remained alone and would thus have saved me the detour of many wasted years through which I was yet to pass before the invisible vocation of which this book is the history declared itself" (*RTP* 2:397; *RTPK* 2:412).

It really seems that the ideal place for the episode is the end of *Le Côté de Guermantes* I, if one considers this part of the novel as the point where childhood and adolescence, represented in space by Combray and Balbec, both being connected with the person of the grandmother, break off and the age of worldly frivolity, perfectly incarnated in the salon of the Guermantes, begins. The death of the grandmother will bring the Duc de Guermantes in person into the narrator's universe, since, in his capacity as a neighbour, he believes himself to be obliged to pay a courtesy visit to the family. It is then that there begins for the narrator a long period of wandering during which the practical fulfillment of his literary vocation is held in abeyance.

Jean Rousset is completely correct in insisting that "This midway point of the work which brings into being so many social groups and characters of every sort is destined to bring us face to face with a truth of which the narrator will only later become aware: all human activity is a snare and engenders a state of spiritual death for anyone who has the vocation to become a creator: the more one gives to the external world, the further one gets from the "graces" without which the artist cannot exist."[12] There is an exact correspondence between the death of the grandmother and a "spiritual death" of the narrator which will only be transcended when his forgetfulness of the grandmother turns into an awareness of his loss: in the isolation of a hotel room.

> Disruption of my entire being . . . The being who had come to my rescue, saving me from barrenness of spirit, was the same who, years before, in a moment of identical distress and loneliness, in a moment when I had nothing left of myself, had come and restored me to myself, for that being was myself and something more than me (the container that is greater than the contained and was bringing it to me). I had just perceived, in my memory, stooping over my fatigue, the tender, preoccupied, disappointed face of my grandmother, as she had been on that first evening of our arrival, the face not of that grandmother whom I had been astonished and remorseful at having so little missed, and who had nothing in common with her save her name, but of my real grandmother, of whom, for the first time since the afternoon of her stroke in the Champs-Elysés, I now recaptured the living reality in a complete and involuntary recollection. (*RTP* 2:755–56; *RTPK* 2:783)

As a sequel to this intermittency of the heart comes the narrator's dream in which he sets out in search of his lost grandmother and only feels pacified on hearing his father say: "She was told you were going to write a book. She seemed pleased. She wiped away a tear." The function of the grandmother is evident: she is there to remind the narrator to be himself, to allow him to recapture his creative personality. She restores him to himself at the cost of her own disappearance.

In contrast to the other characters who change their names several times as work on the rough drafts of *la Recherche* progresses towards a final version, the grandmother, before being introduced by her first name, Bathilde, or in the context of her civil status, Madame Amédée, is always called by Proust "my grandmother". The possessive adjective is systematically attached to the substantive.

One should see in that something different from a brief return to the autobiography which is characteristic of the lack of distancing in *Jean San-*

teuil. If the neo-naturalistic description of the death of the grandmother has as its real basis the attack of uremia which carried off Mme. Adrien Proust in 1905[13] and if the grandmother herself shares the literary tastes of Mme. Nathé Weil,[14] "my grandmother" remains the grandmother of the narrator and does not participate in the process of demystification of names which is chronicled by *Le Côté de Guermantes*.

When Proust notes in 1908, right after having indicated for the first time that his grandmother was going to die: (left hand side of leaf 44) "Names Pontaven etc. Journey to these towns. But they are not their name" he outlined the theme of *Le Côté de Guermantes* which will be slipped into *A l'ombre des jeunes filles en fleurs*.[15] One could say drawing the parallel, that we are confronted once more with the outline: "Names Guermantes etc. Visits to these *people*. But they are not their name."

Alone in *Le Côté de Guermantes*, the grandmother *is* her name, hence the necessity of her disappearance in a world where the narrator will have to learn that names no longer correspond to people any more than to towns and, by the same token, will have to set out himself in search of his name ("for that being was myself and something more than me") lost in the midst of his false notions. So it is difficult to share the point of view of Maurice Bardèche when he claims that "the grandmother's death is an admirable 'painting' that can be hung just about anywhere."[16] Very much to the contrary, for genetic and structural reasons, the grandmother's death must, as Proust wished, conclude *Le Côté de Guermantes* I, since it is an account of the death of illusions concerning the reality of names. In order that the narrator should find himself as a novelist, in order that the text should inscribe her forever "in the form of a young girl" (the Muse) it is necessary that the grandmother should die once she had accomplished her mission as guardian of the Name.

Notes

1. Marcel Proust and Jacques Rivière, *Correspondance 1914–1922*, edited by Philip Kolb, (Paris: Plon, 1955) p. 157.

2. Ibid, pp. 4–5.

3. Marcel Proust, *Lettres à André Gide* (Neuchâtel: Ides et Calendes, 1949) p. 45.

4. Quoted by Léon-Pierre Quint in *Proust et la stratégie littéraire* (Paris: Gallimard, 1932) p. 148.

5. Marcel Proust, *Lettres à la NRF* (Cahiers Marcel Proust VI) Paris, Gallimard, 1932, p. 148.

6. Maurice Bardèche, *Marcel Proust romancier* (Paris: Les sept couleurs, 1971) vol. 2, p. 140.

7. Marcel Proust, *Le Carnet de 1908*, edited by Philip Kolb, Cahiers Marcel Proust Nouvelle série 8 (Paris: Gallimard, 1976), pp. 119–120.

8. Ibid, p. 56.

9. Ibid, p. 124.

10. "with that strange indifference which we feel towards our relations so long as they are alive, and which makes us put everyone before them, I thought it very selfish of her to take so long" (*RTP* 2:308; *RTPK* 2:319).

11. First typescript N.A. fr., 16737 p. 11.

12. Jean Rousset, *Forme et signification* (Paris: José Conti, 1962) p. 164.

13. George D. Painter, *Marcel Proust: A Biography,* (London: Chatto & Windus, 1965) vol. 2, pp. 47–49.

14. Painter, vol. 1, p. 3.

15. Proust, *Le Carnet de 1908,* p. 107.

16. Maurice Bardèche, *Marcel Proust romancier* (Paris: Les Sept Couleurs, 1971) vol. 2, p. 140.

INDEX